728

TIMM

KAL
3 11 08
3410
PP

G000140952

The Miegunyah Press

This is number one hundred and seven
in the second numbered series
of the Miegunyah Volumes
made possible by the
Miegunyah Fund
established by bequests
under the wills of
Sir Russell and Lady Grimwade.

'Miegunyah' was the home of
Mab and Russell Grimwade
from 1911 to 1955.

PROPERTY OF THE LIBRARY
OF CONGRESS

PRIVATE LIVES

Australians at home since Federation

PETER TIMMS

PINE RIVERS LIBRARIES
P.O. BOX 5070
STRATHPINE 4500

THE
MIEGUNYAH
PRESS

THE MIEGUNYAH PRESS
An imprint of Melbourne University Publishing Limited
187 Grattan Street, Carlton, Victoria 3053, Australia
mup-info@unimelb.edu.au
www.mup.com.au

First published 2008
Text © Peter Timms 2008
Design and typography © Melbourne University Publishing Ltd 2008

This book is copyright. Apart from any use permitted under the *Copyright Act 1968* and
subsequent amendments, no part may be reproduced, stored in a retrieval system or transmitted
by any means or process whatsoever without the prior written permission of the publishers.

Every attempt has been made to locate the copyright holders for material quoted in this book.
Any person or organisation that may have been overlooked or misattributed may contact the publisher.

Designed by Peter Long
Printed in Singapore by Imago
National Library of Australia Cataloguing-in-Publication entry:

Timms, Peter, 1948-
Private lives : Australians at home since Federation /
9780522855029 (pbk.)
Includes index.
Bibliography.

National characteristics, Australian.
Australians-Dwellings-History.
Australia-Description and travel.
Australia-Social life and customs-20th century.
Australia-Social life and customs-21st century.

305.824

The out-of-town family house is a sanctuary of pure joy, a respite from all the troubles, pre-occupations, worries, and sadnesses of which life is woven.

OSCAR COMETTANT, *IN THE LAND OF KANGAROOS AND GOLD MINES*

It was not, as it has been claimed a house should be, a machine to live in. It was a material substance that absorbed life from the lives and feelings of those who lived in it, and which gave out again, to console them for vanished time, the life that it had absorbed.

MARTIN BOYD, *OUTBREAK OF LOVE*

Contents

Conversion Table

CURRENCY (APPROXIMATE FIGURES ONLY)

1 penny (d) = approx. 1 cent

1 shilling (s) = 12 pennies = approx. 10 cents

1 pound (£) = 20 shillings = approx. 2 dollars

1 guinea (gn) = 1 pound and 1 shilling (£1 1s). The guinea was a favourite of retailers wanting
to make prices seem lower than they actually were.

LENGTH

1 inch (in) = 25.4 mm

1 foot (ft) = 30.5 cm

1 yard (yd) = just under 1 metre (0.914 m)

1 mile = 1.61 km

WEIGHT

1 ounce (oz) = 28.3 grams

1 pound (lb) = 454 grams

AREA

1 acre = 0.405 hectares

VOLUME

1 pint (pt) = 568 ml

1 gallon (gal) = 4.55 litres

Preface

This book will take you on a guided tour of the Australian detached house (with occasional forays into the apartment and inner-city tenement), criss-crossing back and forth in time between the end of the nineteenth century and the present.

Having first explored the verandah and patio, we will enter through the front door into the hall, then move on to the livingroom, diningroom, kitchen, bedroom, bathroom and laundry. Passing through each room in turn, we will witness changing fashions in furniture, fittings and colour schemes. We will note the impact of telephones, radios, refrigerators, televisions and computers, along with some less spectacular, but still significant, innovations such as can-openers, bedlamps and washing detergents. We will try to rekindle the thrill our grandparents felt at their first encounters with electric stoves, inner-spring mattresses and instant hot water.

However, the real purpose of this tour of inspection is not to outline the history of the house itself, but rather to observe the private lives of the people who have occupied it: to understand changing perceptions of family and solitude; work and play; discipline and indulgence; hardship and ease. After all, architecture, design and domestic technologies do not develop in isolation. They are a response to (as well as a trigger for) human needs and aspirations, even when the professionals deliberately ignore what people actually want, as was frequently the case last century.

In essence, this is the story of how ingrained habits of self-sufficiency and family independence were gradually whittled away, to be replaced by an almost total reliance on professional providers from outside the home. Whereas at one time people grew their food, made their own preserves and household products, undertook the necessary repairs and, in many cases, even built their own houses from scratch, now we simply pay others to supply everything for us. The days of the amateur potterer are over, thanks not only to unprecedented personal wealth, but also tighter restrictions on what we are allowed to do and the sheer inscrutability of modern micro-chipped appliances. So accustomed are we to thinking that almost any domestic problem can be solved by purchasing a mass-produced product or getting someone in that we forget how odd this approach actually is.

But it's not all bad news. Far from it. One important positive outcome is that the rather defensive preoccupation with privacy and seclusion that characterised the domestic lives of our grandparents and great-grandparents has slowly melted away. Domestic life today is more outward-looking, more various in its manifestations and less hemmed in by social and cultural conventions. Today's houses, with their open-plan interiors, glass walls and outdoor entertaining areas, are, as much as anything, a sunny reflection of our changed frame of mind.

Yet questions remain. Why, despite their obvious enthusiasm for sleek modern cinemas and department stores, did suburban mums and dads for so long ignore reformers urging them to adopt the new style for their homes? Was it simply a matter of innate conservatism, as is generally assumed, or did they have sound reasons? Why did householders immediately warm to some technological innovations (radio, television and the flushing toilet, for instance), while remaining steadfastly resistant to others (such as telephones, refrigerators and washing machines)? What motivated widely differing responses to the provision of professional child-care services and the heady seductions of the beauty industry, and what impact did these things have on home life? Finally, why, in spite of everything, is privacy at home still pursued with such determination, albeit in a somewhat different form to that of the past?

The twentieth century, despite its many marvels, was not an easy time, even for those fortunate enough to be living in relative peace and prosperity on the periphery of world events. While they may not have been making history, such individuals were nevertheless profoundly changed by it. Their lives during the worst years of economic depression, warfare and social upheaval—their struggles, disappointments, enjoyments and achievements—can tell us much about who we are today and what has shaped us.

The playwright Louis Esson declared in 1912 that Australian suburbia was 'dull, cowardly and depressing'. On the basis of what he glimpsed of Sydney's outskirts from a train window in 1922, DH Lawrence pronounced them 'utterly uninteresting' and devoid of 'inner life'. How many times have we heard such complacent dismissals? While this book does not specifically set out to refute them, it will, by unveiling something of the 'inner life' of suburbia, at least put them into a proper context as well as holding to account those who, even today, seem intent on upholding the great Australian intellectual tradition of suburbia-bashing.

＊　＊　＊

I am particularly grateful to the following people who agreed to be interviewed and to share with me their personal recollections: Betty Salomon, Margaret Stafford, Margaret McGregor, Arnold Grodski, Rose Harrex, David Coombes, Patricia and Colin Climie, Rita Timms, Marjorie Roberts, Shaz Harrison-Williams, Peggy Heywood, Cynthia Coombe, Bert Jones, Lily Chan and Michael Abbott. Helen Page gave me access to an unpublished memoir by her father, Cliff Page. My thanks also go to Matt Stephens, Reference Librarian at the Historic Houses Trust of New South Wales, and to Daniel Dennis, Michael Dysart, Christopher Lawrence and Gwen Ford, all of whom provided valuable reference material and advice. My friend Jarratt Walker, along with my literary agent Lyn Tranter, my publisher at Melbourne University Publishing Tracy O'Shaughnessy, and my partner Robert Dessaix all read and commented on the manuscript, which led to immeasurable improvements.

Fortress
orFishbowl

Private and Public

On paper it was perfection itself: a superbly proportioned rectangular box sheathed in glass. The client, Dr Edith Farnsworth, had asked the world's most famous architect, Mies van der Rohe, for a weekend retreat where she could contemplate nature undisturbed. The result was stunning. So were the bills. The Farnsworth House, built in a meadow outside Chicago in the late 1940s, ran $16 000 over budget, at a time when $16 000 was a lot of money. Lengthy litigation followed. Yet it wasn't just a problem of cost. Mies had wanted to bring nature, houses and human beings into a higher unity, but his open-plan glass box was impossible to keep warm, attracted clouds of insects at night and, most disturbingly, afforded no privacy at all. Dr Farnsworth could contemplate nature alright, but nature could also contemplate her. 'The truth is', she complained, 'that in this house with its four walls of glass I feel like a prowling animal, always alert, even in the evening.' [1]

Today the Farnsworth House is regarded as an architectural masterpiece, despite its sublime impracticality, and the ideals it expresses of transparency, simplicity and openness have calcified into holy writ. In an urban setting, however, what you are likely to be contemplating are not meadows, rivers and trees but freeways and your neighbour's bathroom, while your neighbours, in turn, will find themselves exposed to a lot more of your private life than they expected.

Our house is, to one degree or another, our refuge. It must enfold and protect us without closing us off completely. A windowless cell, no matter how luxuriously appointed, will quickly become oppressive, but so can one with too many windows, as the unhappy Dr Farnsworth discovered. Perhaps the degree of privacy or transparency we want in our house mirrors our psychological responses to other people: our longings for intimacy on the one hand, or admiration on the other. If that's true, then the houses in which we

feel most at home will be those that best reflect the balance or harmony that we as individuals seek between the internal and external worlds, which is to say between our private and public selves.

A house, after all, is not just a practical assemblage providing shelter and the means to perpetuate life—not just 'a machine for living in'. It must give us emotional protection and fulfilment, too. It must satisfy the needs of the spirit as well as those of the body.

Privacy (or at least having a choice about it) is the privilege of the financially secure. Generally speaking, the poorer you are the less of it you are entitled to expect. Slum dwellers in Sydney's Paddington or Melbourne's Richmond in the early 1900s, crammed with ten or twelve others into two-room sheds with dirt floors and leaky roofs, could hardly afford to be fussy.

In fact, one of the main complaints about the lower orders was that they lived communally on the streets, something respectable folk would never do. Early photographs often show poor people clustered on footpaths before their open front doors. Although this was partly because the interiors were too dingy for the camera, there was something about lingering in doorways that suggested abjection. Middle-class families wouldn't be seen dead outside their open front doors in this way.

Yet, even if we do have a choice, we don't all desire privacy equally. The history of the Australian middle-class house over the past century-and-a-half is one of at first striving for—and achieving—a good deal of family seclusion, then

MIES VAN DER ROHE'S FARNSWORTH HOUSE, COMPLETED IN 1951, ESTABLISHED IDEALS OF SIMPLICITY, OPENNESS AND TRANSPARENCY THAT HAVE LAIN AT THE HEART OF MODERN DOMESTIC ARCHITECTURE EVER SINCE.

willingly giving it up again as the social standing of the family weakened and the world beyond the home grew ever more enticing. Bringing the outside in is only an option if you like what you see outside, and that wasn't always the case in times past.

The decorated façade of the respectable 1880s suburban villa, with its fluted pillars, elaborate bay windows and cast-iron trim, was a mask, an exterior display that gave nothing away, like the nervous party guest who overcompensates with too much swagger. As a cynical journalist sneered in 1887,

> The villa architect takes a cathedral front and slices it up longitudinally; then an Elizabethan house, or a Chinese pagoda, a railway station, a hen-house, a dovecote, a pigsty—for art knows no distinctions—and ... has an infinite number of phrases to work with and can vary the air to any extent ... The inside, like the meat in a penny pie, is generally an afterthought.[2]

THERE WAS SOMETHING
ABOUT LINGERING IN
DOORWAYS THAT SUGGESTED
ABJECTION. ONLY THE DOG
LOOKS HAPPY AND ALERT IN
SALI HERMAN'S DEPICTION
OF INNER-CITY TERRACE-
HOUSE LIVING.

SALI HERMAN
SATURDAY MORNING 1968
OIL ON CANVAS MOUNTED
ON PLYWOOD
38.8 X 51.4 CM
NATIONAL GALLERY OF
AUSTRALIA

Well, perhaps not quite. In fact, the inside carefully maintained the preoccupation with separation and seclusion so clearly articulated by the outside, each room accorded its own degree of privacy and able to be sealed off from the others as required. While to modern eyes this might seem a bit straitlaced, the Victorian house did at least afford its occupants protection, both physical and psychological: a comforting feeling of togetherness which, at the same time, catered to those who occasionally sought out a quiet spot to read or think (at a time when households were bigger and more diverse than they are now). Generally speaking, the collective privacy of the family unit took precedence over personal privacy.

In complete contrast, the fashionable residence of today—the one that wins architectural awards and gets itself into the colour supplements—bares its heart to anyone who might be interested. It is a permanent *Big Brother* house, with glass walls, flexible spaces and outdoor living areas where almost everything is on display. You can't do much in such a house without thinking about how it will look from outside. Yet, while we shamelessly display ourselves to the world, we do our best to avoid fellow members of the household by retreating to our bedrooms or studies. They might have walls of glass too, but to be seen from the street or the neighbour's backyard is acceptable, even gratifying, whereas having to physically interact with those who share the house is not. Today, the need is not so much for family privacy as for privacy from the family.

'If the "union of opposites" sought by Jung is to be achieved in architecture', writes the English critic Stephen Gardiner,

> a building has to be treated rather like the mind: the part concerned with the external world and the part concerned with the instinct must be encouraged to develop at the same pace, not one at the expense of the other, but in such a way that one supplies energy to, and derives inspiration from, the other. The two parts must be integrated and a bridge formed.[3]

Have we built such a bridge or simply swung from one extreme to the other? 'What has been described as the masterly use of open planning and integration, the flow of one space to another', complains the Melbourne architect Peter Corrigan, 'has in a way compromised our ability to find an individual space, to take on different moods, different costumes'.[4]

What turned the house from fortress to fishbowl? As you might expect, it was a complex interweaving of social, environmental, economic, psychological and, most noticeably, technological factors. For a start, the house got itself connected—first by the telephone, then radio, television and the internet. Gradually they whittled away the idea that we were inhabiting a self-contained unit separate from everything around it. The refuge became a base-station, from which the entire world (or the bits of it we wanted, anyway) could be summoned in an instant.

As if in response, the house's architecture started looking outwards, casting off its shading verandahs, opening up its interiors and ridding itself of extraneous embellishments to face the world in all its nakedness.

The weather had a lot to do with it too, or the belated realisation that heat and sunshine should be welcomed, not shunned. Once Australians had sloughed off their old English skins, they realised there was no need to huddle behind thick walls. Health campaigners in the late 1800s made quite a fuss about clean air and light. Large panes of glass, lightweight construction materials and new building techniques would eventually allow us to embrace this ideal which, as luck would have it, proved cost-effective as well.

Finally, fashion played its part, as it inevitably does. To be light, airy and open was not just to be healthy and happy, but *modern*. It marked you as worldly, sophisticated and up-to-the-minute, more 'Continental' (before World War II) or more 'Californian' (after it) than the stuffy Anglophiles around you in their closeted brick villas.

Fresh Air and Sunshine

Fresh air and sunshine! This was the mantra of health reformers everywhere. Fresh air and sunshine would banish infirmity and torpor, dispel the miasma that brought illness and death, and make enfeebled urbanites virile and happy again. Stale air in houses, it was widely believed, caused all manner of medical complaints.

When we call to mind how many people sleep in little, dark, sunless bedrooms', said the authors of *Home and Health* in 1909, 'with the windows rigidly nailed and covered with shades and curtains, night and day, is it any wonder that the constitutions of such people are being weakened by slow poisoning, and that morning finds them with coated tongues, aching heads, no appetite for breakfast, and 'as cross as a bear'.[5]

Fresh air was a major motivation for moving out from city to suburbs, where you could sleep under an open window confident that you wouldn't die as a result. Betty Barnett, interviewed by the historian Janet McCalman, remembered her father moving the family in 1913 from the fug of inner-Melbourne Brunswick 'to the bracing heights of Balwyn': 'Father was mad about fresh air—they had both been brought up in small, poky little houses—so fresh air, coming out to Balwyn—it was almost like a religion.'[6]

Indeed it was, in more ways than one, as witness the fact that *Home and Health* was published by the Seventh-day Adventist Church (although nowhere in the book is this acknowledged). The campaign for healthier, fresher and more efficient homes was largely initiated by middle- and upper-

A STRIKINGLY MODERN FLAGSTONE TERRACE IN CHURCH POINT, SYDNEY, FEATURED IN *THE HOME* IN 1941. IT FLOODED THE LIVING ROOM WITH WINTER SUNLIGHT, SOMETHING THAT WOULD NOT HAVE APPEALED TO EVERYONE AT THE TIME.

IN THE 1960S, HAPPINESS
MEANT (OR WAS SUPPOSED
TO MEAN) BEING MARRIED
WITH A CHILD OR TWO AND
A PLACE OF YOUR OWN.
EVEN THE MOST BASIC OF
PROJECT HOMES WOULD DO.

class Christian reformers and philanthropists, convinced that cleanliness was next to godliness, who secretly feared a working-class revolt if living conditions weren't improved. Although bubonic plague scares in Sydney and Melbourne had galvanised the authorities into cleaning up slums and improving public sanitation, tuberculosis, typhoid, diphtheria, scarlet fever, measles and influenza were still major killers in the early 1900s and thousands of children died each year as a result of diarrhoea. Clearly something had to be done, and the best way to accustom people (especially working-class people who were known to be dirty and ignorant) to the habits of cleanliness and good health was to start with the home. The housewife would lead the way.

To the anguished cries of religious reformers were added the sober arguments of health professionals and experts in domestic management, a rapidly growing breed in the 1910s. Fling open the windows, they urged, get rid of all that heavily padded furniture and those dusty fitted carpets; clean, simplify and renew; bring to your home all the sound rational principles that have been adopted so successfully by industry. Thus the home, which previously had been thought of as a comforting refuge from the commercial and industrial worlds, was now to be run on similar principles.

The campaign quickly homed in on domestic architecture. It would be up to the well-designed, efficient, modern house to deliver the benefits to society. Although the moral connection between good health and modern architecture wasn't as clearcut as it was often assumed to be, at the very least it was symbolically important.

Arguing in 1934 for larger north-facing windows in livingrooms, architect Kingsley Ussher acknowledged that,

> At one time we would have been afraid of that north window, and considered that nothing short of a verandah would have made it safe; but experience has shown that with well-designed eaves and the proper

placing of the window the sun will not enter at all at mid-summer, but will have unrestricted access at mid-winter.[7]

Although such principles had been known since ancient times, Australian builders had been slow to catch on.

The fact remained, however, that if you wanted a light-filled, open-plan modern house, you had to employ a top-flight architect to design one for you and many of its components had to be custom-made. Such designs were not available by the usual means, for the simple reason that, despite their elegant simplicity, they were prohibitively expensive. Besides, as everyone knew, flat roofs leaked. Ordinary homeowners could only look on with envy, or puzzlement, until such time as the modern house became as cheap as, or cheaper than, the traditional brick bungalow.

That time came in the mid 1950s, with two revolutionary innovations. One was the 'window wall', which, for the first time, made expanses of glass cheaper than the equivalent area of weatherboard.[8] Window walls were not just large windows. Instead of filling a hole in the wall, they were prefabricated, load-bearing structures capable of replacing it altogether. They might even incorporate a sliding safety-glass door. The mass-produced, standardised units had only to be dropped off at the site and nailed into place, and their slim mullions and glazing bars gave the whole building a new, lighter look. They helped transform the design of the suburban house.

After that, the problem was how to keep the outside world out. Having got their ultra-modern glass walls, residents then had to find ways to cover them up again. Fortunately, the manufacturers of curtains, sunshades, venetian blinds and awnings rushed to the rescue.

But the really pivotal 1950s innovation was the display home. Instead of the complicated and time-consuming business of having plans drawn up, then negotiating with local authorities, builders, subcontractors and suppliers, you could simply visit a 'village' of well-presented, architect-designed project

It was a spectator sport to rival the footy,
and it allowed people to experience the work
of Australia's best architects at first hand.

homes to select the one that best suited your needs, which would be built on your own land with a minimum of fuss and bother. It was almost as easy as buying a car and, as with cars, new models were released each year. Every weekend, thousands flocked to view them, whether they were looking for a new house or not. It was a spectator sport to rival the footy, and it allowed people to experience the work of Australia's best architects at first hand.

Sharp competition among building companies, along with off-site mass-production of kitchen and bathroom fittings, meant a fully furnished house for as little as £3000 on terms of £7 per week. In 1958, 90 per cent of Australian private houses were bought from speculative builders or built after direct negotiation between client and builder. Just six years later, project homes had seized more than 40 per cent of the market.[9]

So it was thanks to pre-fabrication, standardisation and commercial competition that Best Overend's dream of a light, clean, rationally designed house for almost every Australian could finally be realised. By lowering costs with light-weight materials, window walls, open planning and outdoor living areas, the project home did more to open up the interior of the Australian house than all the stern finger-wagging of the reformers. Although your Sundowner or Prestige might be identical to all the others in the street, it was clean, practical, affordable and, once you'd got the furniture in, not quite as spartan as it first appeared.

In the 1960s, Pettit and Sevitt in Sydney, along with Melbourne's Merchant Builders, brought the outside in with a range of 'natural-looking' houses, featuring exposed wooden beams, clinker-brick interior walls and earthy colours. The so-called 'nuts and berries' style of architecture blended well with wattles, grevilleas and old railway sleepers, which were gaining in popularity, at least among sophisticated Pettit and Sevitt types. To emphasise the point, Merchant Builders employed well-known garden designer Ellis Stones to set their display homes in rugged native gardens. For the first time, environmental consciousness was chic.

Custom Design: Four Craig Davis 'Originals' -for people who can afford to be different.

If you've got ideas of your own about the kind of home you want—we've got the system that makes sure you get it. It's called Craig Davis Custom Design.

We created it for busy people who have the means, but not the time to deal separately with architects and builders—and all the lengthy processes building a home involves. The result: a home that's **made for you alone,** not a run-of-the-mill project house.

From the moment you tell our architect your ideas and thoughts on the way you and your family like to live, until the time when you are well and truly settled in your new Custom Design home, we work with one aim in mind: to make sure **you** are satisfied. It sounds simple. And, as our Custom Design clients have already found, it is. Beautifully simple. Our consultants, Mr Bill Park and Mr Graham Alcorn are the people to call for information. Phone them personally at Melbourne 34 8261. They'll show you why, if you're thinking of moving to a new address, it makes sense to consider this very special way of getting exactly the home you've always wanted.

CRAIG DAVIS
Custom Design.
237 Rathdowne St, Carlton. 34 8261

BY THE EARLY 1970S,
PEOPLE WERE TIRING OF
THE SAMENESS OF PROJECT
HOMES. 'CUSTOM DESIGN'
ALLOWED FOR INDIVIDUAL
VARIATIONS ON THE
STANDARD MODELS. AS THIS
AD MAKES CLEAR, HOWEVER,
IT WAS ONLY FOR THOSE
'WITH THE MEANS'.

Yet, despite the high standards set by companies such as these, an awful lot of cheap, shoddy, poorly designed houses began to give 'modern' a bad name again. 'Chook-sheds', they were being called, and they seemed to confirm all the doubts people had been harbouring about the new style. A backlash was inevitable, although it proved to be less than total, for rather than sacrificing the practical advantages of new techniques and materials, a neat compromise was reached that could deliver you a house with Georgian portico out the front for status and substance, and a window wall overlooking a sunny terrace at the back for sunshine and fresh air. Modernism could be married to sentiment with no loss of amenity.

So you could remain contentedly conservative while still enjoying all the latest innovations. Craig Davis Homes' Colonial was light, airy and spacious, just as the architectural reformers had insisted a house should be. But it also sported Doric columns, fake shutters and cute little attic windows set into the pitched roof. This infuriated the purists, because it cheerfully—and, worse, successfully—subverted all their dearly held moral principles. Yet the company could proudly boast that the Colonial was the 'car stopper' at its Dandenong Road display centre.[10]

The hundreds of satisfied buyers who settled on the Colonial and others of its kind could sleep peacefully in their Jacobean beds, confident that they had achieved the best of both worlds.

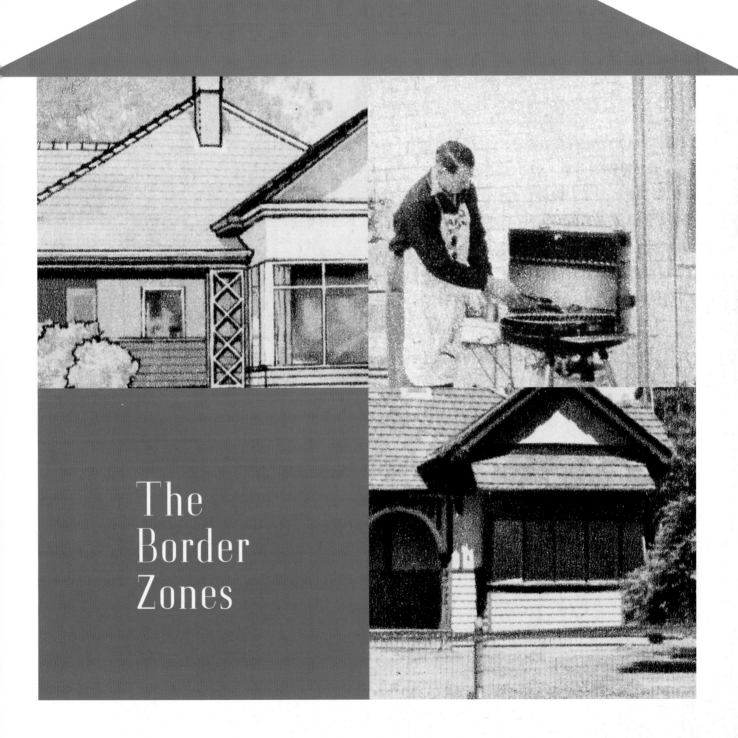

The Border Zones

The Theatre of Arrival

To judge the character of a house, we first look to its front door. Is it crisply utilitarian or cloying? Modest or pretentious? Does it welcome or intimidate? As the principal mediator between outside and inside, the front door is the part of the exterior most likely to be embellished, so as to make this link architecturally evident, although it can be difficult, sometimes, to strike the right balance. A classical portico on a tiny weatherboard cottage will be more comical than imposing, while, at the other extreme, the front door of many a modern glass-box house, tucked away at the side under a severe little steel canopy, can come across as unnecessarily mean-spirited. In combination with the huge areas of impenetrable glass on the façade, it says, 'You may admire us, but keep your distance'.

On the neat symmetrical front of the Georgian stone cottage (still common around Hobart today) the six-panelled front door occupies pride of place in the middle, with a matching window either side and a fanlight above to illuminate the hall. It is quite perfect in its way: welcoming yet reserved. Later, the front bedroom or parlour was projected forward from the main facade to form an L shape, with a protected yet eye-catching corner for the front door to nestle into.

As embellishments multiplied on the nineteenth-century housefront, door cases grew ever more grandiose. By mid-century, technical advances allowed glazed panels to be put into doors without the risk of breakage. Fanlights were now elegantly sandblasted with 'Parnassus' or 'Braeside' (names whose pomposity the lower-middle classes would later satirise with their 'Emoh ruo', 'Thistle-doo-us' and 'Castel Fiasco'). Stained-glass side-lights were flanked by fluted wooden columns and deeply panelled reveals. The maid might spend hours a week keeping this elaborate ensemble dust-free, but it was worth it for the prestige.

With the regularisation of postal services, the house name was joined by a big brass street number* and a letter-slot, with 'LETTERS' embossed on

* A house numbering system was necessary for provision of the services on which suburban dwellers increasingly came to depend, but the decline of the practice of naming them also suggests that houses were increasingly being viewed as economic investments rather than emotional attachments. Several attempts were made to also replace street names with numbers, in the American style (Mildura, Victoria, is an example), but Australians were rarely inclined to go that far.

the hinged cover in case the letter carrier (they didn't become 'postmen' until 1915) should miss it. The popularity of electric doorbells from the 1890s (aside from lighting, they were the only electrical devices that many homes had) did nothing to curb the exuberance of the traditional brass or cast-iron knocker, which was kept on for its symbolic and decorative values. The simple Georgian S-shaped knocker survived into the nineteenth century but, to status-hungry Victorians, the lion or Medusa head made a bigger impression.

All this was the culmination of an elaborate theatre of arrival which, during the boom period of the 1880s, reached sublime levels of refinement. Your stately progress to the front door began with a substantial gate, hung between stone or brick piers, which opened onto a path that curved gently to spice your anticipation with a hint of deferral. The short flight of steps to the verandah, announced by matching urns, tapered gently so the parapets seemed to gather you in as you ascended. And, after you had crossed the shaded boards or tessellated tiles and been admitted to the cool, dark passage beyond, that heavily embellished front door clicked shut behind you with solemn authority.

As approaches go, it could be highly intimidating, which was, of course, the intention. The aim was to impress upon you that you were leaving behind the vulgarity of the mundane world to enter a more orderly, sophisticated and cultured one.

It's easy to be judgmental, but the Victorians needed all the psychological bulwarks they could get. For them, city life beyond the limits of home could be anything but pleasant. Streets were dusty, smelly, noisy and disease-ridden, overrun with beggars, pickpockets and the dreaded larrikins, who enjoyed throwing stones and bottles at 'toffs' and spitting on their clothes.[1] No wonder many respectable women ventured out only when absolutely necessary, preferring to have the essentials delivered by itinerant tradesmen, to whom, of course, the front door did not open. They were sent to a tradesmen's entrance at the side or back, where, if she was sufficiently well-off, the woman of the house could avoid coming into contact with them altogether by leaving negotiations to a servant.

It is hardly surprising that, in their (in many ways admirable) efforts to raise themselves above the primitive conditions of earlier times and disengage from the squalor of their chaotic cities, Victorian middle-class homeowners developed something of a fortress mentality.

The theatre of arrival survives to this day albeit in a less dramatic form. The concrete-brick McMansions of our outer suburbs provide its most exuberant expression, with their baronial wrought-iron gates, their arched loggias and Greek

THE THEATRE OF ARRIVAL

pediments, although if the late Victorian version was Verdi at la Scala, this is Madonna at the Palladium. Yet even the most severe modern house will try to add some sense of occasion to your approach, if only by means of a cantilevered canopy and a pair of potted pencil-pines.

The theatre of arrival is also, of course, a theatre of departure, helping to soften the transition from private to public space by means of graduated steps. Closing the front door, we pause for a moment on the porch to adjust to the light before crossing the front garden to the gate. Thus gently eased from private reverie into civic consciousness, we turn with confidence into the street—'our' street, familiar and reassuringly local—and move from there to progressively more alien territories.

From front porch to garden, to street, main road, suburb, city, nation: home is the hub from which we situate ourselves in a huge unknown space, 'the point we start from', as TS Eliot put it. (Do children still write on the covers of their books 'Jennie Smith, 10 Oak Street, Burwood, Melbourne, Victoria,

Unburden the Queen Anne

AFTER the bursting of the land boom of the 1890s, Australian house fashion swung round to Queen Anne. This example has almost, but not quite, all the gimmicks of its period. There is the turret-like spire, broken roof, ridge ornaments, ornate chimney, arches and wood in-fill, false half timbering, weatherboards cut to imitate shingles, and colored leadlight windows. Missing are the terra cotta gargoyles.

With a dominating feature such as the turret, which is so much out of harmony with modern architectural ideals, very little can be done aesthetically without removing the feature altogether, as has been done here.

The sun-room extension to the room on the right hand side might have been given a gable roof, but it is not always possible to match the color of the old tiles, and those which were retrieved from the removal of the spire-like roof feature were used to patch up the existing roof. Therefore, the new portion has been given a flat roof.

The removal of the arches has given a broader and less closed-in effect to the right hand part of the house.

IF YOU WERE SADDLED WITH A DOWDY OLD HOUSE LIKE THIS, YOU COULD MODERNISE IT BY RIPPING OUT THE TURRET, FRETWORK AND CHIMNEYPOT AND INSTALLING AN ALUMINIUM WINDOW OR TWO. THE IMPROVEMENT WOULD HAVE BEEN SELF-EVIDENT TO MOST *HOME BEAUTIFUL* READERS IN 1960.

Australia, the World, the Universe', as once they did in those innocent days before 'virtual' space?)

A Shady Canopy

'A verandah', writes David Malouf, 'is not part of the house. Even a child knows this. It is what allows travelling salesmen, with one foot on the step, to heave their cases over the threshold and show their wares with no embarrassment on either side, no sense of privacy violated'.[2]

Although it is by no means an Australian invention, we have nonetheless adopted the verandah as our own. Historian Robert Irving has traced it back to the courtyards of the Iberian peninsula in the Middle Ages (although they are predated by the quite impressive one encircling the Parthenon in Athens). From there it was introduced to Brazil, the West Indies and southern India, where it proved very effective against tropical heat and downpours. The Dutch built verandahs in South Africa against the hot sun, as did the British in India.[3]

The simple, unadorned Georgian style of architecture the British brought to the Australian colonies was suited only to cooler places such as Hobart, where it survived quite happily without the need for add-ons. In the rest of the country, it soon became apparent that an external wall left unprotected made the house unbearable in summer. Sydney was full of worldly men who had served in India, the Mediterranean and Central and South America. They knew the benefits of a shady canopy around the house. Substantial verandahs, intended as much for show as for practicality, but ideal for elegant summer parties, were appearing on Sydney's grander houses from the very earliest years of settlement. The fashion quickly spread, to the extent that the verandah became 'perhaps the outstanding contribution to the distinctive architecture of Australia in the nineteenth century'.[4]

However, Australia's climate was not like India's. Even Sydney was cold and gloomy at times. So, by the latter part of the century, it was realised that verandahs had to be made narrower to admit the winter sun.

On farmhouses, the 'high crowned roof and drooping verandah ... became as familiar and typically country Australian as a midday dinner of roast mutton and steamed pudding', as Robin Boyd put it.[5] In the suburbs, narrow blocks and milder coastal climates restricted verandahs to the front and rear of the house, although they were sometimes very usefully extended part-way down one side.

A side verandah, especially a north-facing one, was the perfect spot to relax and entertain at a time when the backyard with its privy, clothesline, wash-house and woodshed was not something you wanted visitors to see. Here you could be relatively cool and, with the addition of a lattice screen at the front end, out of view of the street. A clutch of wicker chairs, a small table and a hardy palm in a brass jardinière meant you could enjoy an alfresco lunch or Devonshire tea without sacrificing civility.

The front verandah was not so often used, since relaxing or entertaining in full view of the street was not thought proper. Relaxing on the front porch is more of an American than an Australian habit, although it was acceptable for grandma or grandpa to sit there of an evening watching the traffic. The front verandah was also a convenient trysting place, where young Violet could hold

People were driven to live and sleep on the verandah partly because the verandah itself made the interior less bearable.

hands with her beau after dinner, well away from inquisitive younger siblings, yet public enough to ensure that holding hands was as far as it went.

The 1890s depression put a dent in the confident expectations of the middle-classes. Ostentatious displays of prosperity were much less in evidence after 1900 than they had been during the boom years of the 1880s. Houses, on average, were much smaller and verandahs could no longer justify their expense. Perversely, this turned them into status symbols in the better suburbs, where, according to *Home Beautiful*, a substantial entrance porch, with concrete columns and wrought-iron balustrade, singled you out as civic-minded. 'Its architectural charm will raise, as its lack of charm will lower, the tone of its entire neighborhood and, incidentally, the spirits of all who pass by.'[6] Which was all very well for some.

Meanwhile, the popular press tried hard to put a positive spin on the straitened circumstances of the majority. 'Like folk songs, native costumes and customs,' chirped one journalist hopefully, 'small houses more intimately express the character of the people themselves than the environment of the wealthy and superior upper classes, particularly in a young nation'.[7]

Whether or not they expressed the character of the people, small, utilitarian houses certainly revealed the state of the economy. In 1924, the Commonwealth Government released some new designs under the War Service Homes scheme: modest two-bedroom cottages that could be built cheaply and quickly to overcome the housing shortage. While the Western Australian house sported an extensive verandah across the front and half-way down both sides, the New South Wales design could boast little more than a porch. It was a realistic response to climate differences.

Needless to say, the warmer and more humid the weather, the more prominent the verandah was likely to be, and the more often it was used. In Queensland and the Northern Territory, it was, writes John Archer,

a dining room, a recreation centre, playground for the young on wet or scorching days, store room and vantage point ... Suspended from its rafters were the meat safe, the water bag, the clothesline in bad weather, swings for the children, bird cages, the Christmas hams and numerous pieces of wire or hooks on which to hang hats, bags and overcoats. At night it was the coolest place to sleep, with a mosquito net carefully tucked in for protection from the abundant tropical insect life.[8]

Yet even here it was less popular than it had been. Addressing the Queensland Auctioneers and Land Agents' Association in 1924, the architect AH Conrad conceded that,

> Formerly a verandah entirely round a house was considered a necessity—now the tendency is to place a large roomy, more or less square, verandah like an open-air room on the most favored side, and use large over-hanging eaves to keep the sun off the exposed walls. These open-air rooms can be made most attractive if they are designed so as to be reasonably proof against storms, and be furnished with seagrass furniture and floor covering.[9]

By this time it was acknowledged that an encircling verandah 10-feet deep not only made the house gloomy in cool weather, it actually impeded the circulation of air through the interior. Lattice screens, which increase the velocity of breezes, helped a little, as did the alignment of doors and windows, but, paradoxically, people were driven to live and sleep on the verandah partly because the verandah itself made the interior less bearable.

By the 1920s, however, with terracotta tiles on the roof, flywire screens on windows and doors, and (if you were really up with the latest) an electric fan suspended from the ceiling, you could remain quite comfortable inside in hot weather, especially if your house had been designed for cross-ventilation. In the popular imagination, the big verandah was now a symbol specifically of rural life.

It was not just a question of health, comfort and financial benefit, but of fashion too. Modernising old homes in the 1930s and 1940s meant replacing the dowdy old front verandah with a smart Art Deco porch (that is, if you were reduced to living in an old house in the first place, which was definitely not the preferred option). 'Australia wants bright, clean, fresh-looking homes, simple and pleasing in design', declared *Home Beautiful*. 'We can't all build new homes, but we can all at least make the most of what we have to live in.'[10] A couple of decades later, when 'old' had been reborn as 'heritage', all those ugly concrete porches would have to be knocked down and replaced with replicas of the original verandahs.

Out Back

The back verandah was much more utilitarian. It was where the dog slept on a flea-ridden potato sack. It was where firewood or bags of briquettes were stacked ready to be taken inside. Mud-caked gardening boots and old raincoats waited there beside the flywire door, gathering colonies of redbacks over summer. If you weren't careful, the back verandah might even be the death of you. 'Wash water, dish water, and all kinds of slop and refuse are thrown out in one spot at the back door,' warned *Home and Health* darkly in 1909.

> The dirt is washed away until a sink-hole is formed. Weeds and grass grow rank in such places; filthy worms and insects multiply on such a feeding ground, and under the summer sun the filth festers and steams, and throws off myriads of disease-producing germs, endangering the household. Frequently such a pest-hole as this is the cause of a neighbourhood pestilence, with death and the grave following after.[11]

Half a century earlier, the back verandah had served to separate the kitchen from the rest of the house. The kitchen would not be admitted under the main roof until the cast-iron stove with sealed firebox came into widespread use around the mid 1800s.

The copper in the wash-house was a fire risk too. Even after gas or electricity had been connected, wet clothes still had to be put through the wringer, then carted outside to the clothesline, so it made sense for the wash-house to remain outdoors. From the early 1900s it was tacked on to the back of the house with a door off the verandah.

The lavatory also paused by the back verandah for a while on its way from the bottom of the yard to the interior. For the middle-classes, that process began in the early 1900s, although working-class households held out longer, mainly because they couldn't afford flushing systems. Although *Home and Health* was steadfast in

IN 1886, THE ARTIST
FREDERICK MCCUBBIN
PAINTED THIS VIEW OF THE
BACK OF THE OLD BAKERY IN
INNER MELBOURNE WHERE
HE WAS BORN AND GREW UP.
THE KITCHEN, SEPARATED
FROM THE REST OF THE
HOUSE, OPENS ONTO A SMALL
COURTYARD.

FREDERICK McCUBBIN
*GIRL WITH BIRD AT THE KING
STREET BAKERY* 1886
OIL ON CANVAS
40.7 X 46.0 CM
NATIONAL GALLERY OF
AUSTRALIA

its belief that the healthiest place for the lavatory was off the back verandah, it had to acknowledge that inside near the bedrooms was more convenient.

In short, the back verandah was a rough-and-tumble all-purpose access point for the necessary animal functions.

Traditionally, the family came and went through the back door, leaving the front for visitors. A subtle protocol reigned, whereby the immediate family, neighbours, tradesmen and the kids' playmates went around the back, while aunts and uncles, doctors, ministers of religion and visiting strangers (in fact, anyone who had to be protected from the grubby realities of daily existence) were expected to go to the front. To make the wrong choice was to court social embarrassment, for to be granted regular use of the back door was a sign that you'd been accepted into the family—that, for you, the barriers of formality had been lifted. (This did not apply to tradesmen, which is why, to avoid confusion, larger houses provided them with an entrance of their own.) The rules were put aside for wedding recep-

Meanwhile, at the wealthier end of town, architects were latching onto the 'outdoor room' idea and investing it with a bit of class.

tions, wakes, christenings and other ceremonial occasions, when everybody got to use the front.

As the backyard utilities moved inside or became redundant, back verandahs lost much of their purpose. They too began to shrink. Those that remained were filled in. For young couples who'd been able to afford only the basic minimum when they married and wanted to extend once a family was on the way, a sleepout was the answer. Boys, it was thought, would be toughened by the bracing night air that whistled through the closed louvres. Besides, his relegation to a makeshift room at the back of the house reinforced a lad's position at the bottom of the family pecking order, which gave him something to strive for and helped to build his character. Filling in the back verandah became such a common practice, in fact, that sleepouts began to be incorporated as features on new house designs: sometimes weatherboard to waist height with the rest flywire. As well as satisfying the fresh-air brigade, they allowed speculative builders to boast of an extra bedroom without the expense of actually having to provide it.

Eric and Doris Fairs bought 1½ acres at Embleton, outside Perth, for £27 10s soon after their marriage in 1949. Like many others at the time, they built their own house in their spare time, using asbestos sheets on a timber frame. It comprised just two small bedrooms, kitchen, bathroom, hall and front porch, with a lounge and diningroom to be added later when shortages had eased. By 1958, with four children in tow, they had built a sleepout for the three boys, Stephen, Trevor and Neil, while privileged Cindy kept the second bedroom to herself. Wardrobes were positioned between the boys' beds for privacy.[12]

If you had no need of an extra bedroom, the verandah might be enclosed with glass as a utility room or, in cooler areas, an ersatz greenhouse, alive with rubber plants and red geraniums lined up on shelves or artfully arranged on wrought-iron plant stands.

Meanwhile, at the wealthier end of town, architects were latching onto the 'outdoor room' idea and investing it with a bit of class. A Californian

ANY HOME HANDYMAN COULD CONVERT AN UNWANTED BACK VERANDAH OR SLEEPOUT INTO A RUMPUS ROOM FOR CASUAL ENTERTAINING AND INDOOR GAMES. THIS ONE, WITH A PLYWOOD FEATURE WALL BEHIND THE BAR, REPRESENTED THE LAST WORD IN SMART 1960S STYLING.

THE BACKYARD BARBECUE
AT ITS MOST BASIC: A
CONFIDENT ASSERTION OF
MASCULINE VALUES OVER
THE PRISSY SOPHISTICATION
OF THE DININGROOM. THIS
PHOTOGRAPH WAS TAKEN IN
MELBOURNE IN 1968.

bungalow designed by the Melbourne firm of Knight and Harwood in 1927 featured a glassed-in 'verandah lounge' at the rear, which opened directly off the sitting room, to which it offered a sunny, informal alternative.[13] 'Another matter that greatly affects the attraction of a house is plenty of doors to the garden', advised *Home Beautiful*. 'French doors opening on to verandahs or loggias help quite a lot, and are very easily provided in old walls.'[14] Modern sanitation was at last making possible a back garden worth stepping out into.

In the radical home of architect AJ Le Gerche in Melbourne's Heidelberg, completed on the eve of World War II, all the principal rooms faced the back, with glass walls opening on to a paved terrace that made up fully one-third of the building's total floor area.[15] 'There can be no doubt', declared one critic confidently,

that great changes are imminent. Deplore it as we may, it seems inevitable that the day of the picturesque 'period' house is done, save for a small proportion of the population. The day of concrete, stainless steel and

> glass is at hand, together with planning based on almost purely scientific,
> as apart from social, considerations. Efficiency is the keynote.[16]

The influential architect Best Overend agreed, predicting in 1938 (wrongly, as it turned out) that the home of 1960 would be as efficiently designed as a car or an aeroplane, 'where everything is cut to the minimum except the material. There are no gable fronts on Boeing bombers', he added, as if that clinched the argument.[17] His timing wasn't good, however, since bombers would not present a particularly reassuring image over the following few years.

Overend was perceptive enough to realise that inexpensive new materials such as asbestos sheeting and large panes of industrially-produced glass would eventually become a practical alternative to bricks and mortar, thanks to advances in insulation and passive-solar design, providing all the advantages of the open-air house without the associated discomforts.

Outdoor Living

'Outdoor living' is a term few people would have understood, let alone used, before World War II. The occasional picnic in the country was diverting, of course, and corned beef and salad on the verandah might be acceptable of a summer evening, provided it was kept in the family. Otherwise, eating outdoors was thought uncivilised. Social historian Mark Thomson says that 'during the depression, ... the sorts of people who ate outside were people who'd lost their houses ... the unemployed people. I had one old bloke saying to me, it was something that drovers, people on the dole and Aborigines did, ate outside. He just thought it was disgusting'.[18] In any case, exposure to the sun risked ruining a lady's fashionable pallor. Pale skin had always been a sign of refinement. Only labourers had suntans.

In the 1920s, however, with beach-going newly popular, 'tanned skin became the golden emblem of beauty and freedom', although obviously only among the well-honed young.[19] Given that the house was being opened up to the elements, why not get out of it altogether and enjoy the fresh air, just as Hollywood stars did? They all looked healthy and happy enough. A swimming pool was almost certainly out of the question but there was nothing to stop you reclining with the latest issue of *Home* in a canvas deckchair under the clothesline.

A prize-winning small-house design at Melbourne's Exhibition of Domestic Architecture in 1928 included a stone-paved outdoor 'dining terrace' opening from both the formal diningroom and the breakfast nook.[20] It was unusual because terraces were generally thought to be for private relaxation rather than eating, so not everyone would have been impressed.

The word 'terrace' signified class. 'Patio'—derived from Spanish—was more down-market. Patios first appeared on the Spanish–mission style house of the early 1930s, whose rounded arches and candy-twist columns conjured up the carefree, outdoorsy Californian lifestyle. The patio was like a verandah without a roof—inexpensive, practical and adaptable—and it quickly made itself at home in the suburbs.

Although eating outside was more acceptable after the war, it usually meant a light luncheon brought out on a tray from the kitchen. When eating outdoors, advised *Women's Weekly* primly, 'minimise table appointments but carefully preserve table niceties'.[21] Advertisements for outdoor furniture, which started to appear in women's magazines at this time, showed men seated comfortably on folding canvas chairs around a wrought-iron or wicker table in open-necked shirts and jackets, while their womenfolk, in gay cotton frocks, served tea, soft drinks and canapés. Never wine: only foreigners drank wine with their meals. Being 'Continental' had its limits.

What really gave the patio a sense of purpose, however, making it something everyone had to have, was the barbecue. The home barbecue was something we picked up from the Americans—it had been a cultural tradition in the southern United States since Civil War days—which may be why polite Australians

The portable barbecue turned the demure alfresco luncheon into the backyard booze-up.

dismissed it as vulgar. American servicemen billeted in Brisbane and Sydney during World War II may have helped by giving it an edge of sexiness.

It first manifested itself as a bulky brick construction in an out-of-the-way part of the backyard, often plonked quite inappropriately beside the incinerator. While dad fought off the engulfing smoke at the bottom of the yard, the family waited expectantly at the kitchen table for his charred offerings to be brought in. The brick barbie was a DIY favourite because it required some basic design skills and provided bricklaying practice, even if it generally turned out to be useless.

It was not until portable models appeared in the early 1950s—the iconic Weber Kettle was one of the earliest—that the weekend family barbie became an Australian institution. The Weber was efficient and trouble-free. You just wheeled it out onto the patio and put it away again when you were finished: no mess, no fuss. More to the point, however, it altered the whole perception of mealtime. So long as the kitchen remained the centre of operations, the housewife reigned, but outdoor cooking was a bloke thing (even if the ladies still had to prepare the salad indoors). Sausages, steaks and beer became the staple fare. The portable barbecue turned the demure alfresco luncheon into the backyard booze-up.

Mr Morrison of Turrumurra had the 'perfect culinary setup', according to *Home Beautiful* in 1959. His entire back garden had been turned into a barbecue area, opening off the livingroom via sliding glass doors, boldly tiled and fully equipped with colourful banana lounges, an elaborate metal grill, plant tubs and bamboo blinds that could 'be drawn right across to give protection from a too-hot sun or from heavy dews at night'.[22] While Mr Morrison pokes happily at the coals, his wife (whose name the magazine does not think to mention) and Brian, his son, wait at a respectful distance with plastic plates poised for his offerings. Like hordes of males who followed, he is the big-game hunter, the masculine provider, cooking the day's kill at the mouth of the cave. The whole ritual was a corrective to the prissy sophistication of the diningroom and a stern rebuke to the effeteness of 1960s counter-culture. It reasserted the Australian bush myth, as expressed so succinctly by Paul Hogan's 'I'll slip another shrimp on the barbie for you' campaign for the Australian Tourism Commission in the mid 1980s: an affectionate dig at Australia's masculine self-image, glossed for an urban American market (Australians call them prawns and, in any case, are more likely to be slipping a slab of beef on the grill).

Swimming at Home

The barbecue's reign as the centre of backyard attention was short. Soon the swimming pool would relegate it to the status of mere accessory. Everyone aspired to a backyard pool but hardly anyone could afford one. A pool with landscaped surrounds and bathing pavilion was the supreme symbol of wealth and glamour. In 1935, Beverley Hills Mansions, a block of flats in Melbourne's ultra-fashionable South Yarra, boasted one worthy of Hollywood, with a smart Art Deco footbridge, outdoor lighting and sphinxes moulded in concrete. It's still there, heritage protected, if a little worse for wear. Not only were such extravagances expensive to build but, in the absence of efficient filtration systems and chemical decontaminants, an absolute nightmare to maintain.

If you were really keen, you could try building your own, by excavating the hole with a shovel and hand-mixing the tons of concrete required. *Home Beautiful* swore it could be done for just £25, but anyone taking it on would have found it not quite as straightforward as they'd been led to believe.

By the late 1950s, however, Australians had a lot more disposable income and pools were cheaper. 'The idea of a personal pool for the family has struck an instant response from thousands of Australians who have been brought up to accept the daily or at least week-end trek to the baths or beach as part of their summer existence', enthused *Home Beautiful* in 1959.[23] Parents who had long harboured doubts about sanitation at public baths, along with children tired of being bullied by the young toughs who hung about at the deep end, were more than eager, but, as is so often the case, the realities didn't live up

THIS FAMILY'S POOL WOULD
HAVE BEEN THE ENVY OF
THE NEIGHBOURHOOD IN
1969, SINCE FEW COULD
AFFORD SUCH A LUXURY.
SO FEW, IN FACT, THAT NO
POOL-SAFETY REGULATIONS
HAD BEEN INTRODUCED.

to the promises. For £10 10s you could get a Hill's Paddlepool, but that was only for toddlers to sit in. The Port-a-Pool, which was 21 feet in diameter and 3 feet 6 inches deep—big enough to swim in so long as you didn't want to swim far—would set you back a hefty £250. Made of reinforced plastic over a wire mesh, it could be folded up and put in the garage over winter. If you wanted filtration, however, you had to rig something up yourself.

Only with the advent of full-size pre-fabricated fibreglass shells in the late 1960s did backyard pools really become a practical proposition for the well-off family, and only a decade after that—when initial teething problems had been ironed out—would they become even moderately popular.

Like the lavatory and the wash-house before it, today the pool is inching its way indoors. First it is encircled by a wooden deck that comes right up to the glass doors of the family room, then it is roofed over, with dressing room, spa and shower provided nearby. The heated pool in its own glass-roofed pavilion is today's supreme status-symbol, and solar heating will add an affirming dash of environmental responsibility.

Do people really entertain outdoors as often as estate agents and television lifestyle shows claim they do? The statistics suggest otherwise. Outdoor entertaining is probably more a feature of glossy magazines than actual backyards. It's a symbol: of our relaxed attitudes; our supposed love of the great outdoors; our affluence; and our fantasies of social equality (after all, it's not easy to put on airs and graces when you're standing in wet bathers with a burnt sausage in one hand and a can of beer in the other). Our relaxed outdoorsiness is supposedly what sets us apart from those staid and less-blessed folk overseas.

In the real world, meanwhile, Australians are more than ever spending their home-time indoors, playing computer games and watching the cricket on television. Oblivious to the backyard pool—dry all summer in any case because of water restrictions—and the Weber rusting in the garage, we gravitate instead to the home theatre to be entertained by Brad Pitt or the Simpsons. It is far less strenuous and it saves us having to make conversation.

Once
Inside

The End of the Passage

Diana thought for a moment and said: 'Are you dining anywhere? Would you like to stay to a picnic supper? The servants are out' ... They were in the drawing-room and she asked him: 'Shall we have supper in here? We often do on Sunday night. The dining-room is so large and gloomy for two people. But it means carrying the trays all the way up the passage.'[1]

That was the trouble with passages: they necessitated an awful lot of traipsing up and down with trays. At least the wealthy socialites in Martin Boyd's novel had servants, even if they were inconsiderate enough to go out occasionally. After World War I, however, those with servants were in the minority. For everyone else, the long passage was just a burdensome remnant of more affluent times.

It had been adapted from the long gallery in the grand house, which provided a convenient means of getting from one room to another without having to intrude upon the rest. The long gallery, in turn, was adapted from the medieval cloister, which served much the same purpose.

Except for the draught of cooling air it created in summer when the doors at either end were opened, the passage in the Australian house had never been practical. Unlike the cloister, which circled around the inside of the building, enclosing a courtyard, it was little more than an alimentary canal that started self-importantly at the front door only to splutter out in a messy rear end. It created a dreary first impression and divided the house into two halves.

Although the working classes in inner-city terraces had never enjoyed the luxury of servants, they had to put up with the inconvenience of the long passage anyway, because this was the easiest way to organise a deep, narrow floorplan, despite the fact that it consumed a quarter of the width of the house. The various rooms opened off it in orderly progression, with some kind of decorative arch or fretwork screen about half-way down to mark an important point of transition. The front rooms, to which visitors were usually confined, constituted the civilised part of the house, and this little archway gently signalled where civility gave way to the animal: that is, the kitchen, bathroom, lavatory and other parts associated with the base bodily functions. Beyond them lay the backyard, which was quite literally animal.

Long passages, complained one working-class South Melbourne house-wife before World War I,

> are enough to give a woman varicose veins in these single fronted houses running up and down for the butcher and baker, as every one of them must come to the front door ... She may be at the back of the house and if a tap is running she cannot hear anyone at the front door until perhaps a neighbour calls out 'Mrs so-and-so, your front door is being knocked down' ... That means she must keep her mind upon both her work and the front door and race up and down the passage perhaps six times in a morning, which is a great waste of energy.[2]

The *Age* suggested helpfully that a 'receptacle for parcels, letters and cards would save a good deal of the weariness of answering doorbells.'[3]

The respectable middle-class house in Melbourne's eastern suburbs in which Cliff Page was born in 1911 had 'a wide hallway with a carpet runner its full length. At each of the four doorways letting on to this passage was a small mat, tasselled each end'. On the left were the drawingroom and diningroom, and on the right two large bedrooms.

THE ENTRANCE HALL IN THE EDWARDIAN-STYLE HOUSE AT LAST ALLOWED THE STAIRCASE A STARRING ROLE.

At the end of the hall was yet another solid door similar to that at the front and like it with coloured glass panes each side. I think that, when the house was built, there would have been a small porch or walkway from here to the right where the kitchen was situated. By the time I arrived on the scene a vestibule had been built at the end of the passage. It was in this room that we normally ate the evening meal.[4]

It was typical of the period that the family gravitated towards the back near the kitchen while the rest of the house languished. The passage did more to impede the flow of people through the building than to facilitate it.

A radical rethink was long overdue, and tighter economic times provided the impetus. Smaller, less affluent modern families couldn't afford such a waste of space and in any case were far less constrained by social protocols. The demand was for compact, easy-care homes. Priding themselves on their modern, scientific attitudes, architects and builders responded with new, more flexible ways of arranging rooms. A 'daring innovation'[5] around 1911 was the side entrance, opening onto a short lateral hall behind the livingroom.

If, instead of a long, straight passage, you had an entrance hall or foyer, it was much easier to make your guests feel at home. They could mill about in a foyer, as they couldn't in a passage. It made greetings and farewells more relaxed and convivial. On the other hand, if you wanted to delay your hospitality for any reason, you might ask your caller to wait in the hall on the hard wooden settle provided for the purpose, although, depending on who you were, that might have been considered pompous. More often than not, the settle was used as just another dumping place for umbrellas and handbags.

To our eyes today, the entrance halls in these old houses might seem rather gloomy, but that was the point. 'Dark tones usually look well', advised *Australian Home Builder* in 1924, 'in contrast with the more colorful rooms opening off it'.[6] The dimness of the hall added a touch of drama: what architects refer to as 'compression and release'.

The erotic allure of Gloria Swanson
gliding down the stairs in a low-cut silk
nightie had not gone unnoticed.

Often virtually a room in its own right, with its decorative stained-glass window, tessellated-tile floor and dark-stained wainscoting, the hall at last allowed the staircase a starring role. In the Victorian terrace house it had been steep and narrow, jammed against the wall to one side of the passage as just an inconvenient necessity. Now it had room to breathe, and its beautifully crafted banisters and newel posts greatly enhanced the romantic, if sometimes ponderous, Arts and Crafts atmosphere.

While most houses built in the 1920s may have been smallish and unassuming, the economic outlook was sunny for the first time in years and people naturally wanted to let their hair down and enjoy themselves. The erotic allure of Gloria Swanson gliding down the stairs in a low-cut silk nightie had not gone unnoticed even in the suburbs of Melbourne and Sydney. It was a great way to make an entrance.* So, if you could afford it, you got yourself an elegant staircase, and even if you couldn't, you understood its symbolic importance. It was a bit of a tease, though, for while it beckoned, it also rebuffed. Everyone understood that the rooms above were private and out of bounds, no matter how inviting the staircase might look.

An entrance hall was like a shop window. It had to make an impression. 'Let the hall be an index to your home', advised *Home Beautiful* in 1931. 'Visitors receive first impressions from it, and the effect of faultlessly decorated and furnished living rooms will be spoilt if entered through an ugly and carelessly treated hall.'[7] Here you presented a summary of your taste. The pictures, vases and items of furniture in the hall were an indication of how you saw yourself, or, more accurately, how you wanted others to see you. Even with something as casual and insignificant as a couple of flowery straw hats on the hall-stand you could deftly paint yourself as a sun-loving free spirit. The colour scheme, advised *Home Beautiful*, should complement that of the livingroom, although 'this rule does not apply to any bedrooms opening off an entrance hall, for the doors of bedrooms placed thus should always be kept shut'.[8]

* But not so good for an exit. Descending was more erotically charged than ascending because it allowed you to flirt with whomever was waiting below.

The entrances photographed for the magazine article were clearly a cut above the average: an object lesson in taste for others not so blessed. Elegantly, if sparsely, furnished with side tables, lamps, a chair or two and some carefully chosen ornaments and pictures, they stand as the very embodiment of decorum and restraint, hinting enticingly at luxuries beyond.

Even at this late stage, however, no telephone receivers disturb the urbane atmosphere. An ugly mechanical object that was difficult to conceal, the tele-

PROTECTION

So safe . . Home dangers disappear with a telephone. The surest protection—the speediest summons for help . . doctor . . nurse . . police . . fire brigade . . friends are **all** at the other end of the wire . . you get them instantly. In **every** emergency the telephone is your very first aid. For this reason alone it is worth the rental of a few pence per day.

It is the greatest convenience your home can possess. It maintains friendships, keeps you posted in all affairs . . saves journeys near or far, and is a satisfactory personal form of contact. It eliminates distance and makes your home a haven of comfort.

INSTAL A
TELEPHONE

CALL OR WRITE TO THE SUPERINTENDENT, TELEPHONE BRANCH.   (Telephone BY4443).

IN THE 1930S, PEOPLE STILL HAD TO BE CONVINCED OF THE TELEPHONE'S BENEFITS, EVEN IF THAT MEANT PLAYING ON THEIR FEARS.

phone had yet to be successfully integrated into the refined parts of the home (mechanical things being mainly restricted to kitchen and bathroom), so attitudes to it remained ambivalent. Although there could be no doubting its usefulness, it stuck out like a sore thumb. Eventually, for better or worse, the entrance hall would become the natural home of the handset, but it took time for telephones to make an impression.

Suburbia gets Connected

The telephone was the first technology to disembody the human voice, initially an alarming prospect that took some getting used to. It heralded a number of life-changing technological innovations that would transform Australian domestic life during the twentieth century.

Australia's first switchboard opened in 1880, a mere four years after the man credited with inventing the telephone, Alexander Graham Bell, had been granted his patent. It says something about the brash self-assurance of the governing classes that such a startling and untried new technology should have attracted investors so quickly. Not that everyone was seduced, Sydney's superintendent of telegraphs dismissing it as 'another Yankee toy'.[9] As it happened, the majority of Australians agreed, and decades would pass before they overcame their antagonism.

But it was never actually intended for them anyway. Initially, the telephone was marketed solely as a tool of government and business. It was too expensive for home use and the idea that it might be handy for sociable conversation among friends and relatives had not really occurred to anyone, or was at least too frivolous to be taken into account. In any case, there was little point in owning a handset unless others you wanted to contact had one too, even if it could be useful in an emergency, or to check with Anthony Hordern and Sons about the dress material they'd ordered in for you.

Although the direct line established between Melbourne and Sydney in 1907 was hailed as a boon to politicians and businessmen, hardly anyone foresaw any benefit to the householder. Much progress was being made. For instance, automatic exchanges meant that you no longer had to call up an operator and ask to be connected. Nevertheless, by 1912, when the first automatic exchange was opened in Geelong, there were just 102 654 subscribers in the entire country, only a small proportion of them domestic, which even federal government ministers had to concede was disappointing.[10]

Not until the late 1920s might you expect to find a telephone in the better class of home. Even so, the handset—of the pedestal type with an earpiece dangling from a hook on one side—would most likely have been installed on father's desk in the den or home office, where he could keep an eye on it. Growing up in the eastern suburbs of Melbourne in the 1920s, Rita Reaby was quite accustomed to the wall-phone at the end of the passage by the kitchen door, which must have made her the envy of her school friends, but it was there for the use of her father, who ran a printing business from a shed in the backyard. 'There was an outside bell on the back verandah so he could hear it ringing over the noise of the press', she remembers. 'I never took any notice of it. It was just there for dad and the business. I don't think the family ever used it for social calls.'[11]

Only very gradually, as home-bound women realised its value for 'keeping in touch', did the instrument's real potential come to be appreciated. This, claims social historian Judy Wajcman, was an early example of how consumers can determine the use to which a new technology is put, despite what its manufacturers intend: that is, of the way society affects technology as opposed to the way technology affects society.[12]

Once it had been accepted not only as a social convenience but also as a status symbol in its own right, the telephone gravitated to the entrance hall. Here you could hold a conversation without disturbing the household and without being overheard. It was also nice to be able to announce to visitors that you were sophisticated and wealthy enough to own one. Telephones were great indicators of class. As late as 1937, there were, on average, only 87 telephones for every 1000 people in Australia, a figure that includes all business connections.[13]

The photograph on this page shows the ultra-modern entrance hall of a very superior home in Sydney's Vaucluse, designed by architects Fowell, McConnel and Mansfield in 1936, that appears to be centred entirely on the telephone receiver. There it sits, the centre of attention, on its own custom-made desk, a leather-covered notepad and comfortable chair in attendance.[14] Some wealthy folk went even further by installing a telephone booth—glazed, of course, so as to encourage envious guests to peer inside as they passed.

As in so many other aspects of life, the telephone system's development was slowed almost to a standstill by the depression and the war that followed, and, of course, by government bureaucracy. By the time consumers could afford to take up the telephone with enthusiasm, the authorities found themselves unable to cope with demand. As a child on Sydney's inner North Shore in the early 1950s, Bert Jones remembers having to share a party line:

Lines were hard to get. We had one of those black telephones with a dial on the front and we shared the line with a number of houses on the other side of the valley. You'd pick up the phone and someone would be talking on it. They'd hear the click and there'd be an embarrassed silence until you hung up again, or else they'd have to ask you to get off the line, not always politely. As a child, I rather enjoyed hearing

UNIQUE AND RARELY LOVELY WOODS, DOMESTIC AND EXOTIC, A WORLD-FAMOUS COLLECTION AT THE ARCHITECTURAL SHOWROOMS AND FACTORIES, BEALE AND COMPANY LIMITED, ANNANDALE SYDNEY.

FLUSH DOORS AND PANELLING
by Beale

RESIDENCE, VAUCLUSE, FOWELL, McCONNEL & MANSFIELD, ARCHITECTS

IN THE FOYER OF THIS FASHIONABLE HOME IN SYDNEY'S VAUCLUSE, PHOTOGRAPHED IN 1936, THE TELEPHONE TAKES PRIDE OF PLACE.

ERICOFON MAY NOT HAVE
BEEN VERY PRACTICAL, BUT
ITS SMART, MODERN DESIGN
MADE IT PERFECTLY AT
HOME IN THE LIVINGROOM.

snippets of people's conversations, their arguments and complaints and so on. I used to imagine what sort of lives they led, since we never met any of these people.[15]

Ericofon, a one-piece plastic handset from Scandinavia, was the last word in chic in the early 1960s. It looked rather like a duck sticking its head out of water, and its dial was on the base, so when you put it down the line cut off automatically, which led to a lot of prematurely truncated conversations. Telephones had not generally been thought of as designer objects before, but Ericofon was just that. It helped bring the handset out of the closet—or out of the draughty hall—and into the livingroom, on the coffee table beside the favourite armchair, where you could talk in comfort without having to leave the TV.

However smart it seemed, Ericofon was clumsy in use and never very popular. But its Australian-made counterpart, the 800-Series Automatic Color Phone, combined practicality with modest good looks and would find its way into millions of homes over the next couple of decades. Lacquer Red and Topaz Yellow were strictly for the adventurous (and tended to fade), Light Ivory being by far the most popular colour. Anything but black, which had been virtually the only choice for phones until then.

From 1975, when telephone services were taken from the old Postmaster General's Department and put under the control of Telecom, a new government-owned company, the aim was for every home to have at least one telephone with national and overseas direct dialling. That would be more or less achieved by the turn of the century.

Telecom's business ethic—as distinct from the old governmental approach of having technocrats decide what was best for people—opened up all kinds of possibilities. Pay an additional annual rental fee, for instance, and you could be happily pressing buttons instead of having to dial. You might choose to buy your own telephone and avoid paying rent altogether, which had not been possible in the past. Even a cordless phone was available, so long as you were prepared to fork out the considerable sum of $400.

It remained only to cut the umbilical cord altogether, freeing the telephone from any necessary connection to the house. That process began in the mid-1980s, although the mobile phone made little initial impact for the same reason that the telephone itself had struggled to find acceptance a hundred years earlier: it was very expensive and was marketed as a business tool.[16] But not for long. The mobile would prove a godsend to a generation that no longer thinks of the house as home, whose concept of community is centred

on peer groups rather than family, and for whom the division between leisure and working-life is less clearcut than it once was.

Highly mobile people want highly mobile communication systems. It makes life much simpler for those who often move house to avoid constant reconnections, with a change of telephone number each time. Lily Chan and the three other students with whom she shares a house rely exclusively on their mobiles. 'We wouldn't bother getting the landline connected. It just creates so many hassles about phone bills and whose name it's listed under and all that. This way, when someone moves out or moves in, there's no problem.'[17]

So quickly has the mobile taken over that the relatively new term 'landline' has already assumed a vaguely archaic ring, like 'gramophone' and 'ice chest'. Today we have the novel experience of needing to ask people where they are when we call them—it might be the corner shop or it might be Alaska— as well as the less enjoyable one of being force-fed the private, yet voluble, conversations of complete strangers wherever we go.

Portable and car radios, mobile phones, laptops and iPods are helping us to sever the ties that once bound us to the home, allowing us the luxury of having all to ourselves devices that once we would have had to share.

Putting Things Aside

Beyond the entrance hall, in the passage that led off it or perhaps on the upstairs landing, was the linen cupboard. This was an early nineteenth-century American idea that had proved so practical that it was adopted all over the world. The linen cupboard, or 'linen press' as it was known, was often built into the wainscoting as a standard fixture, and any house plan that omitted it would have been thought deficient.

In Victorian times, when linen (commonly known as 'manchester' because most of the cheaper kinds originated in that city's cotton mills) played a central symbolic role in married life, it warranted a small room of its own, 'opened by an important-looking key picked from the big bunch out of the housekeeper's basket by the lady of the house',[18] as *Home Beautiful* put it, adding a little embroidery to the tale. Each neatly stacked shelf, redolent of lavender or naphthalene, was carefully labelled: guest-towels; single and double sheets (Irish linen for mum and dad and the guest room, coarser manufactured linen for the kids, and plain cotton twill for the maid); napkins (single damask for everyday and double for special occasions); tablecloths (checked for breakfast, patterned for lunches, cream or white linen for formal meals); all the way down to pudding-cloths, which were washed, ironed and folded just as the more precious things were. An inventory on the back of the door carefully recorded every purchase and repair.

Every girl was expected to begin sewing for her trousseau while still at school, from fabric bought by the yard, with the aim of having at least a dozen of everything by the time she married. It was an essential rite of passage that might well involve all the women of the extended family. With regular darning and careful laundering, those items would last a lifetime.

As stocks multiplied at the big emporiums and prices for industrially-made cotton goods fell, even the moderately well-off housewife was saved the bother of having to sew them herself. And when they wore out, which they did much more readily, they could easily be replaced. Linen lost its ritual significance, becoming just another household commodity, although each new item might still have to be embroidered with the family name or monogram to ensure its safe return from the Chinese laundry.

Although brand names were common before World War II for household medicines, cosmetics, cleaners and so on, manchester (along with clothing) was rarely if ever advertised this way. What you were looking for was good quality weave in the right colour at the right price. If you were choosy, you might insist on Irish, Czechoslovakian or French linen, but you would never specify a particular 'make'. The branding of softgoods was a post–World War II American innovation.

By the late 1920s, the organised, well-stocked linen cupboard had almost gone. *Home Beautiful* mourned its passing, deriding 'the scantily-filled shelves of the small built-in cupboard of the average middle class home of today',[19] but the fact is, it had served its purpose, and few women missed it.

THE COSTANZO EMPORIUM IN COBURG, MELBOURNE, WAS POPULAR AMONG ITALIAN WOMEN FOR DOWRY ITEMS. THIS PICTURE WAS TAKEN IN THE LATE 1960S.

It did, however, enjoy a brief revival as post-war Italian and Greek immigrants brought their own dowry traditions with them, even strengthening those traditions in the face of new and unfamiliar social pressures on the family. For centuries, the dowry had been an important part of the marriage contract in these cultures, serving as a kind of pre-nuptial agreement. Linen held particular significance because, unlike the money, land, furniture and other goods that made up the dowry, it alone remained under female control.

In Australia, migrant women often went out to work, which allowed them a degree of independence. The garment industry was particularly appreciative of their sewing skills, which it exploited mercilessly. Paradoxically, as social historians Maria Tence and Elizabeth Triarico point out, this left women little time to use those skills in the preparation of their own family's dowry linens.[20] They were reduced to purchasing high-quality, ready-made goods from local Greek and Italian emporiums, which their daughters were likely to stash away in the linen cupboard without ever using, as being either too special or just too old-fashioned.

Flats and the Decline of Civilisation

The 1920s may have been a decade of relative prosperity between the awful depressions of the 1890s and 1930s, but it brought with it a profoundly changed society, less cohesive, less bullish and more apprehensive. While they revelled in material progress, many people feared for the loss of traditional moral and spiritual values.

One cause for moral concern was the proliferation of flats, particularly in Sydney. No normal family wanted to live in a flat, only young couples and working singles with doubtful reputations who had nothing better to do with their money. A young David McNicoll, whining in 1939 about the 'appalling decline' in Sydney's home-life, put the blame firmly on foreigners and flats, in that order. 'Where are the big homes?' he asked rhetorically:

Gone, gone. Razed, most of them, one after another, and on their lawns huge blocks of flats towering to the skies, modern prisons, in which twenty families sleep in pigeon-holed regularity ... Flats, flats, flats, the end of home life, the regimentation of the individual, the end of privacy, the breeding of curiosity. And like a canker, the flat evil grows, so that now it can never be checked.[21]

On this matter, at least, McNicoll's aristocratic snobbery chimed perfectly with the moral alarm of the suburban mum and dad. One problem was that you could not own a flat,* and renting carried a decidedly second-class connotation. In fact, most people did not own their own house, either (not until the early 1950s would the number of house-owners begin to overtake the number of house-renters), but the important thing was that you should aspire to ownership.

It was the entrance hall that was called upon to put a bit of shine on the tarnished reputation of apartment living.

McNicoll was right about the numbers of flats around Kings Cross and Elizabeth Bay. By the late 1930s they dominated the landscape. Conscious of the image problem, developers graced them with aristocratic English names such as 'Chesterfield', 'Macleay Regis' and 'Beverley Mansions'. Their 'entrance vestibules' (after the war, when a jazzy American feel was more in order, they would be called 'lobbies') were a glitzy amalgam of Hollywood and Buckingham Palace, dignified-looking stage-sets intended to counter those vile perceptions of loose morals. It didn't hurt that they also helped to justify high rents.

'Alighting from one's car beneath the porte cochere' of Birtley Towers in Elizabeth Bay, reported a magazine at the time,

a large spacious vestibule is entered, which, panelled with Queensland walnut flush panelling ... adorned with horizontal strips of golden tone,

* An exception was The Astor in Macquarie Street, built in 1923, where the apartments were owned on a company, or share, basis. One or two others followed. Generally speaking, however, own-your-own flats are a product of the 1950s, when the offices of titles in New South Wales and Victoria ruled that blocks of flats could legally be subdivided, allowing residents to hold individual (or 'strata') titles. That legislation prompted a boom in apartment building.

forms a delightful wall treatment. It is pierced by large windows infilled with 'Luxfer' glazing of modern design, while a modern radiator recess surmounted by a mantel and clock with a frosted glass surround illuminated from behind is an interesting piece of design in the modern manner. Immediately opposite this is what is known as the 'Fountain Mirror', that takes the form of a large mirror upon which is etched a formal fountain design. The ceiling is in the shape of a circular saucer dome, which, treated in a special plaster finish ... and illuminated by concealed lighting, is very effective.[22]

The mantle, although unconnected to any chimney, added a homely touch to all this showy modernity. Many of these elaborately decorated foyers survive today, with some of their former glory intact.

Twenty or thirty years later, when government housing commissions in Victoria and New South Wales started razing inner-city slums for high-rise apartment blocks, they were working on the reasonable-enough assumption that clean, efficient flats equipped with modern amenities would be welcomed by folk from derelict old cottages with outside dunnies and rising damp. But the euphoria didn't last long. It wasn't so much the flats themselves that proved to be the problem, but rather the lobbies, lifts and corridors leading to them, which quickly degenerated into grubby, dangerous wastelands. In the interests of economy, the social, psychological and symbolic importance of the entrance had been ignored. Government bureaucrats might have learned something from the developers of Birtley Towers.

The apartment buildings being put up by developers on Sydney's North Shore at this time suffered the same problem. Your apartment was no doubt a little oasis of elegance, with glorious harbour views, while outside, the streets of North Sydney remained leafy and pleasant, despite the proliferation of tower blocks. But between the two lay a grim negative space of concrete stairs and bunker-like lobbies to be scurried through as quickly as possible. They

DESIGNER BLEAKNESS:
THE FOYER OF HORIZON
TOWER IN SYDNEY

were areas that nobody felt any particular responsibility for, so nobody could be expected to waste their affection on them.

Today, at least at the top end of the market, lobbies are again sending strong signals: not of stately comfort and moral reassurance, as at Birtley Towers, but something altogether more hard-headed and unsentimental.

On entering Harry Seidler's Horizon Tower* in Darlinghurst, for example, one's first impression is of vast, bright, empty space and immaculate surfaces. A square of carpet with a clutch of leather and chrome chairs are the only concessions to comfort, marooned as they are on a sea of polished black marble with a big abstract by the American artist Sol Lewitt dominating the vast expanse of wall behind. According to one resident, 'the hard surfaces may stifle the emotions but they certainly amplify the sound'. The concierges, he has noticed, 'seem to overcompensate for the bleakness of their environment by turning up their chipperness to a cartoonish degree'.[23]

This bleakness is not the result of carelessness or false economy, however. It is designer bleakness. Horizon's awe-inspiring lobby is an antiseptic bulwark against the seediness of the streets outside, virtually indistinguishable from the foyer of a major bank or mining company, in recognition of the fact that many of its residents will be modelling their private lives on the corporate ethos. Whereas the foyer of Birtley Towers, despite its nods to modernism, looked backwards to a more stable world of established wealth, that of Horizon extols the acquisition of new wealth. The former is about having money, the latter about getting it.

* Unlike houses, apartment buildings have retained their names. This is partly because a glamorous-sounding name is a useful sales tool, but also because it gives residents a sense of group solidarity and belonging. There is kudos in being able to say 'I live in The Horizon'. In many ways it is the equivalent of a street name, the individual apartments within being assigned numbers. Today, apartment towers are likely to bear names that signify corporate optimism and technological progress, although the aristocratic English reference is still good for a touch of class.

The Adaptable Hall

As the apartment-tower lobby segued from old-world charm to new-world entrepreneurialism, the entrance hall in the suburban house was withering, a victim of quite different economic imperatives and the fashion for open-plan living. In earlier times, when extended families and paid employees crowded together under one roof, passages and halls, for all their faults, did at least form useful buffer zones, ensuring some privacy and segregation. Now that it was just mum, dad and a couple of kids, a lot more freedom was possible.

Although it dwindled from an independent room into just a screened-off corner of the livingroom, the entrance hall never entirely disappeared in Australia, as it did in the United States. But it did come perilously close. In 1968, the Casa Valenti, a medium-range project home at just over $10 000, made the best of economic necessity while muddling its nationalist metaphors with something optimistically called a shoji screen shielding the front door from the livingroom. It represented the entrance hall at its meanest and most depleted extent.[24] People on tight budgets willingly sacrificed these unnecessary elements if it meant having a well-equipped kitchen.

More salubrious was the Contemporary L3, marketed by Craig Davis Homes in response to a brand-new problem—the worrisome independent teenager. In effect, it revived the old passageway down one side, giving it a modern twist by glazing the outside wall and calling it a gallery, although on most suburban blocks it would have looked out onto nothing more interesting than a paling fence. Still, by separating parents from their noisy offspring, it helped preserve family harmony, which was every parent's goal in this time of generational conflict.[25] The Contemporary L3 was just one of many designs that tried to keep the family together by keeping it apart, with a hall or passage enlisted as a no-man's-land between the warring factions. They were a tacit acknowledgement that, when young Bobby was teaching himself the electric guitar, open-plan living didn't work.

EXTENSIVE USE OF GLASS MAKES FOR A BRIGHT, TRANSPARENT ENTRANCE, BUT DRAMA MUST BE SACRIFICED.

At one time, only a limited number of people would be admitted through your front door. Your circle of friends and relatives remained relatively stable. Today's social networks are generally wider and more fluid, meaning that many more people will be entering our houses for the first time, and that gives us added incentive to make a good first impression. As a consequence, the entrance hall is enjoying something of a comeback. We certainly have the space, with houses, on average, bigger but with fewer residents than ever before. And we can afford it: over the past decade, our disposable incomes have gone up by a massive 50 per cent.[26] So why not make a splash?

It may be, however, that while we long for the ceremonial trappings, we are not quite sure how to realise them. Our preoccupation with transparency and openness tends to dissipate drama. In advertising its Adobe Collection, for example, AV Jennings apparently sees no contradiction in simultaneously offering 'dramatic entrances' with 'a seamless indoor to outdoor flow'.[27] Is it possible to have both?

Instead of artfully choreographing the progression from dark to light, or subtly manipulating space for compression and release, today's expensive show-home piles on the eye-catching architectural features. Modern buyers would surely reject a half-lit hall as gloomy and depressing rather than seeing it as part of an experiential narrative. So water features, Doric columns, feature walls, sculptural reliefs and pink marble floors are enlisted in an attempt to compensate for a lack of atmosphere.

Call it flamboyant, call it kitsch, call it Tuscan or just bad taste, the grandiose hall is once again a part of suburban life (or some suburban lives anyway), still serving the function it has served since ancient times: that of creating a favourable first impression by announcing its owner's taste, wealth and sense of self-esteem.

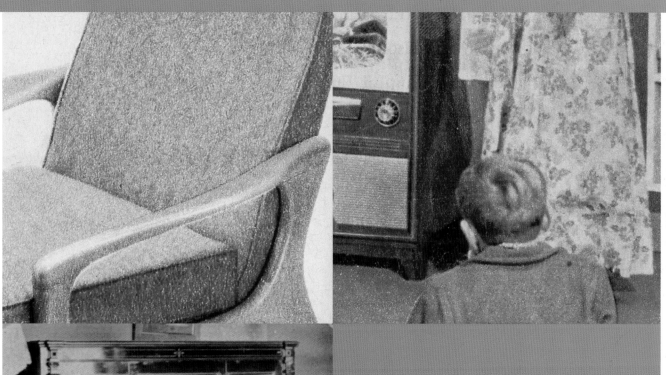

Come
into the
Parlour

The Small Family

When the master of the house arrives home from work, tired, cold and hungry, he is gratified to find his bath ready, a pot of water simmering in the chimney, and a set of warm, dry clothes laid out for him. After a dinner of mutton, baked potatoes, baked apple and toasted cheese he retires to the livingroom for:

> forty winks in peace on the sofa while you remove the dinner things, and set them carefully away for the morning's cleaning up. He wakes to find his pipe and tobacco ready by his side on a little table, with the beer jug handy likewise, if he be given to that form of refreshment, and sees you neat, smiling, cheerful, opposite to him, ready either to go on with your knitting in silence, while he smokes and thinks, or to chatter to him as much as he will ... The home, which is his paradise, is your handiwork, your refuge, your pride, your castle, your very, very own, your actual self, a part of you inseparable.[1]

JACOB OCHTERVELT'S
FAMILY PORTRAIT OF 1663
HONOURS THE UPRIGHT
MORAL VALUES OF MIDDLE-
CLASS DOMESTICITY.

JACOB OCHTERVELT
PORTRAIT OF A FAMILY 1663
OIL ON CANVAS
101.6 X 89.22 CM
HARVARD UNIVERSITY
ART MUSEUMS, FOGG ART
MUSEUM

Well, that was the ideal anyway. Was domestic life ever thus? Of course not, but it was vital to keep up appearances—not just for the well-being of the family but for the prosperity and security of the entire nation.

A woman's task was to make the home a sanctuary for her husband and children, with the livingroom as its symbolic core. Here the ideals of comfort, charm and refuge were most clearly evident. Here the dutiful and devoted housewife demonstrated to visitors her nest-building skills. The livingroom established the character of both the home and those who lived in it, defining the family that gathered around its hearth in shared intimacy. This, in essence, was what made Australia a moral and coherent nation (and apparently still does, if certain politicians are to be believed).

But where did such notions originate?

The idea of the house as a family sanctuary, divided into various rooms, each with its designated function, arose in the Netherlands in the seventeenth century and was refined in France and England during the eighteenth. It was the natural outcome of an increasing concern with privacy, something that people in the Middle Ages had virtually no conception of. Then, households of twenty or more people shared a single large space for eating, sleeping, washing and entertaining. Medieval beds were enormous because they had to accommodate hordes. 'Before the idea of the home as the seat of family life could enter the human consciousness,' writes the architectural historian Witold Rybczynski, 'it required the experience of both privacy and intimacy, neither of which had been possible in the medieval hall'.[2]

Although no great admirer of the Dutch, Sir William Temple, English ambassador to the Hague in the late 1660s, was, like many outsiders, astonished at the spotlessness and orderliness of their houses. The Dutch cult of cleanliness had several sources, chief among them a Calvinist belief in moral purity which centred on the home as 'both a microcosm, and a permitting condition, of the properly governed commonwealth', as Simon Schama puts it so succinctly.[3] To an extent, it reflected what some commentators have called the feminisation of the house—a belief, almost unheard-of elsewhere in Europe, that home was a special place of family safety and togetherness with the woman as its guiding spirit.

Although smaller than its counterpart in other countries, because land was scarce and expensive, the typical middle-class Dutch house had a greater number of rooms. It accommodated not an entire extended family with its servants and retainers, but just husband, wife and a small number of children: what we today would call a nuclear family. Largely unaided by servants, the wife did most of the work herself, even though she might be of high social rank. We have the Dutch to thank for turning the large public household into the private family home. It was a revolution that changed not only the way Europeans lived, but also the way they thought. And, given the close ties between the Dutch and the English, it should hardly be surprising that its effects were felt most keenly in Britain, and thence in her colonies.

For better or worse, the close family unit comprising mum, dad and a couple of kids became the basic building block of Australian social, political and economic life during the twentieth century, so much so that most people could not even imagine any other options. Not until very recently would the preoccupation with privacy and segregation that sustained it begin to relax, allowing the emergence of a more inclusive, varied and outward-looking society.

As an institution, the private family is at once robust and fragile. Considering all the challenges thrown up against them—depressions, wars, epidemics and the scorn of those who, for one reason or another, felt excluded—one can only admire the way Australians of all social classes held so stubbornly to its ideals. Admittedly, they had a lot of financial encouragement. 'The first small nuclear families', as historian Mark Peel points out,

> were middle class because only professional and business men could reasonably expect to earn enough to sustain their dependents in a separate household. For others, the security of husbands' earnings was entrenched later, during the 1890s and the first decade after Federation, in a family wage system which guaranteed that male breadwinners could support their dependent wives and children.[4]

That all Australian families were, in theory at least, entitled to own their own homes became an article of faith for successive federal and state governments, which poured vast amounts of money into creating and maintaining the infrastructure to make it possible, while working hard to starve the alternatives.

Despite this, the institution of the small family always seemed to be vulnerable, and always racked by fear. Working women, bohemian intellectuals, migrants, coloured people in neighbouring countries, Aborigines, homosexuals, rebellious teenagers and the irreligious were all, at one time or another, seen as dire threats and punished for their failure to conform. The family's self-identity as a refuge from the dangers of the outside world demanded (as it still demands) a constant supply of bogeymen.

Something of these anxieties can be seen in the way social and technological innovations were contradictorily pressed into service as evils that would destroy family life or saviours that would keep it together. Birth control is an obvious

No longer are people forced into marriage
against their will for reasons of financial
security and social acceptance.

example: on the one hand, the smaller family would be more prosperous and its children better cared for; on the other, a drop in the numbers of decent folk might see them overrun by Asians from somewhere up north, or by the immoral poor within their midst who were less susceptible to the wisdom of social planners. Given that the family was, above all, an economic unit, any changes in the labour market were also bound to raise worries about possible upsets to family normality: the disappearance of paid domestic servants is an example, and their gradual replacement with unpaid mechanical and electrical ones. Even the introduction of seemingly innocuous things—the movies, radio, television, computers—has been eyed warily for its positive or negative impacts on the family. In the mid 1960s, backyard pools were seen by one hopeful commentator as 'contributing greatly to the solution of the current social problem of keeping the family together'.[5]

Today, despite the proliferation of backyard pools, considerably less than half of all Australians live as part of a heterosexual nuclear family; 31 per cent of currently single men and 26 per cent of single women have no intention of marrying; and even if they do, one-third of them can expect their marriages to end in divorce.[6] Economic prosperity, employment opportunities for women, the secular state, social tolerance and political stability have opened up alternatives that were not admissible in the past. No longer are people forced into marriage against their will for reasons of financial security and social acceptance, only to live out their lives in misery and regret. A family today might be a pensioner with a horde of cats, a single mother and her children, a group of young people sharing, two partners of the same sex, an unmarried man and woman without children, or an extended family of three generations under one roof, perhaps with other relatives—the very arrangement that earlier Australians feared was under threat from the rise of the nuclear family.

Those who rail against the breakdown of what they call the traditional family are still with us, just as they have always been. In actuality, however, the family is simply evolving to accommodate itself to new circumstances, just as it always has.

Resisting the Modernist Package

A Melbourne real estate agent recently advertised a 1930s Californian bungalow as having 'advanced present-day period spaces'. It's not as silly as it sounds. For, while the history of the twentieth century, like that of the nineteenth, is one of dizzying technological change, what is remarkable is how little those changes affected the design and layout of the house. Even the advent of electricity and, a century later, computerisation, both of which revolutionised people's lives, had little direct impact on the house's appearance. It is perfectly possible to lead a fully automated twenty-first century existence in an inner-city Victorian terrace without major disruption to its heritage values.

While reformers were keen to promote the benefits of logical, scientific planning, which, they rightly insisted, would make life better, they didn't stop there. When they imagined the house of the future, it was essentially an unadorned white box with floor-to-ceiling glass and a flat roof, containing a minimum of simple, functional-looking furniture—that is, the standard repertoire we now recognise as 'contemporary'. The house should not only *be* technologically advanced, it had to *look* it as well. The same went for its contents. There is a nice irony in the fact that, just when innovations promised to make life really comfortable, architects and designers began

YOU'D NEVER KNOW IT WAS THERE! THIS AUSTRALIAN-MADE RECORD PLAYER FROM THE 1920S IS NEATLY CONCEALED IN A SIDEBOARD. DISHONEST, PERHAPS, BUT NO LESS PRACTICAL FOR THAT.

to insist on what the American psychologist Joan Kron calls 'conspicuous austerity'. What they failed to acknowledge is that the new technologies were essentially discreet. Electricity hummed away in the background without needing to announce itself. Technology had been divorced from style. So a house full of neo-Regency armchairs, with dados, cornices and floral carpets, was not necessarily any less efficient than a shiny glass box with minimal decor. From a practical point of view, it didn't matter.

Suburban homeowners knew that although the spare, glass-and-steel rooms they saw illustrated in design magazines were eminently photogenic, they were not comforting. This is why modernist interior decoration was accepted, even admired, in public buildings while taking much longer to penetrate the home. And when it did, it was not so much in the livingroom that its influence was felt as in those parts of the house—the kitchen in particular—where utility and efficiency made the most sense and comfort was less important.

Reformers were annoyed that people wanted electric lights in the form of candelabras, gas heaters that imitated coal fires, and radiograms like miniature Greek temples. 'Dishonest', they called it, yet these things were no less workable because of that. The reformers had demanded a marriage of form and function, but consumers realised that no such match was necessary. They were happy to enjoy the material benefits without the ideological trappings. Putting the wireless into a Regency-style cabinet was a perfectly sensible way to absorb the initial shock of this alien object's invasion.

In fact, it was precisely because new technological marvels were not expected to completely transform the home that they were adopted so readily. From the very beginning, electric irons, washing machines, refrigerators and stoves were not promoted as life-changing, but more modestly as making life easier, more pleasant or more efficient. In other words, they did what people were already doing, they just did it better, so they could be absorbed into the life of the household without major disruption to it.

THE DRAWINGROOM WAS THE BEST-FURNISHED BUT LEAST-USED ROOM IN THE HOUSE.

The Liberation of the Drawingroom

THE 'AT HOME' WAS NOT
A PARTICULARLY JOYOUS
OCCASION.

James Maclehose, an enterprising Scottish merchant who settled in Sydney, was proud to record in 1838 that:

> although many of the houses ... are of the humble order of wooden huts, such as Sydney was almost entirely composed of, ... a number of respectable stone houses have been erected, and every month is adding to the number of stone and brick cottages, while the number of the unseemly wooden huts of bygone days is evidently on the decline.[7]

Maclehose could not have foreseen the remarkable changes to come. Just fifty years later, after the gold rushes, there was, on average, more than one room for every individual in the country. But of course they were not distributed equally.

The inner-city and rural poor still crowded into their two dirt-floored rooms, while the well-off in their suburban mansions could indulge in a bedroom for every member of the household as well as a drawingroom, billiard room, conservatory and ballroom. Even the respectable villa of the middle-income earner rejoiced in separate sitting- and diningrooms, kitchen, bathroom and quarters for the maid.

Such profligacy couldn't last and, sure enough, by the 1920s, the average suburban house had been reduced to just five rooms.* Yet, while this was not as many as before, the number of occupants had also been reduced, both because grandparents, adult offspring and domestic help were less likely to be sharing and because birth control programs had led to smaller families. In short, there was a larger number of smaller houses with fewer people in each.[8] (Compare this to the situation today, where we have a greater number of *larger* houses, each with fewer people still.[9]) Australians, it seems, were prepared to sacrifice some comfort and social status in order to maintain their privacy.

One outcome of the trend towards smaller houses was the liberation of the drawingroom or front parlour, which traditionally had been kept for best, 'in case the queen drops in', as mums liked to quip. The drawingroom was the best-furnished but least-used room in the house. However, if you had only five rooms, you could hardly afford to cordon one off, queen or no queen, so the drawingroom was rechristened the livingroom and began to shrug off its reserve.

In the late nineteenth century the drawingroom—originally the 'with-drawing room', where the ladies withdrew after dinner, leaving the men to smoke around the diningroom table—had given the woman of the house a chance to show off her decorating skills, free of her husband's influence. It was very much her territory, and here she could, at certain stipulated times, declare herself 'at home' to her female friends and acquaintances.

It was all very well for the home to be the housewife's refuge but, despite the rosy propaganda, this inevitably led to lonely and desolate lives. The original purpose of the 'at home'—sometimes confusingly referred to as the 'morning call', despite being an afternoon event—was to give women a taste of social life, an

* Until World War II, real estate advertisements stated the total number of rooms in the house without differentiating between them, indicating that there was some flexibility in the layout. Today, in contrast, we want to know the number of bedrooms, bathrooms and car-parking spaces, suggesting a greater interest in both privacy within the household, and escape from it.

aim effectively thwarted by rigid rules of etiquette. A lady set aside a particular afternoon for receiving callers, who were expected to stay no more than fifteen or twenty minutes, occupying themselves in brittle repartee over tea and cake. Each visit was announced with a calling card, around which a terrifying set of protocols became encrusted. Any breach of calling-card etiquette might have you branded as 'ill-bred', which was certain social death.

The 'at home' persisted until well into the new century. In 1909, an anxious reader wrote to the women's pages of the Melbourne *Argus* with a bevy of questions:

> What cards should a married lady leave when calling on another married lady? Should she leave them as she is going out or give them to the maid as she goes in? If she leaves them on the hall-table as she is leaving, does she mention them? In some cases a lady leaves two of her husband's cards and one of her own; in others, only two cards, one inscribed Mr. and Mrs. _. Why the difference? In making a first call does the lady give her name to the maid to announce or does she tell the hostess herself?[10]

All these problems were dutifully addressed by the paper's social editor (the maid, as it happened, was supposed to answer the door with a salver in her hand, on which you were expected to place your card 'unostentatiously'). If and when the poor woman managed to get it all sorted out, her name might be entered into a guest book as a suitable recipient of further invitations.

Such elaborate rituals revealed the insecurities of a middle-class still deeply anxious about its social position. Although to modern eyes they come across as ludicrous, they served to impose order and a sense of security on a still raw society in the throes of great upheaval.

The post-war generation found itself occupying a different world altogether: thriftier, more chastened by economic hardship, and far less circumscribed by convention. Although hardly liberated, women had at least been granted the right to vote, they dressed in a more relaxed manner, and they could get out more. Always a progressive paper, the Melbourne *Age* noted with approval the numbers of young ladies now seen in public places without a male chaperone and welcomed the decline of the 'professional paid companion for women'.[11]

No longer was the livingroom the focus of their social life, although it would retain its feminine atmosphere—so much so that the man of the house might feel the need to retreat to a small den or study, where he could put his feet up on sturdy leather armchairs among his sporting trophies and financial

The maid was supposed to answer the door
with a salver in her hand, on which you were
expected to place your card 'unostentatiously'.

papers. Although his wife might occasionally use the den for sewing or as a guest bedroom, there was no question that it was his.

As early as 1885, *The Australian Housewives' Manual* had recommended that those of modest means (with a household income of less than £3 a week and no servants) should combine dining- and livingrooms into one, keeping it 'as nice and attractive as they possibly can'.[12] Needless to say, these were not the sort of people who had ever known the rituals of the 'at home'.

If your house was spacious enough, however, with a separate dining-room—which was the pattern for middle-class housing until well into the 1950s—the livingroom might continue to be kept for best. The habit persisted a surprisingly long time. As late as 1946, for instance, after the Grodski family had moved to a new subdivision in Melbourne's Moorabbin, their diningroom was devoted both to meals and relaxation while the livingroom, with the only fireplace in the house, was kept firmly out-of-bounds, except on Sunday evenings, when Mrs Grodski allowed the children in to listen to the radio.[13]

Mrs Grodski clearly had social ambitions. Had the queen, or anyone else of consequence, popped in, her livingroom would not have let her down, and if that entailed inconvenience to the family, then so be it. But she was one of a dying breed. By this time, with space at a premium and fewer reasons to be standing on ceremony, the livingroom was more often used for living. In recognition of its newfound informality, it was renamed 'the lounge', or, more commonly, since this was not a term sophisticated people cared to use, 'the laownge'.

Although few would have agreed with the radical architect Best Overend in 1938 that the livingroom should be 'at least half the total area of the house ... for then we will have one really large comfortable room where there will be room for the family to sit and still retain some measure of privacy',[14] by the 1990s his wish had not only been realised, but bettered.

In truth, this meant quite a few measures of privacy had to be sacrificed, but now that families rarely gathered together at home, even for meals, this was

AUGUST 1, 1934

The Australian

ONE SHILLING

HOME BEAUTIFUL

Registered at the General Post Office, Melbourne, for transmission by post as a periodical.

not thought to be a major problem. In really smart architect-designed houses, the livingroom has swallowed up the kitchen, dining and entertainment areas, with bedrooms added to one side or hovering above on mezzanines like afterthoughts. The open-plan house, with its one big space for everything, seems to aspire to the condition of the medieval hall. It is for highly mobile, independent people with three cars in the drive, a weekender on the coast, and a wide choice of restaurants nearby, who need a base-camp rather than a family domicile.

The Hearth

No livingroom was ever complete without its fireplace. This made practical sense when it was the only source of warmth, but its importance was symbolic as well, a reminder that a fire had always meant security (the Latin word *focus* translates as both 'fireplace or hearth' and 'family or household'). The fireplace was the household's emotional fulcrum.

When, in the early 1920s, *Australian Home Builder* forecast that gas and electric heaters would soon make fireplaces redundant, it was ignoring their real significance. As it happened, no part of the Australian house proved more stubbornly resistant to the reformers' rationalism. Far from replacing the traditional fire, gas and electric heaters were forced to impersonate it, a sure sign of their secondary status. Brooks Robinson's Flickering Electric Adam-Style Heater, in which a perforated metal disc revolved above a lightglobe under fake coals, was just one of many that provided a psychologically reassuring substitute, despite making no real attempt to look convincing.

Victorian-era fireplaces were deep and high, allowing the smoke to billow into the room while the heat disappeared up the chimney. You could pile on lots of big logs for a rip-roaring blaze, but you had to sit very close, burning on the front and freezing on the back.* Initially, only the well-off could afford coal but, as its price came down, a built-in cast-iron grate became the aim

THE FIREPLACE, THAT PERENNIAL SYMBOL OF COMFORT AND SECURITY, REMAINED AT THE CENTRE OF ATTENTION IN THE 1930S, DESPITE THE ADVENT OF MORE EFFICIENT HEATING METHODS, ADAPTING ITSELF TO MODERN DESIGN TRENDS.

* In his diaries, the early Victorian settler John Cotton describes a nobly-proportioned rural fireplace with doors on either side large enough for a team of bullocks to haul in whole tree trunks.

of every modern middle-class homeowner. Not only was it more efficient, but a slide-out dustpan simplified cleaning and a trapdoor at the chimney entrance could be kept shut during the day to stop draughts. It looked the part as well, with its decorative metalwork surround and a row of brightly coloured tiles down each side.

After the war, an increasing number of people, buffeted by fluctuations in the price and availability of coal, reverted to wood, which had always been the cheaper option anyway, especially outside New South Wales. As usual, fashions quickly changed to put a positive spin on necessity. 'How much more restful and pleasing is an open clinker brick fireplace, surmounted by a heavy wooden shelf on iron brackets, than the traditional iron grate with its glaring tiles and formal mantlepiece', declared *Australian Home Builder* reassuringly in 1924.[15] Rustic charm was all the go, an antidote to years of straitlaced formality, and nothing set the scene quite so well as a cosy log fire. Every evening across the nation, suburban families sank into their Paterson's three-piece Moquette lounge suites to stare fixedly at the grate, leaping up every now and then to poke and prod ('Leave the fire alone, dad!' issued nightly from every livingroom). They sat there even in summer when there was no fire, because that was easier than rearranging the furniture, and even in cities such as Brisbane where fires were rarely necessary. They would not be dislodged until the 1950s, when everything and everyone swivelled around to face that vulgar new interloper, the television set.

The modern flat of Mr and Mrs Collins in Melbourne, to which *Home Beautiful* devoted a special feature in 1931, 'followed the lead given by the Continental decorators—of the restrained rather than the extreme type'.[16]

THE FAKE FIREPLACE WAS NEVER INTENDED TO BE MISTAKEN FOR THE REAL THING, JUST TO MAKE A NICE IMPRESSION WHEN TOPPED WITH A VASE OF GLADDIES AND A MANTLE CLOCK.

In the livingroom, all the furnishings took their cue from the severe horizontals of a black marble fireplace flanked by bookshelves. Paradoxically, despite the availability by this time of oil-fired central heating, the open fireplace had become the modernist decorator's principal flagbearer.

Few were as fortunate as Mr and Mrs Collins. If, like most people, you could just scrape together enough for a fibro cottage, a real brick hearth and chimney was probably out of the question. Artifice would come to the rescue, however, in the form of the simulated mantle of moulded plaster coloured to look like brick or stone, into which a gas or electric heater was fitted. Like Brooks Robinson's flickering electric fire, the fake mantle conveyed the general idea without making any serious attempt to deceive. It was never intended to be mistaken for the real thing, just to make a nice impression when topped with a vase of gladdies and a mantle clock. It said, 'We acknowledge the importance of the fireplace even though it may be beyond our means at present'.

And, sure enough, when the good times rolled again, fireplaces quickly returned to favour. Builders of project homes in the 1950s and 1960s were surprised, and not a little dismayed, to discover that clients demanded a house with a chimney, despite the gas space-heater that had been so thoughtfully provided. Emotional comfort was just as important as the physical kind and, to be frank, few project houses provided much of either. Although the Building Industry Division of the Commonwealth Ministry of National Development promoted modern heating methods (especially oil, at the behest of powerful oil companies), it had to acknowledge that firewood and briquettes were cheap and, 'except perhaps on the higher levels, climatic conditions are not sufficiently severe to produce extreme discomfort. Most of the population prefers to endure some discomfort rather than to pay for the additional cost of insulated construction'.[17]

Early advocates of efficient modern living such as Best Overend would certainly be astonished to find the fireplace still at the heart of the Australian livingroom in the twenty-first century, despite the fact that all their utopian dreams of affordable central heating have come to fruition. An expensive luxury the open fire may now be, but one many of us are prepared to pay for (and to hell with the environmental consequences), particularly when we want to make an impression on visitors. Amid the clean, minimalist lines of the trend-setting modern interior, the open fire blazes on, sole survivor of a primitive urge for magic in an age that has otherwise relegated such things to history.

1924 and 1971

A SMART, MODERN LIVING
ROOM FEATURED IN
AUSTRALIAN HOME BUILDER
IN 1924

THE LIVING ROOM OF PETTIT
AND SEVITT'S LOWLINE H
PROJECT HOME, 1971

The smart, modern livingroom (above), featured in *Australian Home Builder* in 1924[18], has an up-to-the-minute gas heater installed in front of a fireplace which, to judge from the condition of the brickwork, has never experienced a real blaze. There is something distinctly absurd about this unattractive little object commanding centre stage as it does, bolstered by flanking potplants and a very self-important overmantle laden with vases. It is like a midget dictator surrounding himself with burly bodyguards for added stature.

In complete contrast, Pettit and Sevitt's Lowline H project home,[19] designed by Ancher, Mortlock, Murray and Woolley in 1971, has no fireplace (for economy's sake) and the central-heating grill in the wall is so discreet as to be hardly distinguishable. The warmth in this room is pervasive and unvarying. It issues from no apparent source and is supplied with no apparent effort, fulfilling the modern dream of automated, self-functioning technologies.

There are other telling differences between these two rooms. For one thing, Pettit and Sevitt's is brighter and more colourful, even allowing for the fact that the earlier one was photographed in black and white. The 1970s

was not a time for reticence. A fashion in the previous decade for earthy, natural tones had given way to 'new clear colors, vivacious jewel colors with a new boldness, veering away from the recent whim for neutrals, drabs and the "murky"'.[20] Bright Finnish Marimekko fabrics were the last word in chic and they went so well with polished timber and moulded plastics. But then just about anything went with anything. This room's carefree combination of Japanese paper lightshades, folksy shagpile rug, 'biomorphic' and geometric furniture and bold patterns indiscriminately applied, makes it typical of the period. It's a cheery, 'look-at-me' interior, designed for fun. Here you would not look out of place lying flat out on the floor, which, by the look of those chairs, might well be the more comfortable option.

The 1920s room, by comparison, is rather proper. Pastel colours were recommended for interiors at the time because they were tasteful and less likely to become tiresome, but also because brightly coloured paints were difficult to obtain and unreliable in application. This room's pale walls, plain upholstery, polished timber floors and muted oriental-style rug combine to form a satisfying, if somewhat puritanical, whole. It's a pipe-and-slippers sort of place, yet not one to get too comfortable in. Clearly it expects you to behave yourself. This room exemplifies that quality most valued by interior decorators at the time: 'a practical homeliness, fashioned and refined by a sense of art'.[21]

To our eyes, the windows seem small and mean, and the little daylight they admit is further reduced by curtains. Great store was put on curtains in the 1920s. They were said to 'furnish a room', although these, with their prim little matching valances, are much too demure for that. Despite their glass panes, the doors to the passage reinforce the impression of aloofness. In contrast, Pettit and Sevitt's big open lounge has floor-to-ceiling glass with a slatted wooden screen in the garden outside providing minimal privacy. What the photograph does not show is that this room flows into diningroom, entrance hall, kitchen and family room, and together they occupy more than half the house's total floor area.

As if to compensate for what would, in practice, have been rather too much openness, the designers have gathered the furniture around a circular rug to form 'an intimate conversation area'. (A more up-market variation was the 'conversation pit', sunk below floor level and lined with built-in settees, where your feet were always cold and into which you might tumble head first in an absent moment.) In pursuit of privacy, the furniture turns its back on the glassy expanses of wall towards the thicket of lightshades, which, like the rest of the room, is arranged with studied asymmetry. Note how the coffee table has been carefully placed to one side of the rug.

The furniture in the 1920s room, on the other hand, has been thrust back against the wall, as in a spinning funfair centrifuge, leaving the middle of the room denuded, and a careful balance is maintained, even down to the loose cushions on the armchairs. The effect is to draw the eye back inexorably to that central fireplace and its ridiculous little gas heater. Yet, notably, the equally modern and up-to-date electric light fitting is given no such prominence. Its severely functional shade and carelessly exposed bulb suggest that it is, on the contrary, barely tolerated.

Wall-to-Wall

Like any self-respecting 1970s project home, Lowline H is fitted with wall-to-wall carpets. Homeowners demanded them and were prepared to sacrifice almost anything to have them. 'The dear old wall-to-wall has become such a status symbol that it's almost useless (even sacrilegious [sic]) to suggest an alternative', sighed *Home Beautiful* in 1967.[22] Loose rugs on polished timber could mean only one thing—you couldn't afford wall-to-wall—and that was humiliating. Although Lowline H's are plain, reflecting the superior taste of Pettit and Sevitt's target market, bold floral Axminsters were by far the most popular.

The 1924 livingroom, typically for the period, has loose rugs on stained wood. At this time, fixed carpet of any kind would have been thought old-fashioned and unhealthy. Only when vacuum cleaners had become affordable and efficient would it be a practical proposition.

Coconut fibre and sisal mats from the Pacific Islands were popular coverings for floorboards in the second half of the nineteenth century, but they harboured dirt. Patterned floorcloth and linoleum were easier to keep clean, if generally too hard and cold for the parlour, although it was those very qualities that kept them popular in tropical climes.* 'Don't buy felt', advised

* Floorcloth, the most popular floor covering before World War I, was painted and varnished canvas. Linoleum, first patented by the English rubber manufacturer Frederick Walton in 1863, was made from oxidised linseed oil mixed with wood pulp and colourings.

the *Australian Housewives' Manual*, 'because it wears into holes and the patterns are ungainly. Don't buy tapestry, because it gets threadbare, and looks shabby. But buy a real Brussels, which will wear for ever, and make bedroom carpets afterwards'.[23] Brussels carpet, in a range of colourful mock-oriental patterns, could be bought by the yard and nailed to the floor with brass tacks, wall-to-wall if you could afford a bit of wastage or with a narrow strip left around the edges which was stained with black japan varnish. If dust accumulated under the forest of jardinières and side tables in the Victorian parlour, that didn't really matter, so long as it remained undisturbed and nobody could see it.

Then along came electric light and, in the interests of health and hygiene, down came the heavy velvet curtains. As light streamed in, all that grime was suddenly horribly visible. And where were the servants to clean it up? The livingroom had to be simplified, and the first thing to go was the fixed carpet.

Home and Health, in 1909, firmly recommended loose rugs instead, which could be taken outside every now and then for a good beating. 'Cleanliness

LOOSE RUGS ON STAINED TIMBER FLOORS WERE THE NORM IN THE 1920S, BUT VACUUM CLEANERS, INTRODUCED INTO AUSTRALIA AFTER WORLD WAR I, WOULD MAKE FIXED WALL-TO-WALL CARPET A PRACTICAL PROPOSITION.

gives character to the home and to the nation, and places a healthful mould upon succeeding generations', it declared, according far too much importance to what was, after all, just carpet.[24]

In response, industry got busy supplying the mechanical devices that would bring these bright, clean, healthy interiors to light. 'Faced with the possibility of "a lifetime of drudgery"', writes John Archer, 'the middle and upper classes provided a lucrative market for labour-saving inventions of all sorts designed to replace maids, cooks, cleaners, and even valets'.[25]

Carpet sweepers of various types had been doing their best in the battle against dust since their invention in 1865, but they stirred up as much of it as they gathered. Vacuum cleaners, available in the United States from around 1908, appeared here after World War I, quickly becoming the most popular of the many new electrical appliances on the market. You could get a Rotarex in 1924 for £10, 'half the price of other vacuum cleaners' boasted the advertisements, although still a significant investment for many. Three years later the price had been reduced to such an extent that *Home Beautiful* could claim, a little optimistically, that 'the vacuum cleaner is almost too much of an every-day appliance to mention'.[26] It was certainly so by the mid 1950s, when more than 90 000 of them were being made in Australia every year.[27]

As with all household furnishings, carpets were subject to the frequent ups and downs of supply and price that made domestic life in the twentieth century such an adventure. The Melbourne *Age* rejoiced in 1923 that 'it is now possible to contemplate new

BRIGHTLY COLOURED SHAG-PILE CARPET AND LOTS OF POTTED PALMS: WHAT COULD BE MORE 1970S?

carpets or curtains without dismay. Axminsters are now about 13/6 per yard—more than double pre-war prices yet better than the 27/6 that has been common for the past decade. Linoleums and oilcloths are also affordable'.[28] But not for long. By the early 1930s, although they were cheaper still, wages had been reduced and few people were in a position to buy. Just a few years later, every effort and every penny was going to the war effort and imported goods such as carpets virtually disappeared.

In 1944, *Home Beautiful* told the inspiring story of how a Sydney woman had made all her own furniture and floor coverings from scrap for just £20. There were no men around to do it, she explained, and nothing in the shops.[29] Nevertheless, for the sake of the nation, those on the home front had to be kept optimistic. Women's magazines tantalised potential consumers with predictions of what they might expect 'when peace comes', or, more positively still, 'when Victory comes'. In 1945, with that victory firmly in sight, Thom and Smith electrical in Sydney rashly promised radios, refrigerators, irons, dishwashers, vacuum cleaners, even televisions, and 'all the Household Amenities you hope to acquire very soon'.[30]

It took much longer than expected. In the meantime, those lucky enough to secure a house of their own had to furnish it with local goods made from materials nobody else wanted. Feltex, a floor covering of compressed wool-waste, was cheap, warm and, best of all, *available*. 'Economy is the watchword today', was its attention-grabbing advertising slogan. And, when your Feltex started to look worn (which didn't take long), you could turn it over and start anew.

It's hardly surprising that, when wartime restrictions were finally lifted, homeowners went for luxury, or at least a semblance of it. They turned with relief to the heavily padded, the elaborately decorated and the reassuringly homely: anything that looked solid and lasting and reminded them of happier, more secure times. After all those years of grey-blue Feltex, who could blame them for demanding garish florals?*

Home Entertainments

* The floral carpets that British manufacturers made for export to Australia were brighter and more colourful than those destined for their home market.

Ironically, perhaps, the impact of new technologies has been nowhere more evident than in the ways we choose to amuse ourselves. Victorian parlour games demanded nothing more sophisticated than a box of checkers or a pack of cards. An edifying book and a kerosene lamp were sufficient for any cultivated young lady during those all-too-rare moments when she was free of sewing, mending or other useful work. (The late nineteenth century was the great age

THE ROSENTHAL FAMILY
AT HOME IN CARLTON,
MELBOURNE, WITH THEIR
MUSICAL INSTRUMENTS

of the popular novel.) On the whole, people made their own entertainment, since they had to.

With domestic workloads easing, especially for women and children, leisure became an ever more central component of home-life, and manufacturers were not slow in seizing the opportunity. As the twentieth century wore on, leisure activities within the home became increasingly dependent upon outside providers.

Sometime in the mid 1880s, Mr and Mrs Rosenthal gathered their six sons in the drawing-room of their Carlton house in Melbourne for a photographic portrait. The result, while highly artificial, is touching. The matriarch takes pride of place at the piano. As the only one with sheet music, she would have carried the melody with the others accompanying her. They could easily have adapted for their unusual group of instruments the piano-duet versions of popular classics that sold well in music shops. Dvorak, Brahms and other composers made good money from transcriptions of their symphonic works for home performance. The boy immediately to mother's left appears to be holding a wooden transverse flute,

THE BEST TALKING MACHINES OF 1910, INCLUDING THE PIGMY GRAND, A HORNLESS GRAMOPHONE COMBINING PORTABILITY AND COMPACTNESS WITH PERFECT REPRODUCTION.

very old-fashioned by this time, which suggests that the family's instruments have been handed down through the generations. Their pride in both their skills and their instruments is manifest.

Although not all families were as talented as the Rosenthals, no middle-class parlour was complete without an upright piano and most girls were encouraged to develop a good singing voice. The evening recital could be a rigorous test of endurance for guests.

In 1918, you could expect to pay around £120 for a good-quality upright.[31] This was a very considerable sum, but hundreds of cheaper second-hand instruments filled the classifieds every week. Men of the cloth, horrified by the thought that people might actually be enjoying themselves, urged them to use their money for more worthy things.

If little Millie wasn't quite as talented as mother had hoped, help was soon at hand. 'The young girl entertaining her friends in her home no longer finds it necessary to perform a reproduction of some popular composition, which would make its composer turn over in his grave', enthused *Australian Home Builder* in 1924. 'Instead, she invites her guests to make their own selections from the cabinet of music rolls.' Then all she had to do was pump. Or, better still, 'she chooses from her collection of records those which, by an even more magical process, give forth the very voices of the world's greatest singers— even Caruso himself',[32] although something a little jazzier would probably have been more to her liking.

Whether Caruso or Al Jolson, however, they sounded equally tinny on your Sonora High Class Talking Machine, which could not compete with the sociability and sheer good fun of the piano roll. As the Kiernan's advertisement

JUST TEN YEARS AFTER
RADIO BROADCASTS BEGAN
IN AUSTRALIA, IT BECAME
POSSIBLE TO 'TUNE IN TO
THE WORLD', ALTHOUGH
THE COST WAS HIGH AND
RECEPTION UNRELIABLE.
WHAT MOST PEOPLE WANTED
WAS NOT NAIROBI OR
SAIGON, BUT THE CRICKET
DIRECT FROM LORDS.

put it in 1927, 'For the long winter evenings, what more happy [*sic*] than a cheery fire, a Player Piano—and you—playing your favorite music?'.[33]

What more happy, it turned out, was the wireless, which quickly brought the decline of the livingroom musicale. More than just operetta or popular songs, the wireless offered news, stories, game shows and a raft of other entertainments, and it had the huge benefit of immediacy: for the first time the family sitting at home could hear what was going on in the outside world, more or less as it was happening, and that was thrilling.

Radio was even more thrilling for manufacturers trying to sell products. It brought advertising right into the livingroom, with a force and persuasiveness that no magazine or newspaper could match. It ushered in consumer culture and accustomed people to the branding of products that had previously been sold generically. In other words, the radio helped to Americanise the Australian home.

While the piano had been mainly a girl's thing, the radio had a decidedly masculine air. The news, sport and information it provided was more likely to appeal to men than mere musical entertainment. Furthermore, the thing itself was more accessibly technical. The making of a crystal set (a crude form of radio requiring headphones) was something all red-blooded lads were expected to master, and every boys' magazine and hobby book carried a set of instructions.

'Radio sets keep the boys mechanically interested', claimed *Australian Home Builder* in 1924, just six months after Australia's first radio station, Sydney's 2SB, had begun broadcasting,

Such glamorous machines were
considered 'very Sydney', which was
not necessarily a compliment.

and radio music provides song and dance measures for both boys and girls so that they have no desire to go abroad at night seeking diversion at music halls and dance palaces. Radio news of the day is listened to with restful satisfaction by the house, father seated in his easy chair before his own fireside, so that he does not yearn for the hospitality of the club ... Scientists promise that soon we will have radio picture shows, exhibiting romances and real life scenes from all over the world.[34]

That was jumping the gun by about thirty years, but meanwhile the radio would do its bit to keep the family together in peace and harmony.

It wasn't long before the record player and the radio were combined into one unit, styled as a quality item of furniture. At the height of fashion in the late 1920s was the Centurion All-Electric Phono-Radio, which 'operates direct from your power point or light socket' (since not every home had power points), in a cabinet designed to blend seamlessly with the Jacobean three-piece suite. Elaborate phonograms with automatic record changers, built into mirrored cocktail bars, were the last word in smartness for the 1930s party set, although if the dancing became too frenetic the stylus would bounce right off the record with a sickening ripping sound. Such glamorous machines were considered 'very Sydney', which was not necessarily a compliment.

On 3 September 1939, across the nation, young and old pressed breathlessly towards their radiograms to hear the prime minister, Robert Menzies, announce that Australia was at war. 'Where Great Britain stands', he intoned, 'there stands the people of the entire British world'.[35] The medium came into its own during wartime, as a propaganda tool, a vital source of news, and a solace for those whose loved ones were far away. Radio became the glue that held society together in this time of stress.

Stations proliferated and programming diversified. In 1941, for example, *The Youth Show*, broadcast from Sydney and claiming to be the world's first program wholly produced and presented by young people, was syndicated to thirty-nine stations nationwide.[36] By this time, console, mantle, table and portable models were available (the last mentioned being battery powered and housed in a small suitcase), which meant the radio need no longer be restricted to the livingroom. With a receiver on the kitchen mantlepiece, the woman of the house could enjoy *Lux Radio Theatre* or *Mobil Quest* while preparing dinner. Daytime programs became just as popular as those in the evening and advertisers realised that women listeners were now their main target. As a result, dramas and romantic serials—or 'soap operas' because in America they were sponsored by detergent companies—would be the mainstay of radio networks for the next two or three decades.

The Box

The very fact that you could take your set with you on a picnic or listen in the car helped radio to survive the introduction of television in 1956: that and the fact that FM stereo radio, introduced in 1975, could boast a sound quality TV couldn't match.* However, major changes became necessary in radio programming, with dramas and serials giving way to non-stop popular music that could be listened to on the run. Few people sat down to actually listen to the radio anymore. Even *Blue Hills*, one of the world's most successful serials, finally succumbed in 1976, after 5 795 episodes.

The possibility, even the inevitability, of television had been discussed for years. The fact that it had been available (theoretically anyway) in Britain and the United States since the late 1930s seemed to be accepted without rancour by most Australians, who were prepared to wait for the teething problems to be ironed out and for prices to come down, as they'd been told they must.

Addressing the World Radio Conference in Sydney in 1938, Major General James Harbord, chair of the American RCA network, maintained

* This led to a shortlived phenomenon known as the simulcast, often employed by the ABC for concerts and operas. You could enjoy the picture with the TV's volume turned down while listening to the music in stereo via a simultaneous radio broadcast.

BEDTIME: BUT WOULD THE
KIDDIES BE ABLE TO TEAR
THEMSELVES AWAY FROM
THE TELEVISION? IT WAS
NOT A QUESTION MOST
FAMILIES HAD TO FACE IN
1956, SINCE FEW COULD
AFFORD A SET.

that, although technically a reality, television had no future. For one thing, program production would always be far too expensive to attract commercial sponsors. For another, the complexity of delivering the service was such that only a totalitarian government could achieve it. And then the clincher:

> There is as yet no material indication that the public will fulfil its presumptive part of the bargain, namely, the purchase and constant use of television equipment for the home. Indeed, there is a strong suspicion that ... it may toss the new miracle aside after the first flush of curious interest has subsided ... Nor can I convince myself that a family will sit, evening after evening, gazing with rapt attention at a small screen.[37]

Speaking at a time of world-wide political anxiety following a decade of financial gloom, the major general could not possibly have foreseen the wealth and optimism of the 1950s, nor people's ability to sit, evening after evening, gazing with rapt attention. As Australia's TV age neared, magazines and newspapers were breathless in anticipation. This was the most exciting thing that had happened in many people's lives. Amid the customary promises that it would bring families closer together came warnings from jeremiahs that it would kill off civilised conversation (both predictions proving accurate to a degree). 'How do we go about planning our home to greet the newcomer and gain the best advantages from it?' asked *Home Beautiful* anxiously. 'How will TV affect household routines and family relations? What will TV cost the average family?'[38]

The answer to that last question was, 'quite a lot'. For the first few years, with sets priced at £240 or more, most people's experience of the new medium was limited to standing in the street outside the local electrical shop peering through the plate-glass window (just as they had crowded outside radio stores twenty-five years earlier to listen to the cricket). Or they might cultivate those previously ignored neighbours with the only aerial in the street (although rumours abounded that some folk were putting up dummy aerials just to show off).

THIS FAMILY, PHOTO-
GRAPHED IN 1972, ENJOYS
A SPACIOUS LIVINGROOM
WITH WINDOW WALL, AN
OIL HEATER SET INTO A
SIMULATED FIREPLACE,
A DECORATIVE FEATURE
WALL, MODERN ARMCHAIRS,
A CHANDELIER AND, OF
COURSE, A TELEVISION SET.
NO PREVIOUS GENERATION
HAD EXPERIENCED SUCH A
HIGH STANDARD OF LIVING.

Daily transmission typically began with children's programs at around five thirty in the afternoon, followed by news at seven (although it wasn't long before women's programs were scheduled during the afternoon). Then came light variety, sport or commentaries, and half-hour dramas or 'situation comedies', which provided Australian households with an idealised American view of domestic bliss to try to live up to. Most popular were the live variety shows broadcast later in the evening, before the epilogue and closing time at around eleven. *In Melbourne Tonight* with Graham Kennedy, which began on 6 May 1957 and continued with a couple of name changes until 1975, virtually defined the genre. Although the show itself was a predictable mix of songs and limp sketch comedy, Kennedy's relaxed, occasionally subversive style flattered his audience by glossing the old Aussie larrikin myth with an air of risqué sophistication. *IMT*, as it was affectionately known, was a thorn in the side of the government's Broadcasting Control Board, which complained piously in 1958 about:

> occurrences in which regular programme personalities have introduced jokes, comments or actions capable of bearing a double-meaning; that the less desirable meaning had not been missed was made evident by the audience ... It appears that insufficient rehearsal and a tendency to indulge in unprepared "patter" are often the cause of the trouble.[39]

But it was no trouble as far as most people were concerned. One important outcome was a lively public debate about societal standards which would render the pronouncements of official moral gatekeepers such as the Broadcasting Control Board and the churches increasingly arcane.

Those who complained that television brought too much American influence did have a point, yet local productions made the greatest impact, such as the current affairs program *4 Corners* (which began in 1961); the police drama *Homicide* (1964); the satirical *Mavis Bramston Show* (1964); and the sexy

serial *Number 96* (1972), famous as the first television series in the world to include in its regular cast a sympathetically-drawn homosexual character.

It was because television demanded rapt attention that its impact on home-life was greater than that of the radio. At the very least, the livingroom furniture had to be rearranged. Place a lamp behind your chair, advised the experts, draw the curtains to prevent daylight falling on the screen, stay at least 6 feet away from the set to avoid eye damage, get rid of your bulky armchairs, and so on. There can be no doubt that television hastened the demise of the three-piece lounge suite, not only because padded armchairs took up so much space, but because there seemed little point in settling too comfortably when you had to leap up every now and then to change channels. Remote controls would not appear until colour television was introduced in 1974.

Already in 1956 *Home Beautiful* was warning that, in America,

> TV in the living room tended to shift the focal point of that room from the fireplace or the conversation centre to the set, and thus destroyed the valuable social purpose of the room ... While mum and dad relaxed in their deep cane shell chairs before the screen on one side of the room, high-school Jane and her boy friend were busy on the other side talking—and looking longingly at the record bar.[40]

Despite the novelty of the medium, programming was directed mainly at adults. Until *Six O'Clock Rock* in the late 1950s and *Bandstand* and *Countdown* later, teenagers were likely to find television boring.

One logical answer to *Home Beautiful*'s concerns was for the television set to follow the radio out of the livingroom, perhaps to the kitchen or family room. However, falling prices and higher earnings gave rise to the two- or three-television household. Thus the dilemma was avoided. While the kids watched *Countdown* in their bedrooms, dad could enjoy his footy in the livingroom. As screens expanded into bloated home theatre systems (in sharp contrast to the miniaturisation of almost everything else), there was often nowhere other than the livingroom big enough to accommodate them, so that remained the most common place for viewing. In any case, people realised that the old ideal of the nuclear family gathered around the hearth was already on the wane and that greater mobility as much as the telly had been responsible. Had television really 'destroyed the valuable social purpose of the room', as *Home Beautiful* feared, or merely changed it to be more in tune with the times? In an era of general anxiety about the fragmentation of the family, few would have asked. A scapegoat was needed and television was at hand.

Paradoxically, and disastrously, the proliferation of electronically produced sounds coincided with the fashion for open-plan living. The sub-woofers became more resonant as room-dividers grew thinner and skimpier. Televisions competed with stereos and radios, each family member insisting on his or her personal choice at any time of day or night. Conversation didn't stand a chance. The family dispersed to wage sound wars.

Peace, of a sort, would come only when every individual was personally wired for sound wherever he or she might be, courtesy of the silicone chip and the headset. Less than a century ago, the radio connected the home directly to the outside world for the first time, giving the livingroom an important new role. Now that every human body can be personally connected full-time, the question of where things are sited no longer arises.

The twentieth century saw communications technologies sweep through the livingroom like a storm, only to depart again once they had latched onto a more specific host. They would leave behind nothing more than a slight indentation in the carpet.

May
I Leave
the Table?

The Redundant Diningroom

As the family meal turned from an organised ritual

into something grabbed in passing, the diningroom took its final exit. Many people blame television for the deterioration in eating habits. 'No TV at mealtimes', was every mother's standard rule, but not for long. In fact, 'the box', which lured young and old into the lounge with their steaming TV dinners on tinfoil trays, was merely the final straw.

Few Australians used the diningroom every day even when they had one. It was far less trouble to take casual meals in the kitchen, although as far as urban dwellers are concerned, this is a fairly recent custom. At one time it was not thought proper to eat in the kitchen because that was what the pioneers had done in their wattle-and-daub shanties, and respectable folk had no wish to follow their example. Besides, the wood-fire stove made the kitchen far too hot and smelly for comfort. A breakfast nook in an annexe was a good compromise.

The fact that the diningroom was accorded such high status in the Victorian era was a sign that sharing meals around the table had taken over from gathering around the open fire as the principal focus of family bonding.* Eating was the key ritual of domestic life, with a sharp distinction drawn between formal and informal meals.

Only the diningroom granted the necessary air of decorum to the traditional Sunday roast, with grandparents and one or two stray maiden aunts in attendance to share the occasion. It was also a good place for the kids to do their homework, out of mother's hair but close enough to be supervised. Otherwise, it languished, the curtains drawn, the mahogany table under a plastic protector, the door left slightly ajar. Here the good china and the canteen of silver were stored in the big oak sideboard, with cut-glass decanters of port and marsala gathering dust on top.

Although young couples on low incomes were being advised as early as the 1890s to do away with this room altogether and to put the dining table in

* Today we are less concerned about family bonding, with good reason. However, if anything could be said to symbolise it, the car surely qualifies rather than any part of the house. The family outing or motoring holiday, with all individuals assigned their allotted places and roles and expected to maintain particular standards of behaviour, is as near as we get to the formal situation of the dining table.

the parlour, nobody pretended this was ideal. Even if you were forced into it, however, some formality at dinner was essential. It had to be clear that you'd made an effort.

Apart from the canteen of cutlery and the good crockery, the chiffonier needed to be stocked with, at minimum, a dozen napkins, four white damask tablecloths, a crumb brush, two salt cellars, water jug, six glass tumblers and six general-purpose wine glasses.[1] The accomplished hostess was expected to know at least the basic napkin folds, such as the Mitre, the Flirt and the Neapolitan, although Eugénie McNeil recalls a family retainer named Eileen who, in answer to some frustrated artistic urge, 'could torture table napkins into more shapes than anyone I ever knew!'[2]

'Dinner mats are no longer used, and never were necessary', the *Australian Housewives' Manual* advised. 'It is a very good plan to lay a clean napkin under any dish that has gravy in it in case the carver is clumsy, as he generally is. Another may be laid on the cloth where any careless person sits who slops

EVEN IN SUNNY QUEENSLAND, A FORMAL DININGROOM, COMPLETE WITH FIREPLACE, WAS NECESSARY FOR GRACIOUS LIVING. THIS ONE DATES FROM THE 1880S.

A HEAVILY FURNISHED
FORMAL DININGROOM OF
THE VICTORIAN ERA:
SUBJECT TO RIDICULE BY
THE 1930S.

THIS ELEGANT MODERN
DININGROOM, IN SILVER ASH
AND WHITE LEATHER, WAS
FEATURED IN *THE HOME* IN
1941.

coffee about.'[3] This is down-to-earth, practical advice, even if the dinner guest with the napkin under his plate might quite justifiably have taken offence.

Although a really spacious diningroom had become an unaffordable luxury by the 1920s, no self-respecting hostess could have done without one altogether. Even many people lower down the social scale considered it essential. Historian Nicholas Brown claims that the working-classes were in fact the most likely to adhere to strict room divisions because 'their social identities were, presumably, less secure or reliable' than those of the middle-classes.[4] Alice Harper grew up in a very modest Brisbane cottage between the wars, with 'three bedrooms, a diningroom, a kitchen and a little verandah out the front. The toilet was down the backyard'.[5] Clearly, her parents considered a diningroom to be more important than a livingroom, although it can't have been easy having the family constantly milling around in the kitchen in Brisbane's heat.

In 1931, an article in *Home Beautiful* announced, with a mixture of triumph and resignation, that the age of the small diningroom had dawned. That this

THIS WAS THE PERFECT
1950S DINING SETTING. THE
TABLE AND CHAIRS ARE A
CUT ABOVE THOSE IN THE
KITCHEN, MATS ARE AN
ELEGANT ALTERNATIVE TO
A TABLECLOTH, AND THE
CANDLE BRACKET ADDS
A TOUCH OF PIZZAZZ. ALL
THAT'S NEEDED IS SOME
SOUP FOR THE BOWL.

was the bleakest year of the depression may have been a contributing factor. 'When ground space is being economised, when little entertaining of the formal variety is done in the home, and when servants are at a premium, the dining room is the room that can best afford to be diminished in importance.' This seems reasonable enough under the circumstances, but the writer was keen to put a positive spin on it by mocking the large diningrooms of the past. 'Have you ever seen a Victorian dining room in its full glory?' she asked rhetorically.

> That super-hospitable 4ft. wide table, which, fully extended, will seat upwards of twenty, and costs a small fortune to cover suitably with double damask? Those solidly upholstered chairs, that, once you are 'pushed in' pin you firmly in your place? The incredibly massive sideboard; the dinner wagon that under no circumstances could be induced to run across the floor; the 8ft. glass-fronted bookcase with sets of Scott, Thackeray and Dickens? [6]

In other words, the old days were stuffy and ponderous, whereas today we are free and easy. Yet an undercurrent of jealousy and regret is unmistakeable beneath the self-congratulation. People had good reason to envy the Victorians their '8ft glass-fronted bookcases', even those who had no idea who Thackeray was.

In 1945, with the war almost over but the economic outlook still rather bleak, *Home Beautiful* took the next logical step: 'The modern tendency is to regard it as unnecessary to retain the two typical rooms for leisure or for dining and to say that we can easily dispense with the separate dining room. Used only for taking meals, it seems rather a waste of our valuable space.' [7] 'We' meant middle-class families who had previously thought that only the poor would tolerate such a compromise. Now it was 'the modern tendency'. To avoid crowding and to maintain that essential light, spacious look as you tried to make one room serve as two, drop-leaf or fold-away tables, built-ins and slender-legged chairs were recommended. 'The main thing', the article concluded, 'is to discard

conservative ideas and to follow up intelligently and judiciously the modern trend with its feeling for function, rhythm of space and color'.[8]

As researcher Alastair Grieg has noted of another homemakers' magazine, *Australian House and Garden*, three strategies were typically used to convince a reluctant public to accept the 'modern tendencies'. First, people were made to feel individually stuffy and out of touch: although the new designs might look unattractive and uncomfortable, you were sure to like them once you got over your silly prejudices. Next, earlier designs and fashions were denigrated as self-evidently inferior, as in *Home Beautiful*'s little tirade against the Victorian diningroom, quoted above. Finally, in desperation, the whole Australian nation was painted as a backward sort of place, especially when compared to America.[9]

IN SMART, MODERN HOMES, SUCH AS THIS ONE, DESIGNED BY HARRY SEIDLER IN 1954, THE EMPHASIS WAS ON INFORMALITY, WITH LIVING AND DININGROOMS COMBINED.

Rejuvenation and Decency

Because the public had never ceased to be dubious about zigzags and sunbursts in lapis lazuli and black marble, which were all too redolent of movie theatres and dancehalls, and also just because everyone was tired of upheaval, the word 'modern' in the late 1940s came to denote the simple, the sober and the modestly comfortable. Although wartime experimentation had brought some exciting innovations in construction methods and materials, it seemed tasteless to be too showy at a time when every second family was struggling with bereavement. Flexibility, practicality and muted elegance were called for (the word 'charm', so ubiquitous in the 1920s, had quite the wrong associations and had given way to 'smart'). While ordinary folk sought refuge from troubled times in overstuffed armchairs and gaudy floral carpets, all truly progressive eyes were turned to Sweden. 'The natural home-loving character of the Swede', claimed style guru Nora Cooper, 'together with an abundance of the native material timber, has resulted in the production of furniture which is thoroughly domestic, first rate in quality and not expensive'.[10] What more could one ask?

The enthusiasm shown for all things Swedish at the Festival of Britain in 1951 was a way of avoiding the unpalatable fact that the best modern design was German. The Scandinavians had the distinct advantage of being modest and democratic, and comfortably remote from exhausted, war-torn states in the rest of Europe. As the 1940s swung into the 1950s, something crackled in the air—something about rejuvenation, refreshment and decency—and the Swedes pressed all the right buttons. In any case, if you were going to embrace the post-war enthusiasm for plain, wholesome cooking, it seemed only right that you should eat it from a plain, wholesome-looking table.

As it turned out, this reticent, less utopian approach to new design, its association with economy, well-being and polite good taste rather than radicalism, hastened its acceptance. Since tables, chairs and sideboards were a long-term investment, they had to be chosen with caution. You could always let your hair down when choosing a radio or electric food-warmer because such things were given to glitz, and no doubt you would have to replace them before they went out of fashion anyway. As a general rule, furniture was modern if it looked European while appliances were modern if they looked American.

One exception was the splayed leg, a half-hearted concession to the American passion for streamlining things, even those that were never meant to move. There was no practical advantage in having the legs of your dining table or cabinet set at an angle, but they seemed to defy gravity, enhancing the impression of lightness and adding a touch of pizzazz to some otherwise boringly functional objects. Flying saucers in 1950s sci-fi movies extended splayed legs as they landed in Nevada or San Francisco, and that was enough to recommend them to a generation at once fascinated by and fearful of what the future might hold.

IN THE 1950S, LAMINEX AND TUBULAR STEEL WERE THE LAST WORD IN STYLE.

At few other times in history has the homeowner been presented with such a dazzling range of new building, furnishing and decorating materials. Many post-war innovations must have seemed really quite miraculous, and they contributed immeasurably to the general air of optimism. At the top of the market, for example, aluminium sideboards, dining tables and chairs were causing quite a sensation, although whether anyone actually bought them is open to question. The soft sheen of polished aluminium was terribly twentieth century, combining well with fine timber veneer, which, as one not entirely convinced critic noted, 'somehow makes the furniture more homely'.[11]

Tubular steel chairs were also enjoying a vogue at the smart end of town. Before the war they had been regarded as a bit extreme, especially those cantilevered dining chairs designed in 1928 by the German Marcel Breuer which looked positively dangerous to anyone accustomed to a leg in each corner.* In the parlance of the time, shiny chromium steel furniture was 'mechanistic': all right in the kitchen, perhaps, but unsuited to the feeling of warmth and dignity you wanted in a formal dining area. Standards still had to be maintained.

Later, however, as kitchen, diningroom and livingroom began to meld into one another and domestic protocols dropped away, such distinctions mattered less. Provided it was nicely designed, perhaps with a woven-cane seat and wooden arm-rests to distinguish it from the commoner kitchen variety, the chrome dining chair, with its clean, simple lines, could serve as an elegant indicator of sensible modern living.

For years toys, gramophone records, radio cabinets and telephones had been made of Bakelite, a hard, brittle material that could be moulded into

* They are still in production today and are, apparently, the world's most popular chair design.

MODERN LAMINEX LIVING

TEMPO SET BY TUBULAR STEEL

Table and chairs created by G. A. Whiting, Mitcham, Victoria

In a few short years, Laminex and Tubular Steel Furniture have changed our whole conception of modern furnishing, *now making it possible for everyone* to afford the *best* in furniture. Wonderful things can happen to your home when you choose Laminex and Tubular Steel. Wonderful things in your kitchen, your dining room, in fact every room in your house. Tubular Steel Furniture saves you so much cleaning time. Your Laminex furniture retailer has a full range of lovely Laminex furniture for every room in your home. Call and see it today.

* Laminex is a trade name, often used loosely to describe other more costly, inferior substitutes. Always insist on genuine Laminex.

Guarantee: *Laminex is fully guaranteed against fault in manufacture. Any sheet which is defective as a result of such fault will be replaced without cost. (NOTE that this guarantee does not cover the actual application of the sheet to any surface as this is always outside the Company's control.) Laminex is also guaranteed to resist temperatures up to 275°F. Oven-hot utensils and hot irons exceed this safe temperature.*

ALWAYS INSIST ON GENUINE LAMINEX®

MRS GRIFFITH, OF
MELBOURNE, SHOWS OFF
THE DINING SECTION OF
HER LIVINGROOM IN 1956.
HER HUSBAND BUILT THE
ROOM DIVIDER FROM PLANS
PUBLISHED IN *AUSTRALIAN
HOME BEAUTIFUL*.

almost any form. Invented in 1907, Bakelite had really taken off in the late 1920s when the original patent expired. So everyone knew about plastics. Few, though, were prepared for the revolution that the post-war plastics industry would bring. There seemed to be no limit to the potential of this fabulous new material. In America, by the mid 1940s, designers Charles and Ray Eames had produced a moulded plastic chair. Even mass-produced plastic houses were being proposed, although nobody expected to see them any time soon. What were available, however, and very popular, were plastic-laminated wood veneers, which rendered your fine walnut or maple dining suite impervious to hot plates and cigarette burns.

Generally speaking, 'the plastics age', so long forecast, would not really dawn until the late 1960s, when the average suburban house would contain polythene bags, bowls, detergent bottles and lunch-boxes; polystyrene refrigerator linings, wall-tiles, containers and simulated-wood furniture; PVC shower curtains, upholstery, plumbing fittings and packaging; polypropylene washing-machine tubs, appliance parts, carpet backing, toilet seats and outdoor carpets; acrylic paints, light fittings, sinks, baths, tables, chairs and corrugated roofing; and countless other things made from polyurethanes, melamines, nylons, acetates and polyesters. These are developments of which today we are scarcely aware, so completely have we accepted plastics into our lives.

The furniture featured in *Home Beautiful*'s 'Furniture Plan' for 1951 conforms to all the latest trends. It is, says the magazine (displaying a tentativeness typical of the era), designed to appeal to those who are 'probably fairly modern in outlook and are likely to accept a slightly unconventional solution if it meets their needs'.[12] Most importantly, though, it 'can be built by anyone who has been skilful enough to build the house'.[13] This suggests one reason, aside from its cost and limited availability, that metal and plastic furniture failed to make much of an impact on the average suburban home until at least the mid-1960s. Many people were reduced to constructing their own furniture, and that meant hammer, saw, screws and planks of wood. Even if you could afford to purchase what you needed, you had to be sure that if a leg started wobbling or a corner was chipped, you could fix it yourself. Timber was a familiar material. People knew how to work with it and owned the tools to repair and maintain it. The new synthetic materials would gain real popularity only when Australians became wealthy enough to be able to throw things away as soon as they became worn or damaged (although, paradoxically, chromed metals and the various forms of plastics, being non-degradable and toxic, are among the least suitable materials to be putting into landfill).

With a trestle at each end and a lick of paint, one of the new plywood flush-panel doors made a perfectly serviceable dining table. Caneite, an insulating board made from sugar-cane waste, could, at a pinch, substitute for a plastered wall, at least until the kids pushed the points of their Biros into it. Caneite was so soft and malleable that doing it damage was an almost irresistible temptation.

Masonite hardboard was more robust but, because it lacked insulating properties, it was best for those hard-wearing areas where comfort was not the main concern. Being easy to cut and nail, and very forgiving of the amateur, Masonite was ideal for built-ins and spruced up quite well with the new hardwearing enamels. Dulux, available in twenty-two colours (including Saxe blue, Hydrangea and Zephyr's Breath), dried in a day and could be wiped clean with a damp cloth. If you had to take in boarders to make ends meet, as many families did, a hardboard partition kept them safely at arm's length. Spare bedrooms and redundant diningrooms can be turned into snug apartments, advised *Women's Weekly* in 1945, 'but don't, I beg you, be too matey'.[14] Masonite checked mateyness.

Although advertisements for Caneite and Masonite made every effort to gloss them with an aura of contemporary sophistication, everyone knew they were just for making the best of a difficult situation. A 1945 Masonite promotion suggested overcoming the housing shortage with the three-in-one room: 'you can combine living, dining and bedroom in one room using built-ins and fold-down beds'.[15] Open-plan living might have been the ideal, but harsh reality made this the great age of the stud-wall.

Hardboard was the perfect base for decorative laminates, which were mass-marketed under the brand-names Laminex and Formica from the early 1950s. 'Its glamorous surface never stains, never fades, never wears', claimed the Laminex ad. It was so easy to apply that even a woman could do it and its 'new big range of light-hearted colours and patterns' included Corroboree, Yellow Batik, Woodgrain, Basketweave, and Marble.[16] Soon every Australian family was sitting down to lunch at a woodgrain Laminex table with chrome legs.

Whether cheap or expensive, what all these new materials had in common (Caneite excepted) was a hard, shiny, easy-to-clean surface. And those surfaces reflected a whole new attitude to housework.

Efficiency

During the war, women had been the 'second fighting line', conscripted into the workforce by the inappropriately named Directorate of Manpower. The young serviceman who glared accusingly from the poster pleaded, 'Won't you change your job for ME? What does it matter if the furniture does get a bit dusty ... Come on housewife. Take a Victory Job'. Factory and munitions work may have been hard, but the wages were good (although nowhere near as good as the men's, of course) and many women enjoyed the freedom and camaraderie of working life. They could hardly be expected to just meekly go back to cleaning the house at war's end. Yet that was exactly what they were expected to do. Publicity campaigns that had urged women to go out to work

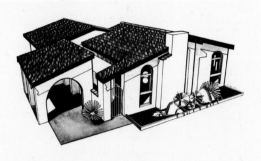

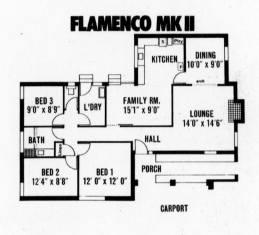

FLAMENCO MK II

were now directed at getting them to stop. Suddenly it did matter that the furniture was getting a bit dusty. Women were selfishly 'robbing the boys' of their jobs. Naturally, this caused resentment, but few women had a choice.

Emotions were conflicted. While women often missed their working days, like everyone else they wanted life to return to normal, which meant a nice house and a couple of kids, with husband in regular employment. Once again, they were called upon to make a sacrifice. Most did so willingly, but not without regret.

Women who had experienced the depression and the war years and were now having to put up with shortages of everything, including houses, would never again accept that housework was an expression of their pure love and devotion. They had other more interesting things to do with their lives. They still took pride in their domestic duties, of course, but they would not allow them to dominate. Accordingly, advertisers of appliances and household products shifted the emphasis from caring and quality to ease and convenience. The aim was much the same—to keep women at home and accord value to the work they did—but the means were subtly different.

Although, as we have seen, campaigns aimed at improving home hygiene and relieving drudgery had been around for fifty years or more, they were given a whole new impetus by American-style consumerism (which unleashed a welter of new cleaning products) and a recognition that women's roles had changed.

Formal occasions were few, and were likely to be held outside the home. People could not afford to entertain lavishly and, in any case, most had no wish to do so. A night of cards with a light supper to follow was much more friendly and relaxed. What you wanted was a house that could be kept clean and tidy

THE FLAMENCO MK II WAS A TYPICAL, LOW-PRICED PROJECT HOME IN THE EARLY 1980S. DESPITE ITS MODEST SIZE, IT INCLUDED A SEPARATE FORMAL DININGROOM.

Never were manners and social customs
more to the fore than in the
diningroom on a Sunday after church.

with minimum fuss and bother. The Good Life no longer consisted of some remote ideal of aristocratic good manners, but of a decent income for all, to be spent on consumer goods that promised ease, comfort and contentment.

No more diningrooms skulking behind half-closed doors and heavy drapes. Down came the dividing walls. From the mid 1950s, project homes and state-government home-advisory services led the way, presenting architects' practical, inexpensive planning ideas to a broad cross-section of the community. For a while, the diningroom clung on pathetically as an intermediate area with little individual character of its own, separated from the kitchen by a laminated breakfast bar and from the livingroom by something optimistically referred to as a 'room divider', consisting of open shelves dotted with china dogs, souvenirs of Rotorua and outsized Mexican pepper-grinders.

But its passing was not without some lingering regrets. In 1967, Aristoc advertised its new cast-aluminium and Laminex dining setting as 'the difference between tea and dinner', a nice play on old-fashioned class distinctions. Aristoc, as the name struggled to suggest, was supposed to 'make a meal quite different, more special'.[17] Sadly, though, it would take more than a Laminex table to do that. Hardly anyone even talked about 'dining' any more. Now it was just 'eating'.

A Civilising Place

The Aristoc advertisement provides a clue as to what was at stake in the elimination of the diningroom, aside from practicalities and economy. More than any other room in the house, it had served a ritual or symbolic purpose. It was for the maintenance of manners and social customs, subjects that had been readily brushed aside by rational planners. And never were manners and social customs more to the fore than in the diningroom on a Sunday after church.

'Sunday we ... all had to eat in the dining room,' recalled one survivor, 'the white starched table and ... I can remember this quite clearly, there was one bottle of DA beer for mum and dad, and this old Aunt Jule ... and one bottle of lemonade for my brother and I ... That was the only bottle of lemonade I can remember we ever had in the house, was Sunday dinner, and Sunday dinner was very important. The big roast sirloin and dad would carve it at the end of the table and all the vegetables would be brought in, the vegetable dish covered up, and mum served the vegetables round, and if you wanted anymore, you could help yourself, but everybody had to sit up and eat their meal correctly. That was the one day that they insisted you did the right thing ... [18]

Carving the Sunday roast, a domestic ritual dripping with symbolism, was but a faint echo of a time when bringing the entire animal to the table to be dismembered before the guests was considered a most enjoyable spectacle. As civility rendered the connections between smelly, snorting creature and what one was committing to one's mouth increasingly distasteful, ways had to be found to disguise them. By the mid nineteenth century, even the joint, whose bestial origins one would have thought were already well disguised, was disdained by persons of delicate sensibility. 'The truth is', declared an English guide to manners in 1859,

that unless our appetites are very keen, the sight of much meat reeking in its gravy is sufficient to destroy them entirely, and a huge joint especially is calculated to disgust the epicure. If joints are eaten at all, they should be placed on the side-table, where they will be out of sight.[19]

Meats could not even be referred to by their animal names. Lamb, beef and pork were acceptable at table, but not sheep, cow and pig. 'In many of our meat dishes the animal form is so concealed and changed by the art of its preparation and carving that while eating, one is scarcely reminded of its origin', notes the German cultural historian Norbert Elias, '... people, in the course of the civilizing process, seek to suppress in themselves every characteristic that they feel to be "animal". They likewise suppress such characteristics in their food'.[20] As far as blood and guts and pain and death are concerned, out of sight, out of mind is the guiding principle of modern life. This is more true today than ever before.

So the diningroom was a civilising place. Its separation from the kitchen was not just a matter of practicality. The kitchen eventually became acceptable for eating meals not only because electricity and gas made it more habitable, but also because the preparation of animal products was increasingly done outside the house altogether. When your sheep's brains and tripe come thoroughly cleaned and neatly packaged on plastic trays, and all traces of bloody slaughter have been banished, cooking and eating may be done in the one room without spoiling anyone's appetite.

Conversation

There was another sense in which the diningroom had a civilising influence. It promoted conversation. Father's insistence that all family members occupy their allotted positions around the table, observing rules of etiquette and not leaving until permission had been given, was not just about the exercise of power, although obviously it was partly that. In essence, Sunday dinner was a scheduled family meeting, structured rather like a business conference, but with the added incentive of food—not just any food, but luxuries such as lemonade that marked it off as special. The table setting, the established order of proceedings, the sense of occasion, all provided a framework that encouraged interaction. As the American journalist Judith Martin says, 'Far from squelching substantive discussion and debate, etiquette is what makes them possible ... Without such rules, there are no exchanges of ideas, only exchanges of set positions and insults'.[21]

In American television sit-coms of the 1950s and 1960s, mealtimes were frequently pictured as opportunities for mum, dad and the kids to work through

PHOTOGRAPHER GLEN
O'MALLEY'S SUGGESTIVE
RECORD OF LUNCH IN A
BRISBANE HOUSE

GLEN O'MALLEY
AUSTRALIA 1948
*14 MARCH 1987, RED
HILL, BRISBANE — THE
O'MALLEYS WERE INVITED
TO LUNCH AT THE POOLES
(FROM 'JOURNEYS NORTH'
PORTFOLIO)* 1987
GELATIN SILVER
PHOTOGRAPH ON PAPER
42.5 X 55.2 CM
COLLECTION: QUEENSLAND
ART GALLERY

and resolve their differences. A lot of important decisions were made around the table. Sit-coms presented an idealised view, of course, but Australians would nonetheless have recognised a core of truth there, and parents, anxious to instil conservative family values in their increasingly distracted offspring, clung to it for dear life.

Yet the almost desperate insistence of *Father Knows Best* and *Leave it to Beaver* on the moral superiority of the happy, middle-class, patriarchal family gathered around the dinner table was, in itself, a sign that the old ways were coming to an end. A bright new world—safe, welcoming, yet pregnant with adventure—had blossomed beyond the family home, and television, radio, the movies and popular magazines were making it irresistible. What dad might have to say as he sharpened the carving knife over the leg of lamb seemed increasingly irrelevant, even oppressive. 'In this decade of James Dean, Bill Haley and Brigitte Bardot', writes the English author Peter Vansittart, 'teenagers—a word now, like student, more often used—were taller, better nourished, better paid, already feeling themselves adult, thus often at odds with adults'.[22] It was the age of self-expression (for adults and teenagers alike), with no shortage of 'forums for debate', most of them among peers and all of them outside the home. Yet there was nothing to quite compensate for the loss of the kind of structured conversations that had previously taken place around the diningroom table. Everyone was free to talk, but in the absence of commonly respected rules of etiquette, nobody was listening.

Basically this is still why we invite friends to dinner today, to indulge in conversation—of the sustained kind you can't have when standing around a barbecue with a can of lager or hovering in the doorway at a party.

Is it cause or effect that the disappearance of formal diningrooms in our homes has coincided with a burgeoning of restaurants and coffee shops? A three-course à-la-carte dinner, if we can afford it—and even a night at the local pizza bar, to a more limited extent—furnishes us with the sense of occasion we need while imposing the necessary standards of behaviour, with the added advantage

that it demands no effort on our part, nor does it require us to put our taste and skills on the line (other than those involved in choosing the venue). This is nothing less than the professionalisation of civility, allowing us simply to pay someone to supply it to us, as people did when they had servants.

The studied formality, the air of ritual and polite good manners that we encounter in a Japanese restaurant, for example, provides the perfect corrective to the vulgarity of the Heat-n-Eat Microwave Dinner plonked on the kitchen bench in front of the telly. Although, on the surface, it may have little in common with the Sunday roast, a meal at the Meiji Palace fulfils a similar role in satisfying our cravings for dining as ceremony, even if it does place us in the position of being mere consumers.

At the same time, however, eating in public can be revealing in ways we might not like. One has only to watch as two people who have been together too long to have anything left to say to each other sit staring blankly across a restaurant table like rabbits caught in the headlights, in order to appreciate what a demeaning experience this can be. They know they are supposed to be enjoying the occasion, especially as it is costing them money, yet they lack the necessary social skills. At home, in private, they might be no less miserable, but at least their misery is not on display for all to see. The formal diningroom, for all its shortcomings, did quite a good job of providing a framework in which boredom, antagonism and antipathy could be kept under control.

MELBOURNE'S SAVOY PLAZA HOTEL WAS A FASHIONABLE PLACE TO EAT OUT IN THE MID 1960S.

The
Heart of
the Home

1910

'An ornate brick villa in the new Queen Anne style',

was how the newspaper advertisement described it, and they were fortunate to have secured it for a very reasonable £1200. It has eight spacious rooms, established flower and vegetable gardens and, as the advertisement was also keen to point out, 'superior modern conveniences'. At six miles from central Melbourne, Canterbury is admittedly rather a long way out. Nevertheless, the railways are efficient these days and the house is well within earshot of the locomotive's whistle, so Mr Ridley can be at his Collins Street dental practice well within the hour.

No wonder this is one of Melbourne's fastest-growing areas. From its hilltops, high above the city's smog, you can see all the way to Hobson's Bay and, on a warm spring morning, the air is sweet with the smell of orchards and freshly mown grass. Unlike the inner suburbs from which the Ridleys have fled, Canterbury is quiet, semi-rural and predominantly Protestant. Yet it's going ahead by leaps and bounds. The new shops along Maling Road provide all the necessities, the footpath outside their doors has been asphalted, and the major intersections are lit by gas. Those moving here are, on the whole, of a better class than one finds in the closer settled areas.[1]

For Mrs Ridley,* the house's main attraction is its up-to-date kitchen. So many places they looked at had kitchens that could only be described as dismal. Some were even outdoors, which hasn't been acceptable for at least the past forty years. Rarely is this room given serious consideration by builders, who just tack it onto the back of the house almost as an afterthought. Mrs Ridley is convinced that this is because houses are designed by men, who have no appreciation of how much time the housewife must spend at the stove. Half the trouble between mistresses and maids arises from dingy, smoky kitchens.

A spacious vestibule at the rear has a large window and glass door onto the back garden.[2] Two maids' rooms open off it at one end (only one of which is now

* Along with the other four women whose kitchen stories are told in this chapter, Mrs Ridley is a fictional figure, conjured up from various contemporary records.

THE DOMESTIC KITCHEN OF
THE BAKERY IN RICHMOND,
VICTORIA, WHERE ARTIST
FREDERICK McCUBBIN GREW
UP, WAS ALREADY RATHER
OLD-FASHIONED BY THE TIME
HE PAINTED IT IN 1884. THE
WALLS ARE WHITEWASHED,
WITH A DADO TO SHOULDER
HEIGHT. THERE BEING NO
PLUMBING, FRESH DRINKING
WATER, PURCHASED FROM
A TRAVELLING MERCHANT,
HAD TO BE STORED IN THE
CERAMIC FILTER BY THE
DOOR. A COLONIAL OVEN HAS
BEEN ROUGHLY INSTALLED IN
THE FIREPLACE. NORMALLY,
IT WOULD HAVE HAD A FIRE
BENEATH AS WELL AS ON
TOP (HENCE ITS NAME: ' THE
TWO-FIRE STOVE'), SO THIS
ARRANGEMENT WOULD HAVE
MADE IT RATHER INEFFICIENT.

FREDERICK McCUBBIN
*KITCHEN AT THE OLD KING
STREET BAKERY*
OIL ON CANVAS
50.6 X 61.2 CM
ART GALLERY OF SOUTH
AUSTRALIA

occupied, since help is so expensive and difficult to procure). A useful feature of the vestibule is the fireplace which, along with a table and some comfortable chairs, makes this an ideal sitting room for the maid. Its walls are covered to waist-height with stain-resistant oilcloth, matching in tone the wallpaper above. A pantry at the other end has doors into both the vestibule and the kitchen as well as a natty little slide giving access to the diningroom. This all makes for a very flexible arrangement. A scullery for the storage of crockery and utensils beside the kitchen features an enamelled sink with hot and cold running water, which these days is considered indispensable in the better class of house (although the hot is, of course, dependent upon the stove being alight).

The kitchen itself, the bustling hub of this ensemble, meets all the modern requirements of efficiency and cleanliness. It is spacious enough never to feel cramped, with the window facing south to maintain an even temperature in summer when the stove might otherwise make it unbearable. The floorboards, painted ferris red and finished with hard oil, look well enough, although Mrs Ridley plans to cover them with linoleum, which the experts recommend for hygiene. Above a dado of vertical lining-boards the walls are plastered. Inevitably they will get dirty, especially around the stove, and will need a good scrubbing from time to time.

THE GIRLS IN THIS
CLASS-ROOM IN 1910 ARE
LEARNING HOW TO COOK,
USING MODERN ACME GAS
STOVES, AND HOW TO
SET A TABLE PROPERLY.

Perhaps the most innovative feature of this room is its built-in dresser and cupboards. Every woman knows that the moving of heavy furniture adds immeasurably to the chore of spring cleaning. However, dirt does not accumulate behind or under these units and they also save a great deal of space. The cupboards, mounted on the wall at a convenient height, have leaded-glass doors that effectively seal out dust and flies. They are so much more effective than open shelves that surely in the future built-ins will be standard features in every kitchen.

Second daughter, Felicity, has taken a particular interest in the built-ins. She is enrolled in the College of Domestic Economy in Lonsdale Street, a recent venture which aims to prepare girls for their special mission in life.

Although, disappointingly, the course is mainly concerned with basic cookery and the proper way to make tea, Felicity is nevertheless gaining some valuable knowledge about how to deal with the servant problem, how to economise in the home, how to manage the household in a rational, business-like manner, and how to use the new equipment that is now coming onto the market in such bewildering variety.[3]

Felicity is already applying at home what she has learnt, reorganising the kitchen so as to save much walking back and forth. For instance, the marble-topped table for kneading and rolling has been placed beside the scullery door so as to be just around the corner from the sink. Its legs stand in tins of water to keep the ants at bay. The big pull-out bins beneath are now clearly labelled 'flour', 'corn meal', 'rye' and 'sugar', and the cupboard above is stocked with basins, measuring cups and baking pans, so everything needed for pastry-making is close to hand. The main work table in the centre of the room is higher than is customary to save constant bending (for years Mrs Ridley has been taking Wincarnis Restorative—'a combination of choice wine, extract of meat and extract of malt'—for the relief of her aching limbs[4]). As soon as the dishes are washed, they can be placed in a drying rack above the kauri-wood draining board, from where they can be put away in the scullery cupboard without needing to be wiped.

Above the big American wall clock on the chimney-piece, Felicity has hung an embroidered motto: 'Always be in time'.[5] This is something Mrs Ridley tries hard to impress upon Maeve, the housemaid, with limited success. Yet, whatever Mrs Ridley might think about Maeve, she is careful to keep it to herself. It is an all too common vice these days to gossip about domestic servants. There are women so constituted that they cannot meet a friend without detailing the housemaid's exorbitant demands for extra hours off, or her inveterate laziness. Such women fail to understand that, although she may be a person to her mistress, a maid is a name only to everyone else.[6]

Perhaps because of the domestics problem, Felicity is distressingly keen on mechanical gadgets, whereas her mother still holds to the sensible view that the old ways are generally best, rarely using Haughton's Revolving Grater or the mechanical apple corer and peeler her daughter gave her, however ingenious they may be. One thing she does make good use of is her old knife-cleaning machine, since the knives must be thoroughly cleaned after every use if they are not to go black, and this is a very tiresome chore to undertake by hand.

It could hardly be claimed, however, that Mrs Ridley's mind is altogether closed on matters of progress. On their visit to the ANA exhibition of

Cleaner Kitchens
and Better Cooking

M^cCLARY'S
ELECTRIC RANGES

YOU can rid your kitchen of fumes and
oppressive heat by installing a
McCLARY Electric Cooker. This will
mean greater comfort whilst cooking, for
the McCLARY Electric Range keeps the
heat in the oven and does not heat the
room.

Write for booklet describing McCLARY
Stoves, or, better still, call and have the simplicity and economy of any model explained to you.

ALL MODELS IN STOCK
FROM £21/10/ UPWARDS.

OUR SHOWROOMS, over 2600 sq.
ft. in area, contain a model kitchen
in which is fitted a McClary Range,
Washing Machines and Water Heaters.
There is also a model bathroom with electric Bath Heaters, Towel Rails and Mirrors. See these ideal rooms and plan your
home on similar lines.

Over 300 Lighting Fixtures, excluding the
many Period Fittings, Pendants, Brackets,
Floor Standards, etc., are displayed for easy
choice.

CALL AND LOOK AT THEM.

Brooks, Robinson's
59-65 Elizabeth St., Melbourne

THE GREAT ADVANTAGE OF
ELECTRIC STOVES WAS THAT
THEY DID NOT HEAT UP THE
KITCHEN. HOWEVER, £21 WAS
A LOT OF MONEY IN 1927.

Australian Manufactures and Products earlier this
year, she was quite astonished by demonstrations
of cooking with electricity. Kettles briskly boiling
with no visible flame beneath them were enough
to make any housewife long for the advent of
the electric stove, with no handling of wood,
coal or hot ashes, nor any smoke or fumes.[7] The
Melbourne Electric Supply Company plans to
extend its services into this area within the next
year or two,[8] although only for the purposes of
lighting. From what she has seen of electric light,
Mrs Ridley is firmly of the opinion that it is much
too hard and bright for the home. All the same, she
has to admit that the gas jet in the kitchen, situated
most inconveniently above the mantlepiece some
eight feet from the floor, is not only difficult to light but of little benefit when
she is cooking. On dull days, she must stand at the stove with a candle in one
hand and a fork in the other.[9]

The demonstrations of gas cooking at the ANA exhibition were of less
interest, since gas stoves have been around (although admittedly not especially
popular) for nearly thirty years. Mrs Ridley has a gas cooker as an accessory
to the main stove and in summer it can certainly save the build-up of heat in
the kitchen. It must be admitted, too, that today's cleaner gas does not taint
food as the old sort did. However, for roasting and baking, only the big IXL
range will do. It is Maeve's responsibility to rise early and have the fire well
alight before breakfast, thus ensuring that the kettle is ready and there is ample
hot water on tap in the scullery. Mrs Ridley is familiar with the big stove's
every idiosyncrasy. By throwing a handful of salt into the oven and observing
whether it sticks to the sides, for example, she can tell when the right baking
temperature has been reached. It's a trick she learned from her mother.

While no less conscious of family health and well-being than any modern woman, Mrs Ridley draws the line at an American doctor's recommendation, enthusiastically relayed by Felicity, that vegetables need only be lightly steamed.[10] She is content to follow the advice of her reliable Australian guide, *Home and Health*, boiling carrots for one to two hours, peas for thirty minutes, spinach for thirty to sixty minutes, cabbage (if young and tender) for fifty minutes and lentils for eight hours or so.[11]

Of course, cooking is a lot more arduous in summer than it is in the winter when the warmth of the stove is of benefit. This summer would have tested any kitchen, with temperatures frequently hovering around the century mark. Under such conditions, a block of ice barely lasts the night in the Snowden Refrigerator, even when wrapped in a blanket, and the drip pan is constantly overflowing across the kitchen floor. Many's the time Mrs Ridley has had to discard milk that had soured because the ice-man failed to arrive early enough—or, even more annoyingly, because Maeve forgot to collect the milk bucket from the front gate before the sun got to it. Half the time, the milk is on the turn even before it arrives, which might be understandable in the inner suburbs, but not out here where dairy farms are close-by. Well aware that bad milk is one of Melbourne's chief causes of serious illness, Mrs Ridley insists on scalding it and sterilising the billy daily. She keeps handy one or two cans of Nestlé's condensed milk in case of emergencies. Recently, she read that a Melbourne firm is planning to dry milk for sale as a powder, which apparently tastes no different from the new pasteurised variety.* Meanwhile, she has hung a Coolgardie safe in the vestibule to help preserve her perishables. Indeed, she is inclined to think that this tried and tested device is rather more dependable than the modern ice-chest, even if one is constantly having to top up the water in hot weather.*

Much to Mrs Ridley's displeasure (although of course she was careful not to show it), Felicity has given her a fan whose blades are propelled by a kerosene burner.[12] Although it creates a gentle breeze, the effect is offset by the

* Pasteurisation was first used for milk in 1889, but the practice was so slow to be adopted that it may well have seemed new to Mrs Ridley in 1910.

* A Coolgardie safe is a wire-mesh enclosure hung where it will catch the breeze. Long strands of hessian or towelling, suspended from a tray of water on top, siphon moisture down the sides of the safe, thus cooling its interior by evaporation.

Rising before six, she takes a vigorous
hand-bath, combs her hair and dons her
apron ready for the day's chores.

heat of the burner and the kerosene smell. Maeve refuses to enter the kitchen while it is working, complaining that it interferes with her breathing, although she regularly uses kerosene for household cleaning without complaint and relies on a kerosene lamp in her room.

Of course, the best way to avoid the heat is by means of a sensible working schedule,[13] the aim being to keep out of the kitchen as much as possible during the hottest part of the day. Fortunately, as Mr Ridley takes his luncheon in town, his wife is spared the necessity of having to prepare a proper meal mid-day, as she did when they lived near the city. Rising before six, she takes a vigorous hand-bath,* combs her hair and dons her apron ready for the day's chores. By this time Maeve has, she hopes, got the stove going and brought in the milk. The table having been set, the family gathers for a breakfast of toast, tea and flaked rice or porridge, there being little necessity for heavy breakfasts these days, especially in the warmer months. When her husband and the two girls have left, she and Maeve do the washing up and get the kitchen clean and tidy, with not so much as a crumb left to attract the flies. Then it is time to close the windows against the heat and draw the blinds.

When the bathroom, hall and diningroom have been thoroughly swept and the beds made, it is time for a brief rest and a welcome cup of tea. Then the evening meal is got underway—the joint and the vegetables prepared so there is nothing more to do later than to put them on to cook, cutlery cleaned and placed on a tray ready for setting the table, and a pudding made, to be served cold.

After the lunch dishes have been washed and put away, the afternoon may be spent sewing, mending, receiving callers or shopping. Mrs Ridley also puts aside half an hour each afternoon to bring the household accounts up to date. By then it is time to get the stove hot again for the evening meal. In the summer, however, Mrs Ridley finds that hot meat and vegetables are not always necessary, a soup or broth making an excellent substitute if accompanied by salad and a cold meat pie. It was, of course, Felicity who introduced

IN THE EARLY 1900S, LAWS HAD BEEN INTRODUCED TO CONTROL MILK PRODUCTION AND TRANSPORT, BUT THEY WERE INEFFECTIVE. BY THE 1920S, WHEN THIS POSTER WAS ISSUED, MUCH OF THE MILK SOLD IN CITIES WAS CONTAMINATED. NOT UNTIL WELL AFTER WORLD WAR II WOULD PASTEURISATION AND REFRIGERATED TRANSPORT BECOME THE NORM.

* For a description of a 'hand bath', see p.184.

Sybil Jason
FAMOUS NEW 6 YEAR OLD FILM STAR
says "I Love Milk"

her to salads, and she finds them so easy to prepare and so nutritious that it's a wonder they are so little known.[14] All the same, she would never serve them if guests were present. In this heat, the lettuces and celery in the shops are likely to be so limp that very little can be done with them, so Mr Ridley's kitchen garden comes in very handy.

All being well, she will have time for a bath in the late afternoon in order to appear bright and supportive when the family arrives home at around seven. After the meal—which they like to linger over, since it is the only time the family has a chance to sit together and talk—the girls help to clean up, wash the pots and pans, and scald the milk pail while Mr Ridley gets in the wood and coal for the morning. Of course, there are other chores for Mrs Ridley beside this regular daily round. The laundry is a major undertaking every Monday, for example, and a thorough cleaning and reblacking of the stove is necessary from time to time, not to mention the myriad minor tasks, such as trimming the lamp wicks, preserving fruit and making laundry soap, which, although they are not onerous in themselves, do take up time.

Nevertheless Mrs Ridley's workload is nowhere near what it was when the children were young and it must be said that her well-designed and well-equipped kitchen makes life so much easier than it might have been.

1934

The kitchen is not something Grace Swan wants to be much concerned about. In the past, women seem to have spent most of their lives in front of the stove, but times have changed. For Grace, it is enough that her kitchen be compact and bright and serves its purpose.

This is one reason she and Dennis chose a flat in Kings Cross after they were married. Well, that and the fact that there really wasn't much option financially after Dennis refused to live with Grace's parents. 'It's part of the solution of the home question at present for young married couples to stay

ARNOTT'S WAS THE
ANSWER FOR ALL THOSE
NERVOUS ABOUT THEIR
SAVOURIES IN 1934.

with their relations', protested her mother. 'If your husband persists in his high-falutin' notions you'll never have a place of your own.' But there will be plenty of time to secure a house when they decide on a family. Meanwhile, the excitement of inner-city life is available for enjoying, and they intend to make the best of it. Most Europeans, apparently, live in blocks of flats, which makes the Australian insistence that everyone should be in a suburban villa all the more difficult to understand.

Through the lifting clouds of the depression, a few sunbeams are at last appearing. Only the other day the state government announced a new Home Building Plan that will make houses more affordable for middle- and low-income earners. Dennis has promised to look into it.[15] Meanwhile Grace maintains her job as a stenographer, despite the general antipathy towards working women and her employer's initial reluctance to keep her on after she was married. A member of state parliament recently expressed outrage at girls going to work even when there was no real necessity for them to do so, just because 'everybody is doing it' and they enjoy being 'in the swim, in the rush and glamour of life'.[16] He doesn't seem to appreciate just how necessary the extra household income is.

MODULAR KITCHENS ARE NOT A NEW IDEA. IN 1934, SUNSHINE KITCHENS OFFERED TO ADAPT ITS STANDARDISED, FACTORY-MADE UNITS TO ANY SPACE. THE ONE SHOWN HERE IS CLEARLY TOP-OF-THE-RANGE, WITH ELECTRIC REFRIGERATOR, LIGHTS OVER THE SINK, A SMART CANVAS AWNING OUTSIDE AND A SEPARATE BREAKFAST NOOK.

IN THIS 1930S INNER-CITY KITCHEN, A GAS STOVE HAS BEEN FITTED AWKWARDLY INTO THE OLD FIREPLACE, WITH A LINE STRUNG IN FRONT OF IT FOR DRYING WASHING. JESUS LOOKS OUT FROM BEHIND THE CANISTERS AND CUT-PAPER VALANCES ADORN THE MANTLEPIECE.

* At the end of 1933, the average weekly wage for adult women was 43s 2d, down from 53s 7d in 1929. The average wage for adult men was 80s 6d, a decline of 1s 4d from the previous year. Dennis' 95s a week would have been just under the average for the printing industry (Commonwealth Year Book, 1934).

Kings Cross is a busy, cosmopolitan, friendly sort of place, full of young professional people who know how to have a good time. Friday and Saturday nights are always lively, although there are a few shady characters around, so one needs to take care. Repins now serves real coffee (not the milky stuff made with coffee essence you get everywhere else) and the White Rose in William Street has the best bread and butter custard in Sydney. You can even get continental brown and wholemeal breads from the mixed business just off Macleay Street, although they are mainly for foreigners and those who like to put on airs and graces. Once or twice a week, however, on her way to work, she drops off a covered dish, which, for just sixpence, they fill with delicious egg salad for her to pick up in the evening. In winter, a hot stew can be had for just a few pence extra.[17]

Look after the pennies and the pounds will look after themselves, as Grace's mother keeps insisting. Yet, however hard they try, it's not easy to make ends meet, with prices on the rise again while wages just keep falling. Grace's forty-five shillings a week is almost entirely swallowed up in rent, while the ninety-five shillings Dennis earns in the printing trade has to cover all their bills and living expenses, leaving precious little to put aside towards a house.* Yet they can still afford to splash out on a movie every Friday as well as the occasional night out with friends. At fifteen shillings a head, Romano's all-night dinner dance is a rare treat, and one they are careful not to tell Grace's mother about.[18]

Everyone knows that modern flats are much better appointed than any speculative builder's cottage. In order to attract tenants, the builders of flats are leading the way in the design of efficient modern kitchens and bathrooms.

SUNSHINE" in your kitchen... a sensible Centenary suggestion!

MANY otherwise charming homes are spoilt by the uninviting appearance of the kitchen . . . or it may be that the kitchen, while being pleasant enough to the eye, is ill-designed or badly fitted. The housewife spends much of her day in the kitchen . . . it is, in fact, her "workshop." It is but fitting, then, that the kitchen should be given greater attention. The equipment to be found in factories and offices is always modern and efficient. The kitchen, too, should be so equipped as to reduce the labor of housework and to make the surroundings pleasant. This may be achieved at surprisingly low cost by fitting "Sunshine" units.

SUNSHINE Kitchen Units are designed especially to suit any room. Large rooms . . . small rooms . . . rooms with no odd corners . . . rooms with too many corners . . . all of these can be transformed into kitchens of convenience and beauty by the use of Sunshine Units. Sunshine Kitchen Equipment is made in standardised units that are quickly and economically installed. Brighten up your home for the Centenary . . . and make the kitchen the first room to have attention! You are cordially invited to call at our Showrooms and inspect the various types of kitchen units available. If you cannot call, write or 'phone for full details.

Call and inspect the displays of Model Kitchens at the Sunshine Showrooms...these displays incorporate "Silva" sinks supplied by

R. H. MYTTON & Co. Pty. Ltd.
Offices and Showrooms, 119-127 York Street South Melb., SC5.

ring SUNSHINE into your home...
stal handy kitchen units made by

SUNSHINE BUILT-IN HOUSEHOLD EQUIPMENT PTY. LTD.

THIS NEAT 1940S KITCHEN
HAS A DOUBLE STAINLESS
STEEL SINK, BENCHTOP GAS
STOVE (THE OVEN WOULD
SIT BESIDE IT, OUT OF SHOT)
AND BUILT-IN FLUE.

* In 1934 an electric fridge
cost around £65, which was
almost a third of the average
yearly male wage. That
would be the equivalent
today of about $17 000.

The luxury apartments now going up along Macleay Street and down into Elizabeth Bay, such as Birtley Towers and Chesterfield, have every amenity, including electric refrigerators, basement laundries equipped with the latest gas coppers, and telephones in the vestibules.[19]

Although it is, as the letting agent put it, 'compact', and offers no harbour views, Grace and Dennis' flat boasts a gas stove, a Goodrid incinerator in the basement with chutes on every landing, and hot water at all hours courtesy of a Briar gas heater over the sink, whose little pilot light stands ready to spring into action at the turn of the tap.[20] Of course, for a rent of £2 a week, one can hardly expect an electric refrigerator,* let alone a lift, but the ice-chest in the hall has an outside door accessible to the iceman, so it is not necessary to be at home when he calls. These are hardly the sorts of luxuries you would expect to find in the average suburban house.

The kitchen is the epitome of the compact, efficient domestic workshop, equipped to save time and effort, to maintain hygiene and to look cheerful.[21]

It is designed in the modern manner for eating in as well as for cooking, although of course formal meals must still be served in the livingroom. The sheer convenience of having breakfast in the kitchen is a real boon when they are hurrying to get off to work.

Electric sockets throughout the building are of the modern three-pin type, thus eliminating any danger of shocks. For a nominal fee, the Haron Electric Company offers a personal course of instruction for new tenants on how to connect and use electrical appliances, but Grace and Dennis opted to take their chances.[22] As yet, the iron and the toaster are the only things they have that need to be plugged in, except, of course, for the radio in the livingroom. Magazine illustrations of General Electric's Model Kitchen offer the enticing promise of 'woman's complete emancipation from kitchen drudgery', with a Hotpoint cooking range, GE refrigerator, electric dishwasher, heater and ventilating fan. Grace dreams that she will have something like this one day.[23]

The flat's designers have made good use of metals and glass, which go so well with the ivory and green walls, compensating to some extent for the tiny window which looks out onto nothing more interesting than a brick wall. Even Grace's mother is impressed by the new stainless steel Monel sink with double draining board. She is always complaining that her enamelled sink breaks plates, and her terrazzo draining board, installed only a year or so back, is already stained.

As is the trend in flats these days, everything here is built-in. An enamelled table, hinged to the wall, drops down when not in use and the bench seat has a lift-up top with storage beneath. Some brightly coloured cushions that

SYLVIA EVANS WAS FORTUNATE TO HAVE A REFRIGERATOR IN HER KITCHEN AT ARNCLIFFE, SYDNEY, IN 1940. IT FEATURES A FREEZER CABINET WITH ICE-CREAM TRAYS AND RACKS IN THE DOOR FOR FRUIT AND VEGETABLES.

Grace is having sewn up at Mark Foy's will make it a little more welcoming. The wall-cabinet opposite is virtually a kitchen in itself, complete with two cupboards with leadlight doors above, a roll-top bread bin, a cool cupboard for perishables, drawers for cutlery and linen, and ample storage space under the benchtop. The cupboard doors have fashionable glass knobs and patented spring latches that snap shut tightly at the slightest touch.[24] An aluminium saucepan stand holding five saucepans and a kettle nestles in the corner next to the stove.

At first, Grace was disconcerted to find the stove standing directly on the linoleum floor without any brick surround or mantlepiece and only a metal flue to carry off the fumes. But she now realises that there is no necessity to contain a gas or electric stove in a fireplace. Old habits die hard. Hers is a Metter's Early Kooka of the new automatic type, with an oven heat regulator that can only be described as a cooking revolution. A dial controls the flame, allowing her to set the desired position and forget her cooking until the scheduled period has

MRS ADRIANA
ZEVENBERGEN, AUSTRALIA'S
100 000TH POST-WAR
DUTCH MIGRANT, ARRIVED
IN AUSTRALIA WITH HER
HUSBAND IN 1958.

FOOD RATIONING WAS
INTRODUCED IN AUSTRALIA
IN 1942. TWO YEARS LATER,
SEVERE DROUGHT MEANT
RATIONS WERE FURTHER
REDUCED TO 60 GRAMS OF
TEA, 450 GRAMS OF SUGAR,
170 GRAMS OF BUTTER AND
A KILOGRAM OF MEAT PER
PERSON PER WEEK. MAX
DUPAIN'S PHOTOGRAPH,
THE MEAT QUEUE, TAKEN IN
1946, CONVEYS THE STRESS
OF RATIONING.

MAX DUPAIN
THE MEAT QUEUE 1946
GELATIN SILVER PRINT
45.5 X 54.7 CM
MONASH GALLERY OF ART

elapsed. She can go out shopping or listen to *The Comedy Players* on 2BL without having to continually open the oven door to check on progress.[25]

Although all the necessary kitchen fittings, along with the furniture in the rest of the flat, were installed by the builders, Grace has added some personal touches of her own, things she can take with her when they buy their own place. For just two shillings at Mark Foy's, for instance, she found a natty little tea silo which attaches to the wall and delivers a spoonful of tea at the twist of a lever.[26] Her polished aluminium teapot and coffee percolator look very good on the window sill above the sink, and a lacquered metal stand with three shelves keeps her vegetables fresh and tidy. Of course, she has also secured the basics—clock-faced weighing scales, a geared egg-beater, a meat mincer which clamps onto the edge of the table, a whistling kettle, a set of enamelled-metal canisters with raised lettering, and so on.

Since, of necessity, she and Dennis rely a good deal on canned foods (an expensive waste of money, according to mother), she was happy to pay a bit extra for one of the new can openers which operate by turning a handle, rather than the sharp lever-action type that invariably cause an injury.[27] Great strides have been made in food canning over the past decade or so, especially as regards its vitamin content. Well over 200 foodstuffs are now tinned and the list, starting with milk, soups, meat, fruits and jams, extends to such delicacies as whole hams and chickens, shellfish and even steak and onions.[28]

Like all sensible young homemakers, Grace reserves a kitchen drawer for coupons. She has already collected six from packets of Fountain Self Raising Flour to claim her free beach towel, which turned out to be disappointingly small. The 100 Sunlight Soap box-tops required for a set of bedsheets will take longer, as will the 72 Rinso coupons for a damask tablecloth. Hardly a product is sold these days without a coupon offer. They permit women to acquire so many things they could not otherwise afford.

To that end, too, the sewing machine behind the bedroom door is proving most useful and her Thursday evening needlework classes are holding her

BY THE EARLY 1960S, A WIDE
RANGE OF CONTINENTAL
FOODS WAS ON OFFER
THROUGH DEPARTMENT
STORES AND SPECIALTY
SHOPS, ALTHOUGH NATIVE-
BORN AUSTRALIANS
REMAINED SUSPICIOUS.

in good stead. At the urging of *Home Beautiful*, she has also taken up asbestos craft, which she does at the kitchen table on weekends. Nock and Kirby's sell offcuts of this versatile material, from which shelf coverings, table mats, cutting boards and many other useful items can be fashioned. As the magazine says,

> the average handy-woman would have no trouble in dealing with the material herself as it can be cut with a saw ... and the edges can be smoothed by rubbing with glass or sandpaper. It is easy to keep clean and, with its greyish-white coloring, it looks efficient, smart and fresh.[29]

1956

Australia is an odd sort of place. Well, she hasn't seen much of it—only Adelaide—so she can't say really. But Adelaide is not like Rotterdam, that she does know. When Marion and Josephus van Heemstra first arrived here with their two children three years ago, it was all a bit of a shock. You couldn't even call Klemzig a real community, just a grid of dusty, unmade roads on the city fringe lined with weatherboard Housing Trust bungalows, all built to much the same design.* Although they are clean and modern, their tin roofs are not insulated, making them fearfully hot in summer.[30] And not a tree in sight! In the mornings, after Josephus had gone to work and the boys were at

* The South Australian Housing Trust, a state government body, provided rental accommodation for migrants and low-income earners.

AN ELECTRIC STOVE MADE
IN AUSTRALIA BY SIMPSON
IN THE EARLY 1950S

school, Marion felt trapped there, so far from town and so far from home. There were periods of such desperate loneliness that she often felt physically ill.

Gradually, though, they've got to know some of the neighbours. The majority are English, but there's a Scandinavian family over the road and an elderly couple from Leiden further down (Calvinist, unfortunately). Yet, whatever their nationality, they are all professional people or skilled workers who, like Marion and Josephus, were drawn to South Australia by generous state government incentives. Being among like-minded folk certainly makes it easier to break the ice. In addition, she and Josephus often go to functions organised by the Catholic Dutch Club, such as the forthcoming pre-Easter Carnival at Hindmarsh Town Hall,[31] just one of the many ways the church has helped them adjust to their new surroundings. It was at one of the club's functions that she first met Marjorie Connolly, who is not Dutch but got involved as a volunteer because she wanted to help the New Australians. Marjorie, who has an elegant older-style house in Hindmarsh, has become a friend, although she can be annoyingly condescending at times. 'I prefer the Dutch to other European migrants', she says, 'because they are more like us. They're prepared to fit in to our Australian way of life'.

As Josephus, always an optimist, has never ceased to point out, here in Australia the family is free from the fear of famine and far from the awful physical and psychological suffering of the war years. Here he has a good job with General Motors–Holden's Ltd., they have a secure place to live, education for the youngsters and the promise of better times ahead.

So Marion has set about turning their three-bedroom house into a real Dutch home*: *gezellig*–cosy and homely–unlike Marjorie's, which, in common with the other Australian homes she's been in, looks frugal and under-furnished, with everything pushed against the walls, leaving the middle of the room bare.[32]

* In her book *The Dutch Down Under*, Nonja Peters shows that Dutch women tended to remain firmly within the domestic sphere. 'Creating a Dutch home in Australia is what Dutch men folk expected of their wives. However, these women perceived their confinement to the domestic sphere as advantageous, rather than oppressive or the outcome of male dominance' (p. 229).

You'll win a cooking reputation...

Do you like to hear your family say, "Ah! That's delicious!" when they sit down to one of your carefully cooked meals? What housewife doesn't? You'll find Dad and *all* the family tackle their meals with a new zest—and you'll get this result with *less* time and trouble with a Hotpoint Electric Range. Models are available to suit every family.

HEAVY CAST HOTPLATES
Even heating eliminates hotspots in simmering

HI-SPEED CALROD HOTPLATE
Fast, reliable, glows red

SIMMERSTAT
Infinitely variable heat control

PRECISION TEMPERATURE INDICATOR

"KICK" RECESS

ONE-PIECE STAINLESS ENAMEL TOP

GLEAMING CREAM ENAMEL FINISH

SIDE-HINGE OVEN DOOR
Saves stretching across hot door

OUTSIZE OVEN

You'll be delighted with the speed, ease and cleanliness of cooking with the Hotpoint LM36 Electric Range—the range with the red-glowing calrod hotplate. Also available with automatic oven temperature control. Hotpoint Ranges are backed by 40 years' experience in electric range manufacture.

Hotpoint

MODEL LM36 ELECTRIC
RANGE

There's a Hotpoint Electric Servant for every domestic need

OBTAINABLE
FROM YOUR LOCAL
HOTPOINT
RETAILER

AUSTRALIAN
GENERAL ELECTRIC
PROPRIETARY LIMITED

SYDNEY, NEWCASTLE, LISMORE, MELBOURNE, BRISBANE, ROCKHAMPTON, TOWNSVILLE,
ADELAIDE, HOBART, LAUNCESTON. AGENT IN W.A.: ATKINS (W.A.) LTD.

Good hospitality depends upon a good kitchen. Although Marion's may be basic, she's made the best of it. The Housing Trust equipped it with little more than a stainless-steel sink under the window that looks out over the backyard, flanked on one side by an electric stove and on the other by a built-in flywired larder. In the corner sits Marion's greatest joy, her Electrolux gas fridge, something she had long coveted and one of the first things they bought when they moved in, despite Josephus's opposition to hire purchase. 'If you want something', he insists, 'then you should save for it'. On the wall opposite the window stands her old Dutch dresser and the table is in the centre, under the fringed lightshade. For some unaccountable reason, Australians all seem to go in for tubular steel kitchen furniture, which, as far as Marion is concerned, looks cold and industrial. Chrome is for cars, not tables and chairs. She much prefers the charm of wood, which she is pleased to see is coming back into fashion, perhaps under the influence of newcomers such as herself.[33]

Recently, at the local newsagent, Marion discovered packs of decorative transfers in gay floral designs, with which she has brightened all the door frames and windows, as well as the canisters, the waste bin and the glass tumblers.[34] The walls are hung with tea-towels and plates depicting Dutch scenes, and a row of hooks Josephus installed beside the stove holds all her pots and pans. It is another of the peculiarities of Australian housewives that they hide their utensils in cupboards, as if they were something to be ashamed of.

Yet, however nice the kitchen may now be, entertaining is made difficult by the scarcity of continental foodstuffs. For instance, the local butcher sells little other than lamb chops, beef steaks and pork cutlets, quite unlike the refined prepared meats she is accustomed to. She has heard of a specialist Dutch butcher who delivers to the door and means to ask if he would be prepared to come this far out.[35] Australian biscuits and cakes she finds completely inedible. So plain and tasteless are they that she is forced to make her own, something she never did at home, with so many excellent bakeries at hand.[36] The one concession she is prepared to make, solely for reasons of patriotism, is a packet or two of Menz Olympic Creams, the ones with the Olympic logo impressed into them.

To add to her troubles, the cost of living keeps increasing: up two shillings a week from last year.[37] Butter is 4d a pound dearer, cheese 2d,[38] and the recent floods have put fruit and vegetables almost beyond reach. Thank goodness for the kitchen garden they've established in the backyard, although it is producing little at present, not only because of the poor soil, but because the weather has been so wildly unpredictable. The government categorically denies that this has anything to do with the atom bomb tests at Maralinga.[39]

BY 1951, ELECTRIC STOVES WERE WITHIN REACH OF MOST MIDDLE-CLASS HOUSEHOLDS, SO EVERY WOMAN COULD COOK A DELICIOUS MEAL FOR HER FAMILY.

SUPERMARKETS WERE
A BRAND NEW CONCEPT
IN 1954 WHEN COLES
INVITED RESIDENTS OF
MELBOURNE'S COBURG TO
SHOP 'THE NEW WORLD
WAY'. THE MANAGER
PROMISED TO BE AVAILABLE
AT ALL TIMES TO HELP
PEOPLE WITH THEIR
SHOPPING PROBLEMS.

Whenever she is planning a dinner party, there is no alternative than to catch the bus into the city. The continental food bar at John Martin's in Rundle Street and the specialty food court at Myers have now been joined by a gourmet shop on the lower ground floor of Charles Birks.[40] It is most encouraging to see that many Australians are patronising these establishments as well as migrants, although Marjorie is apparently unconvinced. She refused to touch the rollmops Marion put out for lunch a week or so back, claiming that she had come down with a wog.

Marion herself has been tempted beyond the familiar Dutch fare to sample some novelties from other cultures as well, with varying degrees of success (that hot Indian chutney was an awful shock). John Martin's has a wide range of imported delicacies hygienically sealed in tins and jars, including fried herrings in mushroom sauce, crème de foie gras with truffles, oysters in natural juice and, from Denmark, smoked fillets of eel in scrambled egg. At Charles Birks, she can buy foods that cannot be found anywhere else in Adelaide, such as preserved fruits in brandy, real turtle soup and calves' foot jelly with cognac, port wine or sherry. Best of all is Charles Birks' coffee bar, with twenty different blends on sale.[41] It was one of the things she missed most when they first came here, a decent cup of coffee.

Just last week, Marjorie invited Marion to look at her brand-new kitchen— she refers to it rather grandly as 'a kitchen work centre'—installed by Hains Hunkin's of Hindley Street.[42] Although to her mind it is rather spartan, Marion is nevertheless impressed by its modernity, and not a little envious, as Marjorie clearly intended she should be.

Instead of a dresser, it has a huge number of built-in cupboards, both at floor level and overhead. The Corroboree-patterned Laminex on the benchtops (specified by Marjorie for its Australian connotations) contrasts excellently with the black and white linoleum floor tiles. When Marion ventured that the green and yellow wallpaper was rather bright, Marjorie produced an article from one of the quality magazines that said colour harmony has now been replaced by colour contrast. It is a new washable plastic-coated paper from America that has only just become available here and is apparently very expensive.[43]

A special feature is the island bench, with semi-circular shelves projecting from one end, which are ideal for knick-knacks. Marjorie has very cleverly trained a potted ivy up the central pillar supporting the overhead glass-fronted cupboards, in which she keeps her best glassware. The food cupboard has pull-out vegetable drawers, and a set of narrow shelves on the inside of the door for herbs and small tins. Everything is within easy reach and all the working surfaces are at the same height as the sink and stove, both to prevent breakages of crockery and to present a pleasingly uniform appearance.[44]

If Marion thought her gas fridge was something to be proud of, she could hardly believe Marjorie's new Kelvinator Space-Saver-10 Delux, with Magic

THE BIG ATTRACTION OF THE SUPERMARKET WAS ITS CARPARK, WHICH ALLOWED YOU TO LOAD A WEEK'S SUPPLY OF GROCERIES INTO THE BOOT STRAIGHT FROM THE TROLLEY. SUPERMARKETS FLOURISHED WHEN OWNING A CAR BECAME COMMONPLACE

* The microwave oven was invented by an American, Percy L Spencer, in 1941, but not marketed until 1967. Among the first in Australia were those installed in the cafeteria of the new National Gallery of Victoria building in St Kilda Road, Melbourne, in 1968. They had to be removed after staff complained of dizzy spells.

Cycle automatic defrosting. The fridge actually defrosts itself, with no drip trays to empty! The inside is pastel blue and gold, with roll-out shelves, a full-width freezer that holds three ice-cream trays and a heated butter compartment in the door that keeps the butter spreadable at all times. No wonder it cost £225, which even Marjorie had the grace to be slightly embarrassed about.[45]

'One of these days', she announced proudly, 'I'll have a garbage disposer in the sink and an automatic dishwasher. I've even heard of an electronic oven that can cook potatoes in just a few minutes and heat coffee in thirty seconds—cup, saucer and all!' Clearly this was preposterous, but Marion said nothing.*

Later, as they sat in the lounge listening to Terry Dear's *Amateur Hour*, Marion told Josephus all about Marjorie's kitchen. Sensing a hint of regret in her voice, he assured her that one day they would have their own home with a kitchen just like it. In fact, that isn't really what she wants at all. Of course, every woman craves a St George electric range with automatic timer and a self-defrosting Kelvinator. Even Marjorie's new appliances—the Semak Vitamiser, the Hecla high-speed electric kettle and the Sunbeam deep-fryer—have their attractions. Yes, all those things would be nice. But what she wants most is *gezellig*. Surely there's no reason that a kitchen can't be modern and efficient yet still cosy and charming, with something of the old world preserved.

1975

Predictably, Mark was scornful. 'Can't you see, mum, it's just another sinister manifestation of global US capitalism', he shouted, before storming off back to Sydney. Well, that may be so but, for Leonie Snape, Woden Plaza is a godsend. She and Eric can drive straight into the carpark at Woolworths Supermarket and Family Centre on Saturday morning and get all their

weekly food shopping done in one go. It saves so much time, and now that she has gone back to lecturing at the university, that is the most important consideration. Although it is, admittedly, a bit brassy and American, she quite likes the sociability of Woden Plaza, which has only just reopened after a major redevelopment, with over a hundred shops, including Venture and David Jones.[46] They sometimes run into friends or work colleagues there and stop for a chat or a quick cup of coffee, although you do have to be a bit careful about who might see you there. Manuka is a much more socially acceptable place to meet people in public.

A SMART 1970S KITCHEN, WITH DISHWASHER, RANGEHOOD, BREAKFAST BAR AND LOTS OF CHEERY COLOURS AND PATTERNS

FLUORESCENT LIGHTING
CONCEALED BEHIND PLASTIC
PANELS DISTINGUISHES
THIS KITCHEN IN
TOORAK, MELBOURNE,
PHOTOGRAPHED IN 1968.

Once she gets home, she just takes everything straight from the car to cupboard, fridge or freezer. When people drop in unexpectedly, there need never be any problem about inviting them to stay for dinner.

Except Mark, of course. He's vegetarian and refuses to eat packet foods, which are also, apparently, part of some capitalist conspiracy. What he does eat in that grubby little Balmain terrace is anyone's guess. Leonie is becoming really concerned at how thin he's getting. Eric tells her to stop worrying. 'He'll grow out of it', he says dismissively. But she can't help it. She knows, as Eric doesn't, that Mark is back on drugs. She confronted him about it when he came down to Canberra recently for a rally in support of Mr Whitlam's plan to decriminalise marijuana. Mark has never really recovered from Vietnam but whenever she tries to talk with him about it he flies into a rage.

Nevertheless, as Eric keeps reminding her, they have their own lives to lead. The university demands a lot of Leonie's time and Eric is working long hours at the department while the restructuring is going on. The house at Garran is now all but complete, with just the landscaping and some interior touching-up to do. Having looked at the project homes on offer, they decided, in the end, to design their own: a more expensive option, admittedly (the cost has now blown out to more than $38 000), but worth it in the end, even if soaring interest rates and a recent stiff hike in property rates are starting to undermine their confidence. Before the election, Whitlam promised to reduce interest rates by 3 per cent, but there's little sign of that so far.[47]

Bedrooms and other private areas have been consigned to the rear of the house, grouped around an enclosed courtyard, allowing the kitchen at the front to get the full benefit of the view. This is, after all, one of the most-used rooms in the house, so there's no reason it shouldn't be in the best position. There's an Insinkerator garbage disposal unit in the twin-bowl stainless-steel sink, which sits directly beneath the sliding aluminium window. An automatic dishwasher is tucked under the bench nearby—something of a luxury, admittedly, but of huge benefit when they are both working full-time. In the centre of the room, a U-shaped island bench with built-in chopping block doubles as preparation area and breakfast bar, while also marking the transition from kitchen to family room.

In keeping with the return to natural materials and earthy colours, they have opted, wherever possible, for furnishings and utensils made of wood, cane, wicker and stoneware, even down to the Danish wooden cereal bowls and hand-hewn Japanese ladles (although these might have to be replaced because they are unsuited to the dishwasher). She and Eric also insisted on natural cork tiles instead of vinyl for the kitchen floor, and timber benchtops sealed with Estapol.[48] The effect, overall, is smart and up-to-date but with a friendly, country-living feel.

In a moment of weakness, Leonie was seduced into purchasing a Frigidaire Caprice double wall oven, which 'lets you cook a roast while you bake a cake',[49] but she now suspects that this is not something she will ever want to do so that was $440 that could have been better spent, although the eye-level oven windows and internal lights are certainly a great advantage. Leonie has been reading about stove tops with clear glass hotplates that are already available in the United States. Until the price comes down, however, they are unlikely to be seen in many homes here.*

According to Eric, impulse buying will become much more prevalent now with the introduction of Bankcard. Like many men of his generation, Eric has never approved of hire purchase, preferring to save for the things he wants, however long it takes. Traditionally, Australians have gone into debt for only one thing—the purchase of a house—and that's as it should be. Diners Club and American Express may be all right for the rich, but allowing everyone to rush out

* Ceramic hotplates first appeared in the United States in 1968, becoming available here, if hardly affordable, from around 1972.

A fondue party certainly helps
to break the ice, providing maximum
effect for minimum effort.

with a plastic card and buy whatever they want whenever they want it, without a thought to their levels of personal debt, will ruin the economy. As an economist, Eric should know. Secretly, though, Leonie rather likes the idea of Bankcard, but apparently it's very difficult for married women to get the necessary approval.[50]

One purchase that has proved its worth is the Westinghouse electronic microwave oven. As soon as she saw it demonstrated at Young's a month or two ago she just had to have one. At $339, it wasn't cheap, but at the end of a long working day it is convenient to be able to take some frozen chicken breasts and a packet of Birds Eye peas from the freezer, pop them straight into the microwave and have dinner on the table in no time at all. It wasn't so long ago that chicken was a real luxury. Now it's one of the cheapest meats you can get, thanks to battery farming. The variety of packaged and ready-prepared foods available in the supermarkets these days is quite amazing, from gourmet dinners to convenient snacks.[51]

On rare occasions when they are very late and tired, she and Eric can arrange to meet on their way home for a quick meal at Colonel Sanders or McDonald's, although this is not something she'd dare to tell Mark about.*

Naturally, these sorts of meals are not ideal. They are purely for convenience when there's only the two of them. Something more substantial and refined is required when they are entertaining, which they quite often have to do. Fondue parties are the smart solution. Many shops in Canberra stock a range of fondue ware. The Provincial Kitchen at Civic, for example, has brown-glazed Swiss fondue pots for $13.95, a set of six fondue forks for $39.95, asbestos mats, and fondue plates divided into compartments for a variety of different sauces. Alison Burt's informative *Fondue Cookery* includes all the traditional Swiss-cheese recipes.[52] When the chaps from Eric's office bring their wives around for dinner, a fondue party certainly helps to break the ice, providing maximum effect for minimum effort. When she serves something more substantial, such as roast meat and vegetables, Leonie dispenses with dessert altogether, simply putting out a board containing a selection of cheeses

* Colonel Sanders (later KFC) came to Australia in 1968, with McDonald's and Pizza Hut following two years later.

CORNING ☀ WARE

THE GIFT THAT OUTLASTS
THE THOUGHT BEHIND IT

The gift that outlasts the thought behind it

When you are buying a gift for
a discerning person–someone with
impeccable taste–then Corning
Ware is more than acceptable
because it is not only attractive
and in the best of taste, but is
versatile and durable.
Corning Ware is strikingly
beautiful, a constant reminder
of your generosity as it moves
from freezer to stove, from stove
to table. It will not break in
extreme changes of temperature.
We guarantee it–in writing.
Having once given a Corning Ware
product and had the satisfaction
of honest appreciation, then you
are never stuck for another gift
idea. There are over sixty different
Corning Ware items to choose
from. But we warn you, it is
difficult *not* to keep it for yourself.

CORNING ☀ WARE

HEATPROOF GLASS WAS
MARKETED IN FRANCE FROM
THE 1930S. CORNING WARE,
AN AMERICAN BRAND OF
GLASS-CERAMIC COOKWARE
SUITABLE FOR STOVETOP
OR OVEN, WAS INTRODUCED
IN 1958. INTERESTINGLY,
THIS SOPHISTICATED 1972
ADVERTISEMENT IS NOT
DIRECTED SPECIFICALLY AT
WOMEN.

(the recent Festival of Foreign Cheeses at Forrest, organised by the Cheese Club of Australia, gave her lots of useful tips).[53] With some savoury biscuits and a big pot of Nescafé, they make a very modern and sophisticated finish to a meal.

Australian table wines are a particular interest of Eric's and the wine rack he has had installed under the kitchen bench is filling rapidly. He insists on showing it off to every visitor. His taste for wines, like those of many people, began with Wynn's cask riesling—the 'bag in a box'—which is always popular at parties.[54] Leonie keeps a cask of white on hand in the fridge for a refreshing glass at the end of the working day. These days, however, Eric's tastes are more refined. Seppelt's Moyston Claret is one of his particular favourites, and Arawatta Riesling, he says, is surely one of the finest wines available for under $2 a bottle. As a subscriber to *Australian Gourmet* since its debut in 1966, Eric has become quite knowledgeable about the latest food and wine trends. He pointed out just recently that Australians are now drinking, on average, around 10 litres of wine a year.[55] 'The Galloping Gourmet', Graham Kerr, is often criticised for quaffing wine on his television cookery show, but he's done a lot to popularise Australian table wines.

As a result of all this enthusiasm, Eric has turned into a surprisingly good cook, although only on special occasions: he won't do any of the day-to-day cooking. Unfortunately, though, his burgeoning epicureanism is turning him into a bit of a grouch when it comes to convenience foods and ready-prepared snacks. 'They are ruining the traditional family meal', he insists. 'They have taken cooking out of the home and into the factory.'[56] Although this attitude doesn't seem to preclude the occasional visit to McDonald's, it certainly ensures that it will be a less enjoyable experience.

2007

Although it was the extensive views of Perth that the selling agents were most keen to promote, the 'dream kitchen' came a pretty close second. Actually, Melissa Price-Scott didn't think it a particularly important consideration at the time. She's not much of a cook, after all. Basically, she was looking for a secure penthouse apartment in the city with generous office space in which to base her public relations consultancy. Nevertheless, she is rather gratified that when she has someone up for drinks they invariably admire this beautifully conceived work station, designed on open-plan principles to be viewed sequentially as one moves around the various living spaces. As one of her clients assured her, it's a stunning lifestyle investment. The smoke-grey Pietro Cardoza stone floor, the cherry-wood cabinets and stainless-steel accents create a layered architectural statement that is elegant without being austere.[57]

Because the kitchen is fully exposed to view, it is important that all its working components be concealed. The flush-panel, floor-to-ceiling cabinet doors have no handles, opening and shutting with a satisfying 'clunk' in response to a sharp tap with the fingers. One of these doors hides the stainless-steel refrigerator-freezer, which dispenses unlimited amounts of crushed ice at the press of a button. Behind another is an integrated kitchen tidy and recycling bin and a wheel-out multi-function work trolley, which can be quickly popped out of sight when guests arrive.

Concealed lighting casts a soft glow over the marble benchtops, every fitting individually adjustable from a computerised control panel which also operates the climate control and integrated sound systems.

As someone who has always been fully committed to doing whatever she can to save the planet, Melissa applauds the developers' decision to install energy-efficient Miele appliances. The cooking zone, for example, features a Miele KM390G gas hob and a H4240B multi-function oven, whose fan-forced cooking system apparently allows food to be cooked at three different temperature levels simultaneously, reducing cooking time and therefore energy consumption. The M8261 microwave features a range of programs, including automatic cooking, reheating and defrosting, as well as a powerful grill element.[58]

Melissa uses the cherry-wood panelling that conceals the five-speed rangehood to display selected items from her extensive collection of Aboriginal dot paintings and artefacts. She has chosen coolamons and other pieces related to native food preparation so as to enhance the culinary

SINCE THE 1980S, COOKING HAS BEEN REVOLUTIONISED BY THE READY AVAILABILITY OF ELECTRIC FOOD PROCESSORS, CUTTERS AND JUICERS, MAKING IT POSSIBLE TO PREPARE DISHES AT HOME THAT WOULD PREVIOUSLY HAVE BEEN RESTRICTED TO PROFESSIONAL KITCHENS WITH LARGE STAFFS.

easyliving

Breville
's the idea™

Class act
Introducing the 800 Class range
for the serious home chef

Life of luxury
Pamper yourself with
our personal care range

Summer breeze

One day she must sit down with a large
whisky and really concentrate on that
complicated-looking instruction book.

theme. Someone once warned her that the heat from the stove might cause them to split, but since she never actually uses it, that shouldn't be a problem. In fact, one day she must sit down with a large whisky and really concentrate on that complicated-looking instruction book to find out how the oven works. On either side of the hob, retractable panels slide open to reveal convenient storage for spices, herbs and other small items. Pull-outs in the storage unit that defines the transition from cooking to clean-up zones provide ample storage for her collection of mint-condition Le Creuset enamelled cookware.

The centrepiece of the clean-up zone is the extra-wide double sink with platinum-finish taps and spray attachment. It is almost a pleasure to rinse the coffee cups here, especially at night, with the entire city laid out beneath her. Any more demanding jobs can be handled by the Miele G1170VI-Plus dishwasher, which comes with a water-saving Eco-Sensor Program. Fully integrated into the cabinetry, its electronic controls are very cleverly hidden in the door rim, so you would never even know it's there.[59]

Electrical outlets in the food preparation zone are located behind flip-down panels, which also hide unsightly appliances such as jug, toaster and juice fountain when not in use. The selling agent referred to this as an 'appliance garage', a term she rather likes. Melissa also finds herself in possession of a rice cooker, a pasta maker and a Breville electric bread oven, among other things, all given to her over the years, and never taken out of their boxes. Since she doesn't like to dispose of gifts (just in case the giver should ask), she stores them well out of reach overhead.

To maintain the minimalist aesthetic that is so vital to the overall look, she keeps her benchtops completely clear, apart from her G Rushbrooke and Co. traditional English cutting board, which in any case is too heavy to move around; a large jar of Spanish preserved lemons, whose colour goes so well against the cherry-wood cabinets; and, most vital of all, the De Longhi Magnifica Fully Automatic One-Touch Espresso Maker with Precision

Integrated Conical Grinder and Programmable Digital Electronic Display. She got it on special at Harvey Norman for $3200 and it is the one appliance here that gets plenty of use. Melissa simply can't function in the morning without copious amounts of coffee and she demands the best. Unfortunately, this means she is unable to buy the fair-trade coffee her local supplier is promoting, which would, of course, be preferable from an ethical standpoint. One of her special little indulgences is a touch-screen beside the bed, which opens the bedroom curtains, then instructs the De Longhi to have a steaming long-black waiting for her in the kitchen when she gets up.

Sometimes, when she has people up for cocktails, she'll put a bowl of fruit, a brioche and one or two vanilla pods on the island bench for atmosphere, just to give the kitchen a softer touch and perhaps help to whet their appetites before they all go down to a bistro for dinner. In addition, some colourful cookery books are displayed on the shelf above the wine chiller: Nigella, of course, and Jamie, Delia and others. Her latest acquisition is a beautifully illustrated volume on tofu, written by one of Japan's major celebrity chefs. These are not just for display. For someone in her position, it is important that Melissa be cognisant of food trends so as to appear confident when ordering in restaurants, particularly when in the company of clients.

Although her kitchen is more than adequate to her lifestyle needs, and represents a valuable financial asset, Melissa is well aware that, in global terms, it can no longer be considered state-of-the-art. Recently, while visiting friends in New York, she was gobsmacked by their fully networked kitchen. The internet refrigerator she was already familiar with, of course, since they have been available here for ages. It has a screen built into the door for watching television, accessing recipes, leaving messages and ordering supplies. But her friends' fridge has, in addition, a thermostat that can be pre-programmed to thaw certain frozen foods by a set time, or to snap-freeze selected items without affecting others.

But what particularly impressed Melissa was that every kitchen operation is controlled by a computerised command station, which automatically checks the status of all appliances, turning them on and off according to a preset program; keeps a record of product use-by dates and warns when they are due to be replaced; automatically orders groceries by internet when stocks are getting low; and maintains and continually updates the personal schedule of every family member. It will even order flowers for a dinner party.[60] 'We don't know how we could possibly keep our busy lives in order without it', they say. 'It has turned our kitchen into the heart of the home.'

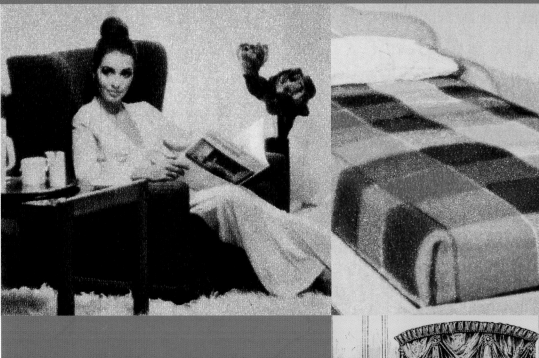

Go to
Your
Room

Lifting the Magic Barrier

'Every bedroom we create is unique, designed specifically around you', declares the ad in a decorators' magazine. 'By taking time to understand you and your home, we can transform your space to give you … the look you've always wanted.'[1]

Yet what is immediately striking about the designs illustrated is just how perfectly anonymous they are. They might be expensive hotel rooms. What the company appears to mean by 'individuality' is not any expression of personal or family history, nor of any distinctive quirks or peculiarities you might have. No allowance is made for the clutter and messiness of everyday life. It is, instead, about people's ability to make the 'right' choice from the limited number of options the interior design industry presents as currently acceptable. If you really wanted a bedroom designed specifically around you, then presumably you would do it yourself.

'The look you've always wanted' (as distinct from, say, 'the comfort you've always wanted') acknowledges that the bedroom, that last bastion of privacy, seclusion and furtiveness, has been transformed into a quasi-public space, just as sex, the bedroom's dirty little secret, has emerged from under the covers to penetrate every aspect of public life. Sex, flaunted as a symbol of glamour and sophistication in its own right, freed from any necessary connection with procreation, is the motivation behind the adult bedroom's recent coming-out.

Not so very long ago, it was thought immodest even to leave the bedroom door open during the day. When showing guests around the house, you would gesture towards it and say, 'That's the bedroom', before breezing on down the passage. If the house lacked an entrance hall, visitors might be allowed to drape their coats across the chenille bedspread, but they wouldn't dream of retrieving them without permission. To the kids, their parents' bedroom was a no-go zone, a quiet, half-lit place harbouring great mysteries.

WHILE WH ROCKE AND CO CATERED FOR THE WELL-TO-DO, ANOTHER MELBOURNE FIRM, WALLACH BROTHERS, APPEALED TO WORKING-CLASS FAMILIES BY OFFERING TO FURNISH A THREE-ROOMED HOUSE FOR JUST £18 10S. THE BEDROOM, AS ILLUSTRATED IN THE COMPANY'S CATALOGUE, IS SPARTAN BUT PRACTICAL.

'We have learned early, my sister and I', recalls David Malouf of his Brisbane childhood, 'that this room is not to be trespassed upon. Its thresholds are magic barriers'.[2]

As befitted its shrine-like status, the aptly named master bedroom occupied a prominent position beside the front door, opposite the livingroom, even when street noise or the house's orientation made that inconvenient. Status overcame practicality. In fact, the relative sizes and positions of bedrooms confirmed the family hierarchy even more decisively than the Sunday roast did: typically, mum and dad in the big room at the front, daughters in the smaller second bedroom, and sons, regardless of their ages, sharing the sleepout at the back.

Although, as private areas, bedrooms were always furnished and decorated more modestly than livingrooms, the master bedroom did at least sport a more elaborate cornice or frieze and deeper skirting boards than the others. Today, despite children and teenagers having gained equal standing with their parents in so many other respects, the size, position and superior furnishings of the master bedroom are still reliable indicators of who is really in charge.

In the 1880s, the Melbourne furniture makers Wallach Brothers appealed to labourers and others of modest means by offering to completely furnish a three-roomed house for £18 10s. For the bedroom, they recommended a double French bedstead with iron frame, furnished with a pair of palliasses,* a flock mattress, flock bolster, two flock pillows, a pair of blankets and a quilt. The only other items of furniture were a cedar chest with four drawers; a rather plain-looking cedar dressing-table with a toiletry mirror atop; two cane chairs; and a wash-stand equipped with a towel-rail, a small curtain at the back to catch splashes, a wash-bowl and water jug, and two chamber pots on the shelf beneath. The company's thoughtfulness extended to a rectangle of matting under the bed to protect bare toes. The result, although spartan, is perfectly serviceable and satisfies the contemporary need for cleanliness and avoidance of clutter.[3]

Some twenty-odd years later, in 1909, the *Australian Housewives' Manual* is recommending much the same inventory of bedroom necessities, which by

* The French bed, as the term was commonly understood in Australia, had head and foot rails of similar height and no fixed hangings. A palliasse is a straw-filled mattress. By the late nineteenth century it was mainly used as a bed base under something a little more forgiving.

A HALF-TESTER FRENCH BED
ILLUSTRATED IN AN 1880
CATALOGUE FOR MESSRS WH
ROCKE AND CO., MELBOURNE

* A thin cotton fabric with
textured stripes or checks
woven into it

this time is estimated to cost only about £5 more. 'A neat, orderly, inviting-looking bedroom, with a nicely draped couch, pretty window curtains, bright furniture, and glittering toiletware, is the ambition and the pride of every housekeeper worthy of the name', enthused the author. In those days, even inexpensive items of furniture were expected to last a lifetime, so 'when you get rich, as you will, if you follow the advice in this little book, they will answer admirably for a guest chamber'.[4]

It was the already-rich in whom Wallach Brothers were mainly interested, however, and they demanded quite a bit more. At the very least, they would have included in their inventory a large, heavy wardrobe, some padded easy-chairs, a chaise-longue, a fireplace with overmantle, a full-length mirror, Brussels carpet and a commode chair. The lady of the house might also have wanted a decorative folding screen, both to protect her modesty and to display her artistic taste.

Aside from a few uplifting landscapes, nothing was recommended that might distract a woman from her solemn marital duty. 'It would be as well', advised one ladies' journal, 'to avoid a [wall]paper with a spotted pattern or one that divides itself into squares or diamonds, or has groups of flowers or other objects that attract the eye and cause one to feel compelled to count them'.[5]

The big four-poster canopy bed was well out of fashion by the early 1900s. Since rooms were smaller and less draughty than before, an enclosed bed was no longer necessary. In fact, insofar as the bed-curtain collected dust and impeded the flow of fresh air, it was considered positively dangerous. The half-tester, with a small (but nonetheless sometimes elaborate) canopy over just the bedhead, was a reasonable compromise: 'a nice light arrangement of dimity* and

A WARDROBE AND A MIRRORED
DRESSING TABLE FOR THE
LADY AND A LOWBOY FOR
THE MAN, IN YOUR CHOICE OF
WALNUT VENEER OR OAK. THE
'MARVEL' SUITE, PICTURED IN
THIS 1934 ADVERTISEMENT,
COMBINES A MODERN ART
DECO-INFLUENCED DRESSING-
TABLE MIRROR WITH 'SMART
CABRIOLE LEGS'.

net around the canopy of a half-tester bedstead', advised the *Australian Housewives'*
Manual, 'looks well and is comfortable. It shades the eyes and prevents draughts
and colds. I should risk the doctor if I were you, and stick to it for the sake of
neatness and beauty … ' [6]

Yet the four-poster, the decorative half-tester and their later, much diminished
descendant, the pastel-green or pink chenille bedspread, were much more than
merely utilitarian or decorative. By making the bed
the centre of attention, they symbolically declared
the sacredness of procreation. If the master bedroom
was a shrine, the double bed was its altar.

The Invention of Cosiness

Unfortunately, there were others multiplying in
the nation's beds besides the mums and dads. Lice,
fleas, bedbugs and mites were constant compan-
ions of both rich and poor. Iron and brass beds
gained favour in the late nineteenth century not
only because they were fashionably lightweight
and elegant (not to mention relatively inexpensive) but also because they provided fewer refuges
for pests. Yet anything soft and warm enough to
sleep on was, by its very nature, an invitation to
them. Occasionally, home-help manuals provided
recipes for fumigants: burning a bowl of sulphur
with the doors and windows firmly sealed was one
not very healthy suggestion. [7] But every housewife
knew that constant cleaning and airing were the
only effective deterrents. A net curtain over the
bed might do for the flying kinds, at least until

flywire came along, but the crawlies in the mattress were almost impossible to shift and they made bedtime quite a trial.

For stuffings, down (the soft breast feathers of a female duck or goose) provided superior comfort for those who could afford it. Ordinary folk had to settle for horse hair, a plentiful product of the knackeries. At the turn of the twentieth century, straw palliasses and horse-hair mattresses were the stock-in-trade of the Australian Bedding Mill in Sydney and would remain so for some years, but the flock favoured by Wallach Brothers, made from wool or cotton waste, was far more comfortable, as well as light, inexpensive and relatively pest-resistant. 'Mattresses made from vegetable products are better than those made from animal products', advised *Home and Health*. 'Straw or coconut fibre are all that many families can afford. Cotton and felt are best. Of animal products, hair is best, but not wool. Do not choose feather beds—they were the most common among good households in the past, but are unhealthy.'[8]

Health was not the only reason plant fibres were being promoted. They were among the few products Pacific nations could sell into Australia, so they were also good for trade. Christian missions encouraged and organised their production. In addition to coconut fibre, there was kapok, extracted from the seedpods of a tropical tree, and pulu, derived from a Hawaiian plant. Kapok mattresses and pillows were a great success, still being advertised—mainly for children's beds and guest rooms—in the late 1950s, when they sold for about half the price of inner-springs. Pulu, on the other hand, was found to disintegrate into dust after just a year or two and was soon forgotten.

The very fact that such a wide variety of stuffings was tried suggests that none was completely satisfactory. They all compacted and sagged, some more quickly than others. Although wooden-slat or woven-wire bases encouraged air circulation, it wasn't long before you felt them poking into your pelvis as the mattress filling worked its way down to your feet. Getting a comfortable, healthy night's sleep was one of life's intractable little problems.

Metal springs were the answer. They were first tried in the 1870s without much success, until the coil spring, originally patented for use in chairs, was satisfactorily adapted for beds towards the end of the century. Australian homeowners, however, would have to wait another forty or fifty years for the supreme comfort and support of the inner-spring mattress to be made available to them.[9] Not for the first time was an important domestic innovation delayed by industry inertia and customers' inability to pay.

The only real challengers to the coil-spring have been latex (introduced in the late 1920s), foam rubber (its successor), the futon, the waterbed and the airbed. All have the advantage of being relatively easy to handle, an important consideration for flat dwellers and those who move house often.

Our brief love affair with the futon was, indirectly, a product of the American occupation of Japan. General Macarthur's policy of promoting Japanese culture in the United States in order to position the former foe as an ally in the fight against Communism translated, over time, into a fashion for Zen, sushi, chunky brown earthenwares and futon-style beds. The futon could be rolled up, popped into its carry bag and flung over the shoulder, making it perfect for peripatetic youth—provided, of course, they were prepared to put up with some discomfort. Although the futon shops that once occupied every second street corner thinned out rather quickly, they popularised a spare Japanese aesthetic that would have a more lasting impact.

Dunlopillo foam-rubber mattresses were sold from the early 1950s for use with day-beds.[10] Although they could never compete with the inner-spring, the company banked on their appeal to those with small houses who could not afford to keep a bedroom in reserve. When country cousins arrived unexpectedly, it was simply a matter of wheeling the Selby Sleeper, Californian Divanette or Put-U-Up out of the hall cupboard.[11] The thin, synthetic foam sprang instantly into shape within its gay sunflower-print cotton slip and was just uncomfortable enough to ensure their stay was brief.

Waterbeds were much more fun, if hardly conducive to a restful night's sleep. But it was generally assumed that anyone who owned one was not thinking about sleep anyway. Waterbeds had no chance of surviving the onslaught of jokes they provoked. Although Harrods in London had been selling bulky therapeutic models from as early as the mid 1890s, they would be accepted, and gain their racy reputation, only in the 1960s, after the invention of vinyl (and sex).

While your houseguests tossed and turned on the folding bed in the living-room, and junior lay engulfed in kapok over a sagging wire base in the

LARGE OPEN-PLAN HOUSES
IN THE 1970S ALLOWED
THE BEDROOM TO DOUBLE
AS SITTING ROOM, STUDY
OR BREAKFAST ROOM.
ESTATE AGENTS SOMETIMES
REFERRED TO SUCH
CREATIONS AS 'PARENTS'
RETREATS'. THE SHAG-
PILE CARPET IN THIS ONE
MAY NOT HAVE BEEN VERY
PRACTICAL, BUT IT ADDED A
TOUCH OF LUXURY.

sleepout, what you were careful to secure for yourself, above all else, were comfort and cosiness. If the nineteenth-century marital bedchamber aspired to stateliness, its successor in the twentieth opted for intimacy. This was largely a matter of economic necessity. After all, it's hard to look grand in a ten-foot-square room with plywood panelling. Yet there's another, deeper, factor at work here as well. Magazines in the 1930s and 1940s repeatedly turn to the word 'cosy' when referring to bedrooms (not a term that today's designers would dream of uttering), because the gloomier and more threatening the outside world appeared, the more cosiness at home mattered. To be tucked up in bed on a cold winter's night with a good book and a hot cocoa was one of life's enduring simple pleasures and, as far as most people were concerned, simple pleasures would have to do.

All manner of inexpensive, practical comforts were devised to make being in bed a pleasure in its own right, something that turn-of-the-century commentators would have heartily disapproved of. Early to bed and early

> Thus the delightful conjunction of
> bed and pleasure—sexual or otherwise—
> slowly gained respectability.

to rise had been their stern moral injunction. While they agreed that a bed should be warm and moderately comfortable, it was purely for reasons of health and bodily well-being. Heaven forbid that you might find it blissful. That was a sign of decadence and effeminacy.

After the experiences of the Boer War and World War I, hard, masculine self-denial lost some of its former shine. To the concern of moral guardians, the 1920s and 1930s were far less anxious about virility. At the same time, sex became something a woman might be expected to enjoy rather than just endure while she counted the flowers on the wallpaper. Besides, it was no longer necessary for the wife to be asleep by ten so as to be up at five-thirty to stoke the stove and scald the milk. Thus the delightful conjunction of bed and pleasure—sexual or otherwise—slowly gained respectability.

In 1933, 6s 6d would buy you an electric bed warmer, 'flat and uninspiring looking', admitted *Women's Weekly*, 'but of unimaginable comfort. You just plug it into the powerpoint'.[12] Although superior to the rubber hot-water bottle, it was more expensive, and there remained the suspicion (not unjustified at the time) that anything electrical between the sheets might burst into flames without warning.

The most important innovation, as far as bedtime pleasures are concerned, was the bedside lamp, which made reading in bed a practical proposition for the first time. 'Who would be without an electric bedside lamp at the small cost of 3/11d', asked a *Women's Weekly* columnist, 'or 6/11d with flex, globe, and shade complete? It was something I had long coveted. It promised hours of cosy comfort, tucked under the blankets with a favorite book'.[13] The really modern bedroom of the 1930s might feature wall-mounted bedlamps, which were less likely to be knocked over and which somehow rendered the luxury of reading in bed a more established and abiding one.

'When the rain swirls down and the wind moans around the eaves', beckoned an advertisement in 1945, 'then is the time to snuggle down and savour in full the soft, restful cosiness of the famous Warrnambool Blankets'.[14] It is an apparently simple statement, but loaded with metaphorical significance.

'YOU NEVER WIND IT–
YOU SIMPLY PLUG IT IN.'
ALTHOUGH THE FIRST
EXPERIMENTAL ELECTRIC
CLOCKS DATE FROM THE
MID NINETEENTH CENTURY,
PRACTICAL DOMESTIC
MODELS WERE NOT MASS
PRODUCED UNTIL THE
MID 1920S. THIS 'GEORGE
WASHINGTON' ALARM CLOCK
WOULD HAVE BEEN QUITE A
NOVELTY IN 1933.

At least there's a CLOCK *that cannot lie!*

ANGUS & COOTE

It's a real "George Washington" *Guaranteed by Angus & Coote.* YOU NEVER WIND IT— you simply plug it in.

From year's end to year's end you have the right time, and a call every morning if you need it.

24/6
Complete with 6 feet of flex and its own adapter.
POST FREE ANYWHERE

IT'S THE CHEAPEST ELECTRIC ALARM EVER OFFERED

You Never Hear The Tick.
This clock is insulated to prevent noise. But it "buzzes" for 30 minutes if you wish to be called. It's a smart, oxidised clock, just 4½ inches tall—with a fine silverplate bezel, good base, and complete with flex and its own adapter. It's a "Westclox" product, Brother to "Big Ben" Electric, at 65/-.
ALL THE MODERN ELECTRIC CLOCKS—BOTH TIME AND ALARM— are DISPLAYED, DEMONSTRATED, and GUARANTEED by

ANGUS & COOTE Ltd.
500 GEORGE STREET, SYDNEY.
CATALOGUES OF CLOCKS POSTED FREE ANYWHERE.
(Please mention "The Australian Women's Weekly.")

To a lonely young woman awaiting her husband's return from the front, it would have been irresistibly enticing. In all probability, however, she would have had to wait longer for her blankets than for her man, because rationing had made them a luxury in more ways than one. The Warrnambool ad was actually a bit of a tease.

Getting Serious about Growing Up

As a baby in Hobart in the mid 1920s, Peggy Heywood slept in a cot in her parents' room, while her elder sister occupied the second bedroom. After their widowed grandmother moved in, both girls had to share a closed-in verandah at the back of the house. 'It had sliding glass windows', she remembers, 'and it opened directly off the sitting room', so presumably they were not afforded much privacy.[15] Just up the road a few years later, Marjorie Roberts and her two sisters were sleeping in a big sunroom at the back of the house, protected only by flywire, the second bedroom being reserved for grandmother's occasional overnight visits. 'It was terribly cold in winter', she admits,

> but then the whole house was cold because, although my father had a good job as a clerk with the AMP, his salary was cut by fifty-percent during the depression so we couldn't afford proper heating. Dad brought home some big pottery ink bottles from work and we used them as hot water bottles. Mum knitted covers for them.[16]

By the standards of the day, both Peggy and Marjorie were reasonably well-off. For poor children, sleeping arrangements could be even more rigorous, although being in a warm climate certainly removed some of the hardships. Recalling her childhood in Brisbane, Dolly Russell says, 'we never had a room to ourselves. My two younger sisters and I were in a double bed, the three of us. We never thought anything of it—none of the kids wanted beds to themselves'.[17]

IN 1947, RUTH PARK'S *THE HARP IN THE SOUTH*, WHICH REVEALED THE HORRORS OF SLUM LIFE IN INNER SYDNEY, WAS SERIALISED IN THE *SYDNEY MORNING HERALD*. MANY MIDDLE-CLASS AUSTRALIANS HAD NO IDEA THAT SUCH CONDITIONS EXISTED IN AUSTRALIA. PHOTOGRAPHERS SUCH AS DAVID MOORE, WHO TOOK THIS PHOTOGRAPH IN REDFERN TWO YEARS LATER, PROVIDED EVIDENCE THAT WAS HARD TO IGNORE.

DAVID MOORE
REDFERN INTERIOR 1949
GELATIN SILVER PHOTOGRAPH
30.0 X 40.3 CM
NATIONAL GALLERY OF
VICTORIA

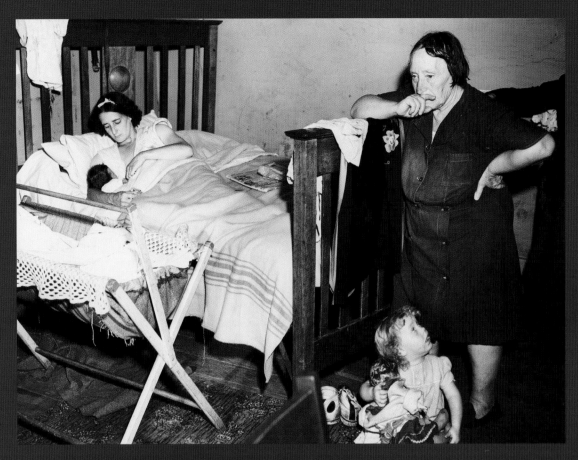

Not that it was usually a matter of choice. For large working-class families, crammed into three- or four-roomed houses, sleeping quarters were bound to be cramped and lacking in privacy, although they were probably an improvement on those of both their British contemporaries and previous Australian generations. Keeping the family fed, clothed and reasonably healthy was the first priority. Conditions did little to encourage intimacy between the generations. A high infant mortality rate perhaps discouraged parents from forming too strong a bond with their infants, in case they were snatched away without warning. This didn't mean that parents loved their children any less, just that their love was expressed differently.

As the historian Kerreen Reiger has shown, the relationships between parents and their offspring in the nineteenth century tended to be somewhat distanced, regardless of social class. 'From either side, expectations were of adequate role-performance rather than inter-personal intimacy; parents were concerned more with the physical and moral wellbeing of their children than with their individual personal development.'[18] Children tended to be seen as adults-in-training rather than as people in their own right. At the same time, however, they were never simply dependants, but were expected to make a significant contribution to the family's welfare through domestic chores or paid employment.

Despite parental control being stricter than it is now, and children's time more ordered, young people were much more likely to be independent, self-reliant and free of adult influence during what little time they had to

themselves. They spent their leisure hours outdoors, freely exercising their imaginations. They grew up tough, strong and disciplined, and much less conscious of their own individuality than children today. Much of what they learned about life they found out for themselves.

Around 1900, however, the professionals started moving in: the doctors, psychologists, welfare workers and educationalists, guided in their efforts by government bureaucrats. No longer would the raising of children be primarily a private matter. Parents, especially those of the lower-classes, were not to be trusted to take care of it themselves. Certain social standards had to be met. Even giving birth was removed from the home, and from the care of amateur midwives, to be entrusted to hospitals and trained doctors.

Alarming press reports of female factory-workers marrying before they were eighteen and bearing children they could not care for led to the founding of a 'school for mothers' in Richmond, Victoria, in 1909. Not even after a second or third child, claimed the *Argus*, do these girls 'seem to develop any faculty for gathering experience. One Richmond resident', it continued breathlessly, 'related how she found a mother endeavouring to bath her child in a jam-tin, and even then she was doing better than others, who failed to see the necessity for bathing at all. Stories of injudicious feeding are simply appalling'.[19] Typically for the times, the *Argus* gave no thought to the social or economic conditions that might have led to such outrages, preferring to blame the mothers' ignorance.

Yet such revelations did have the effect of focusing government concern for children and their welfare. Although well-intentioned and usually beneficent, such interest was, by its very nature, patronising and therefore often resented, especially by the poor, who had every reason to be suspicious. It would, nevertheless, quickly impinge on all levels of society.

During periods of economic prosperity—the early 1910s, the 1920s and the decades following the mid-1950s—when it was not so necessary for children to go out to work or to contribute significantly to the family's material needs in other ways, childhood became unprecedentedly privileged. Parents' relationships with their offspring grew more caring, more respectful and more sentimental, partly because much of the responsibility they had had previously could now be entrusted to outside providers.

As children's domestic workloads decreased and playtime increased, more attention was given to how they were filling their leisure hours. Idle hands were the devil's workshop, so all that idleness had to be put to proper use. It was no longer acceptable to send little Johnny out into the street to amuse himself tying jam tins to dogs' tails or gluing coins to the footpath, safe in

IN THE MID 1960S, *HOME BEAUTIFUL* ENVISAGED A BOYS' ROOM THAT WAS BRIGHT, BUSY AND SUITABLY SPORTY, WITH SPACE RESERVED FOR STUDY. NO CHANCE OF THESE WHOLESOME LADS TURNING INTO SISSIES.

the knowledge that his onerous domestic responsibilities would provide a suitable corrective. Little Johnny's domestic responsibilities were now far from onerous. Therefore play would have to be not just a way of letting off steam but also an essential part of his education, and his parents were expected to supply him with the appropriate toys and books.

Paradoxically, then, the increasing interference of the authorities in children's upbringing, by setting standards which parents were expected to meet, tended to increase mothers' anxieties rather than alleviating them, while making their little ones more, not less, dependent.

At one time, kids' bedrooms were places to sleep and nothing more. *Home and Health* recommended only that the young should have adequate rest, that their beds be comfortable, clothing light and warm, and the room aired and free of dampness. A 'hearty romp' before bedtime is suggested to tire them out.[20] It's all strictly utilitarian. But already things were changing. Just a year later, in 1910, the *Argus* was bewailing the:

> elaborate preparations now made for the comfort of children in both their homes and at school … Not so many years ago quite severe discipline prevailed in such houses as boasted nurseries. Mutton and vegetables had to be eaten without a grumble, and complaints as to the variety of jam supplied were not permitted … Nowadays the nursery only exists as a playroom, and it is very often a most beautifully appointed apartment with every hygienic luxury to hand … punishment, even of the milder sort, has gone quite out of fashion, and … many mothers endeavour to carry out their duty in the matter of bringing up their offspring by means of argument and philosophic reasoning. This is, of course, one of the outcomes of the small family.[21]

It was partly that, yes, but also the result of children having been relieved of some of their responsibilities as mechanical aids and outside services such as electricity began to make home-life less demanding. Although she may have been exaggerating the extent of the problem, and seems to be considering only the educated upper-middle classes, the *Argus* writer has nevertheless caught the trend.

By the 1920s, however, parents were fretting about losing control. Motor cars were making it less safe for little Johnny to be playing in the street and, more worryingly still, his scruffy neighbourhood mates were now exerting more influence on him than his guardians. 'One of the great problems that

It was vital, for both the continuation of the family and the vitality of the nation, that men should be men and that women should know their place.

parents are facing today', warned *Australian Home Builder* in 1924, 'is that of "How to keep the child at home".'[22]

The answer lay not in force or discipline, as it might have a generation earlier, but enticement. The bedroom was no longer to be just a place of rest: it was the child's own domain. 'If the anxious parents would properly furnish and drape their homes,' advised *Australian Home Builder*,

> … instead of the children running to others, others would come to them. The parents then are given the opportunity of meeting and knowing the associates of the family's junior members, and can judge for themselves if the acquaintance should continue … Encourage the boy to have his friends call; fix him a den in which he and they can retire to enjoy themselves in their boyish ways … The modern girl likes to have girl friends call. Furnish her room so that she can entertain her guest there should she so desire. Let the daughters and sons, advised by their parents, select their furniture, for some time they will have homes of their own, and thus they learn how the correct piece of furniture makes a correctly appointed room.[23]

Thus the stated aim of making children's leisure more enjoyable was underpinned by a host of ulterior motives.

Avoiding Sex

Boys and girls had to be trained for their differing roles in life. It was vital, for both the continuation of the family and the vitality of the nation, that men should be men and that women should know their place. Even in the nineteenth century, people had worried that Australia's mild climate encouraged idleness in young fellows, which led straight to effeminacy. By the 1920s and 1930s, a growing lad faced the added enticements of too much

THE SEX HYGIENE
FILM *SECRETS OF LIFE*
ATTRACTED LARGE CROWDS
TO THE PARAMOUNT
THEATRE, BUNDABERG, IN
THE 1950S. AS THE POSTER
SAYS, 'TO MISS IT IS A SIN.'

leisure and the immoral distractions of modern city life. Meanwhile, girls were going out to work, smoking cigarettes, leaving home before they were married and even wearing trousers.

Corrective measures had to be taken early, before the rot set in, and the home environment was where they began. Thus your son's room should be simple, practical, even austere, with a bench for hobbies and a map on the wall. A sporty theme might be recommended for the decoration and muted, earthy colours for walls and floor coverings. As to curtains and bed cover, *Home Beautiful* recommended a 'virile' fabric such as printed burlap. The most important thing was to avoid 'something that he considers "cissy"'.[24]

For young Veronica, something altogether more feminine was called for. 'Whether she marries or not', advised *Home Beautiful*, 'some day she is almost certainly going to furnish rooms for herself'.[25] A dressing-table with drawers for jewellery and trinkets was essential, as was a full-length mirror (something not found in any boy's room, for vanity was not to be encouraged in males) and a glory chest for her dowry. A framed landscape or ballet print on the wall and a pretty print fabric, perhaps in primrose, would complete the lady-like scene. The decisions having been made, it was then time for a bit of bonding: so, while mother and daughter together sewed the curtains and coverlets, dad could be found in the workshop with young Bobby constructing the built-ins.

The trick was to educate young people about their sex roles without mentioning sex, which was, of course, too delicate a subject to raise in public (or even, very often, in private).

From the early 1900s, some courageous reformers advocated sex education, even for the pre-pubescent, often at great personal cost. Public authorities remained reluctant to trespass on what was thought to be a private family matter, and parents, even when they had no idea of how to broach the subject themselves, resented any suggestion of outside interference. What right had teachers to be talking to their children about such things? 'We entirely differ from the … well-meaning enthusiasts who, in their impatience, would start teaching this subject as a drill sergeant does to a squad of recruits', wrote one righteous defender of parents' rights. 'We see grave dangers in the proposal to at once ask teachers to undertake this teaching, or even to send special teachers into our schools to teach sex hygiene.'[26] Religious leaders, fixated on vice and moral turpitude, scorned the reformers' push for objective, professional, health-based instruction, thus succeeding only in making matters worse. But at least silence had been replaced by discussion and at least, by the 1920s, it was generally accepted that children were not innocents but active sexual beings (or at least potentially so). All agreed that sexuality should be guided along healthy, normal lines, even if they didn't necessarily agree on how to go about it.

One happy outcome of the professionalisation of daily life was that public discussion about sex education increasingly centred on hygiene, leaving matters of personal morality to the family and the Sunday School teacher. Even the fraught topic of masturbation was dealt with 'scientifically', although usually with so-called science co-opted to the moralists' cause. An unhappy result of such rational discourse, however, was that nobody, except one or two of the most radical reformers, thought to mention sexual pleasure. 'In spite of these "modern" ideas', notes Kerreen Reiger, 'running through the advice were older assumptions, that sex was sacred, directed towards procreation, and to be thought of only within the framework of marriage and the family'.[27]

Even in the 1950s, what the majority of high-school students knew about sex was what they had picked up behind the shelter sheds. Their ignorance kept them anxious and miserable under a fragile façade of bravado.

At one time, being sent to your room had been a genuine punishment, since it would almost certainly have been a boring place, even if you did know about the saucy postcards under your elder brother's mattress. By the mid 1950s, however, thanks to the combined effects of youth culture, mass marketing and economic prosperity, the bedroom had been transformed into the centre of domestic life as far as the young were concerned. With the advent of *Playboy*, even the titillation had improved. 'Older boys and girls' and 'young adults' morphed into a new breed called 'teenagers', whose unnaturally long period of adolescence was the product of extended education and social conditions that shielded them from adult responsibilities. The world, it seemed, belonged to them.

Musical entertainment was no longer a family affair—singalongs around the piano being well and truly passé—but instead an essential mark of distinction between young and old, a bold assertion of difference. The transistor radio and portable record player helped turn teenagers' bedrooms into private retreats, vibrating to Elvis and Bill Haley and out of bounds to adults. The difficulty now was in getting the kids to come out of their rooms.

The bedroom-as-livingroom reached its fullest realisation in the late 1960s, when teens and twenty-somethings, making the most of prosperity, free tertiary education and healthy job prospects, escaped from what they saw as the stultifying suburbs to inner-city digs. Abandoning the traditional hierarchical arrangement of rooms, they turned their rented terraces into informal groupings of personal bedsits, all more or less equal in status, gathered as if randomly under one roof. There, through a haze of patchouli oil and sweaty socks, Che, Mao and Shiva gazed down sternly at a dishevelled mattress on the floor, piles of abandoned tee-shirts and a pair of speakers the size of wardrobes. The curtains remained permanently drawn and windows and doors locked to protect the stash. Dust accumulated undisturbed. The denizens of these gloomy wombs would emerge bleary-eyed to use the communal kitchen or bathroom only when necessary.

'The place in St Kilda I lived in during the early 1970s, just after I'd dropped out of uni', remembers Michael Abbott,

> was a huge old ramshackle mansion with rooms and passages every-where. I never really knew who was living there from one minute to the next. You'd come out for breakfast and there'd be somebody there you'd never seen before and you didn't know whether they were someone's squeeze for the night or whether they'd moved in. Often it didn't occur to me to ask. I'd just say hello and fall into conversation as though it was the most natural thing in the world. The fridge was full of bottles and jars of stuff labelled with people's names. 'This milk belongs to Jane. Do not touch', and that sort of stuff. And I'd think to myself, 'Who the hell is Jane?' It was a great time.[28]

Suburbia gets wired

It took genius to invent the computer. It took even greater genius to put computers into every home. Not that this hadn't been anticipated. In 1968, when it was still possible for social forecasters to be unguardedly optimistic, a group of American engineers and industrial designers imagined the fully computerised 'House of Tomorrow'. In some cases, their predictions, reported in Australia with a mixture of scepticism and wide-eyed wonder, would prove fanciful.[29] For instance, nobody actually wanted disposable plastic dishes extruded from a kitchen dishmaker, and vacuum cleaners and sewer pipes have not been made redundant–not yet anyway.

The group did, however, foresee with surprising accuracy how the microchip (then being developed for space programs) would revolutionise domestic life. What we now know as internet banking, internet shopping, e-mail, video recording and computer games were all described in some detail, as was 'an electronic complex that will automatically control all lighting, entertainment equipment, appliances

APPLE SAW TERTIARY
STUDENTS AS A CORE
MARKET IN THE EARLY
1980S, OFFERING THEM
DISCOUNTS ON COMPUTERS
SUCH AS THE 128, SHOWN
HERE. THE COMPANY
HELPED UNIVERSITIES TO
SET UP COMPUTER SHOPS,
CLASSES AND USER GROUPS.

and communications gear in a space the size of a contemporary portable radio'.

Aware that such predictions might panic some women (but not men, of course, who were far more worldly and sophisticated), the designers hastened to reassure them: 'By the time the House of Tomorrow becomes a reality, we hope that we will have been able to convince our homemaker that a computer is a willing and tireless servant and not a competitor that will reduce her importance in the eyes of the family.' They naively assumed that, while the new technologies would make family life so much smoother, traditional family structures would remain entirely unaffected. So it would be 'the housewife' using the 'video shopper' and pushing buttons to dispense meals, while 'the man of the house' checked his bank balance and answered his mail. In other words, they envisaged the technological, but not the social impact.

Electronic games, for example, were pictured as group activities, with children gathered together around the console excitedly competing against one another rather than playing alone with the software. Being of their times, the designers thought of digital technologies as aids to socialisation and family togetherness rather than as essentially anti-social (which would have sounded very scary), hence their frequent references to 'the family computer'.

There would never be a family computer, but in the light of previous experience, they could be forgiven for their mistake. New domestic technologies had hitherto always been intended for the benefit of the household. Even the telephone, initially connected for dad's business activities, was quickly democratised. As we will see, one reason washing machines took so long to catch on was precisely that, although they eased women's drudgery, they were not thought to contribute to the betterment of the family as a whole. But it was in the very nature of the personal computer, from the time it first entered the house in the early 1980s, to remain personal. These were prosperous times, allowing almost all individuals to aspire to having one all to themselves. For privacy's sake, the logical place to keep it was the bedroom.

Thus a peculiar contradiction was established. While movies, rock music, cars and cafe culture were enticing people (especially young people) away from the nest, digital technologies were busily drawing them back again. Curiously, however, this did not have the effect of enhancing family togetherness. Although banking, shopping, searching for information and communicating with friends or potentially interesting strangers could now be accomplished without leaving home, such transactions remained strictly private. The PC, along with the mobile phone, turned the bedrooms of a house or flat into quasi-autonomous modules, each with multiple connections to the outside world but largely independent of one another: the secretive haunts of outgoing solipsists. Although the laptop and the iPod can be taken anywhere, they have as yet made little impression on the bedroom's status as a protective private refuge, from which life may be experienced selectively and at arm's length. The Hikikomori children of Japan, who lock themselves into their rooms for years at a time, are perhaps one indication of what it can lead to.

To earlier generations, the bedroom was a place to sleep, a rather dreary little enclosure, out of sight and mind for the greater part of the day. The very idea that it might turn into the principal conduit between the house and the outside world would have left them dumbfounded.

The personal computer is but the most visible manifestation of electronic technologies. Almost every appliance in the contemporary house or apartment, from the garage door to the heater, must be programmable, to assuage our lust for digitalisation. The doggy-door or cat-flap can be instructed to let pets in and out at certain times. We can turn on lights and televisions in our

Comfort can be taken
entirely for granted. It simply
isn't an issue any more.

holiday house when we're not there to discourage burglars, even when the holiday house is on a Greek island. The digital display on the bedside clock thoughtfully adjusts itself to changing light levels in the room. And, in the morning, the clock radio builds gradually to its pre-set volume level to ensure we are awakened without trauma.

Everything must also be capable of performing infinitely more tasks than we require of it. Few of us (except perhaps the very young) will ever realise the full potential of our CD or DVD players, let alone our computers. Whole sections of the instruction manuals are devoted to explaining features we will never need. There is something seductive in the knowledge that the rice cooker and the answering machine harbour secrets we cannot unlock. Not just 'willing and tireless servants', as the House of Tomorrow's designers thought, they are sentient beings with a will of their own. In the past, turning the wrong knob or pressing the wrong button risked damaging the machine, whereas now the machine will tetchily inform you of your error and insist that you correct it. A plaintive female voice from within the iMac PC, popular in the 1990s, wailed 'it's not my fault', whenever anything went awry. When you press a button on your CD player, it will wait a second or two before responding. There may well be good practical reasons for this, but it's as if it has been deciding whether to ignore you.

'Here, in a newly paranoid form', writes Peter Conrad rather gloomily, 'is one of the twentieth century's most terrifying imaginative scenarios. We treat our machines as drudges. Could they, like the homicidal computer in *2001*, be meditating revenge?'[30] Probably not. All this flamboyantly unnecessary digitalisation is pure theatre, either frightening or comedic, depending on your point of view, but theatre nonetheless.

While it makes our domestic appliances more sophisticated, more versatile, infinitely more complicated and often deeply frustrating, digitalisation does not, in most cases, make them noticeably more efficient. It has not lightened domestic workloads to anywhere near the extent that electrification did. Electric stoves, refrigerators and washing machines transformed housework and electric radios, televisions and record players revolutionised leisure. What digitalisation does is to conceal technology, making it appear as if the house is functioning all by itself, without needing any significant input from ourselves other than the occasional fine tuning. This encourages us to ignore the house and its working components altogether. Yet, as the American philosopher Erazim Kohák warns,

> Our preoccupation with labor-saving, beyond the elimination of soul-destroying drudgery, is … counterproductive. To have without doing corrodes the soul: it is precisely in investing life, love, and labor that we constitute the world as personal, as the place of intimate dwelling … the idea of buying a home is an illusion: it is a house we buy; we make it a home by giving ourselves to it.[31]

If the bedroom design company quoted at the beginning of this chapter fails to consider comfort, concentrating entirely on the 'look', that is because, thanks to central heating, insulation, fluffy doonas, double-glazing and push-button remote control of everything from curtains to clock radio, comfort can be taken entirely for granted. It simply isn't an issue any more.

Belying all this, the fashionable *look* is of spareness, even rigorous self-denial. This allows us to enjoy the illusion of living a simple life in tune with nature, while suffering none of the inconveniences that this would normally entail. Thus, our bare-floored, glass-sheathed, minimalist bedrooms simultaneously satisfy the two opposing impulses of pleasure-seeking and puritanism.

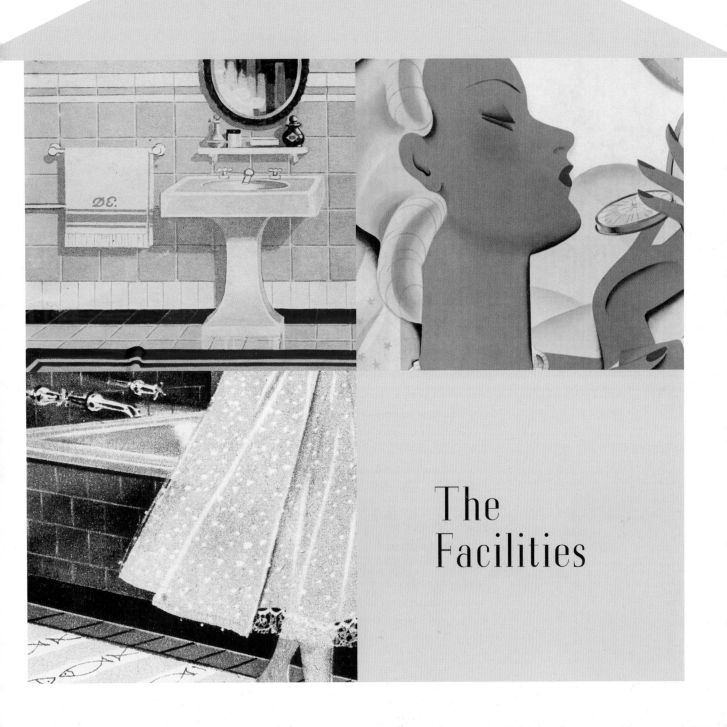

The
Facilities

The Luxury of Sewerage

Tearing yourself from the warmth of the doona, you shuffle to the en-suite, where the residues of yesterday's eating and drinking are flushed away. An invigorating stream of hot water, summoned by the turn of a tap, then washes your dirt and sweat down the plughole in a swirl of suds, carrying them off to who knows where. After a shave and a dab or two of unguent, you emerge from your immaculately tiled bathroom refreshed and invigorated, ready for a new day.

It all takes no more than half an hour, and it seems as natural as eating or breathing. Yet this is a scene that our great-grandparents would have regarded with utter astonishment, and not a little disapproval.

Forget electricity, cars, television and computers: the greatest technological advance of the past 200 years is plumbing.

A century-and-a-half ago, your morning ablutions would have been less inviting. If you were comfortably middle-class, the maid would deliver a jugful of hot water to the wash-stand in your bedroom for you to sponge your face and hands before dressing. She would then discreetly remove your chamber pot for emptying into the cesspit.

No such luxuries, of course, if you were consigned to the lower orders. For hot water, you would have to stoke the stove, then wait half-an-hour or so to fill a wash basin at the kitchen table. It was far easier to endure a cold splash at the water butt by the back door or simply to dispense with ablutions altogether. Pausing on the verandah to don your boots, you then had to trek to the bottom of the yard to a lavatory comprising little more than a seat over a hole in the ground, a haven for funnelwebs and redbacks and a vigorous assault on the senses, especially before breakfast.

But whether you were rich or poor, your bodily wastes were likely to end up in much the same place. Flowing in slimy, stinking streams beneath kitchen and bedroom windows, they made their way into the streets, to combine with

animal carcasses, decomposing vegetable matter, horse manure and other rubbish in great foetid pools in lanes, gutters and waste ground. Even in the best suburbs and in the elegant parlours of the grandest mansions, the stench of raw sewage could be overpowering. As late as 1882, Lady Martin, wife of the Chief Justice of New South Wales, was forced to abandon the family residence in Potts Point because of sickening odours from the drains of Rushcutters Bay. Two of her children had already died of typhoid.[1] Twenty years earlier, it had been estimated that, in Melbourne alone, cesspits were directly responsible for 1500 deaths and more than 30 000 serious illnesses every year,[2] and this at a time when the city's population was less than 500 000.

It was a national scandal, but the situation was well past crisis point before municipal authorities were finally forced to act, and even then their solutions were half-hearted. The cost of constructing sewers was just too great for them to consider but, of course, the longer they delayed the higher it got. The pan system, which replaced cesspits around central Melbourne and Sydney in the

IN 1900, AFTER BUBONIC PLAGUE HAD KILLED 103 PEOPLE IN INNER SYDNEY, A CAMPAIGN WAS LAUNCHED TO KILL RATS, LIMEWASH BACKYARD LAVATORIES AND EVEN TO DEMOLISH THE WORST OF THEM. THIS FAIRLY TYPICAL EXAMPLE, IN THE ROCKS AREA, SERVED A GROUND FLOOR BUTCHER'S SHOP (NOTE THE SAUSAGES HANGING FROM THE SHED ROOF) AND THE DWELLINGS ABOVE IT.

1860s (but not until 1888 in Perth), was only a partially satisfactory compromise. To this day, many of our inner suburbs are honeycombed with narrow lanes built to accommodate the nightman's cart. Dunnies, lined up along back fences like sentry boxes, had a trapdoor onto the lane through which he emptied the pan once a week (if you were lucky) by hauling it onto his shoulder and pouring out the contents, being none too careful about spillage.

No wonder the middle-classes were prone to constipation. Their stodgy diets were a contributing factor, to be sure, but another was the repellent nature of their lavatories, whose existence they did their best to ignore. Nineteenth-century home-help manuals and domestic guides, so voluble in every other respect, coyly pass them by without mention. It was inculcated in children from an early age that there was something shameful about going to the toilet.

Those of delicate sensibility might time their eliminations so as to enjoy the luxury of a newly emptied pan, but since it was returned unwashed, they gained little real advantage in terms of smell or hygiene. The two-pan system, in which the used pan was replaced with a sterilised one, although it cost more, proved much less hazardous for both householders and nightmen.

Another improvement of sorts was the earth closet, of which many ingenious variations were marketed from the 1860s. A tug on a lever released a quantity of ash or dry dirt from a hopper into the pan after use. By eliminating offensive odours and the risk of pestilence, claimed one manufacturer, it would 'save the ladies, children, sick, and infirm from indelicate or unnatural restraint'.[3] Yet the earth closet added to the weight the poor nightman had to shoulder, and of course someone, usually the harassed housewife, had to shovel dust from the road outside and sieve it laboriously into the hopper.

Municipal councils actively discouraged the use of chemical deodorants because they had found, to their great satisfaction, that they could sell unadulterated loads of nightsoil (as sewage was euphemistically called) to market gardeners, thereby almost covering the cost of collection, although that didn't stop them levying householders anything up to thirty shillings a year for the service.

So, happily disregarding typhoid epidemics, scandalous infant mortality rates and the stinking pollution of cities and foreshores, councils saw little reason to commit to the trouble and expense of putting in sewerage pipes. Only towards the end of the nineteenth century, when state governments took over responsibility for sewerage and drainage, did matters begin to improve.

Nevertheless, growth continued to outstrip governments' ability to provide services. As recently as 1960, the nightman was still calling at nearly one-third of all suburban houses in Sydney.[4]

THE SMALLER AND LESS SOLIDLY BUILT HOUSES BECAME, THE MORE SILENCE OF OPERATION MATTERED, BUT WHEN THIS AD APPEARED IN 1955, NOBODY SAW ANYTHING WRONG WITH A TWO GALLON CAPACITY.

Smartest Styling
WITH LIFETIME QUALITY
AND SILENT OPERATION

The PUSH-BUTTON

Delmatic

LOW-LEVEL Flushing CISTERN

Australia's Finest and Most Efficient

★ Handsome modern streamlined case of slim trim proportions
—designed to permit installation of toilet pan close to the wall.

★ Beautifully finished in lifetime quality hard stove baked enamel.
Chrome plated push-button fittings and flushing pipe.

★ Patent outlet valve ensures powerful flushing with silent action
and positive closure. Tested and proved in thousands of homes.

★ Lifetime quality non-corrosive parts. Bowl of 20-gauge
pressed brass, sealed inside with baked aluminium anti-
corrosive coating.

★ Approved by M. & M.B.W. and other water supply authorities.
Available in 3, 2½ and 2 gallon flushing capacities for city or
country homes.

BE EMPHATIC — SPECIFY *Delmatic*

Available from your plumber or hardware store

Another quality product of
DRAFFIN BROS. PTY. LTD. Melbourne
Makers of the famous
EVERHOT Hot Water Systems.

D84 HPC

In Modern Colours to match
all sanitary ware !

If the sewer main had been laid in the back lane, the cheapest option was to leave the outhouse where it stood by the back fence. But not many people were prepared to put up with the inconvenience and gradually, as odours were brought under control, the lavatory crept closer to the house, first hovering beside the wash-house and woodshed close to the back door, then, in the early 1900s, being admitted inside, in its own cubicle at first, for modesty's sake, then as a fitting in the bathroom. This progress towards refinement is largely thanks to an English pottery manufacturer, Thomas Twyford, who, in the 1870s, developed the washout toilet. Made entirely of porcelain and with no moving parts, it was easy to keep clean and, because of an S-bend that trapped clean water in the bottom of the bowl, it stopped smells from rising up the pipes. A slightly later improvement, known as the washdown toilet, with a less complicated S-bend, is still the one we commonly use today.

Far from being unmentionable, the toilet bowl now rejoiced in a wealth of flamboyant decoration, the inside festooned with garlands of printed flowers and its base moulded in the form of a leaping dolphin or crouching lion. Such exuberance was, in effect, the visual expression of a huge collective sigh of relief. Especially popular were aquatic motifs such as fish, water-lilies or Japanese-style wavelets, naive emblems of freshness and cleanliness that proved to be of such symbolic potency that they have never quite gone away. Of course, fish have nothing to do with sewerage, but the connection seems comforting nonetheless. Although today we prefer our porcelain unadorned, they are still a popular motif for shower screens, bathmats and the printed friezes on toilet paper.

Rolls of perforated toilet paper, an American innovation first marketed in the late 1870s, were not always readily available, and in any case were widely dismissed as an unnecessary luxury until well into the twentieth century.* Instead, newspapers, magazines and old sales catalogues were threaded onto string and suspended from a nail on the back of the door, beneath the playful puppies on the butcher's calendar. According to some, however, this was risky. Do not use printed paper such as newsprint, warned *Home and Health*, 'for it is claimed on good authority that printers' ink is often responsible for serious rectal diseases'.[5] That may well have been true in 1909, but few had a choice.

All the major advances in lavatory technology—sewerage, articulated water supply, the flush cistern and the S-bend—are nineteenth-century ones. They were belated responses to a crisis in public health which seriously threatened urban life. Everything since has been a refinement. These refinements fall roughly into two categories: the ones aimed at making the lavatory less distasteful to the fastidious—ever more 'clean and nice looking', as one 'sanitary ware' advertisement put it in 1925—and, much more recently, those that try to minimise environmental harm, a similarly belated response to a new crisis. The two are not unrelated, since it is our collective embarrassment about bodily wastes that has made us so profligate in using resources to get rid of them.

A fixture in the bathroom was certainly convenient, but that ever-present embarrassment factor, which continued to spawn a multitude of coy and jocular euphemisms for the unmentionable 'lavatory',* demanded that it be of discreet appearance and as quiet as possible. The smaller and less solidly-built houses became, the more advertisers concentrated on silence of operation. As advances in plumbing allowed the cistern to be brought down from well above head-height to just over the bowl, designers integrated the two into a single unit, which could then be marketed as part of a suite with matching basin and bathtub. A simple wooden-handled lever replaced the old-fashioned chain until it in turn was superseded in the early 1930s by the push-button flush. Fowler's Marrick Combination Suite was the height of sophistication in 1933, with its Art Deco-inspired 'geometric lines instead of the conventional

* From the mid 1850s, toilet paper could be bought as individual sheets, often printed with the manufacturer's name. In earlier times, moss, rags or bundles of leaves might be used and, especially in Arabic countries, the left hand (which is why only the right was used for eating). Ancient Greeks and Romans used a sponge attached to a handle, which was stored in a jar of salty water to be shared among those using the public latrines.

* The words 'lavatory' and 'toilet' are themselves euphemisms, originally relating to bathing and skin-care, respectively.

curves ... The bevelled corners and edges, relieved with a drop ornamentation, impart an artistic note to an otherwise utilitarian article'.[6]

Yet nobody gave a thought to the amount of water it contained. As recently as 1955, advertisements for the Delmatic Low Level Press-Button Cistern boasted of its three-gallon (or around thirteen-litre) capacity.[7] Was such a vast torrent of fresh water really needed to flush away a trickle of urine? Well, no, but the more water you used, the cleaner, fresher and nicer your bathroom would be. There was something more than a little paranoid about it.

A severe drought across most of mainland Australia in the 1960s, along with a widely reported remark by the Duke of Edinburgh about the amount of water wasted by toilets (which was thought extremely vulgar at the time, especially from a Royal), finally penetrated the wall of awkward silence. Cistern capacities were steadily reduced to around half of what they had been previously, with no loss of effectiveness. Then, in 1982, Bruce Thompson, of the Australian company Caroma, invented a dual-flush system, which some state governments subsequently made mandatory in all new houses. They were the first in the world to do so. Although complicated in design, the dual-flush has been estimated to save 32 000 litres per household each year.[8] Nevertheless, it was not introduced into the United States until the late 1990s and, even in environmentally conscious California, has still not been made compulsory.[9]

Keeping Clean

The need to be 'water wise' is now drummed into us at every opportunity, something quite new to most city dwellers, who have tended to regard an unlimited supply of fresh water as a basic right. It is, after all, the primary requirement for life.

Many early settlers in Sydney and Hobart Town would have been familiar with the idea of a piped water supply, since one had been constructed in London in the eighteenth century, based on ancient Roman examples.

Australians became, and would remain
for the following half-century, the world's
largest per-capita users of soap.

However, the water it delivered was polluted by sewage, a problem that would quickly arise here in Australia as well. Schemes for getting rid of waste water invariably lag well behind those for delivering clean water, which makes it very difficult to keep the two separated.

Not until cities were ringed by dams feeding a maze of underground pipes did Australian householders secure a clean, reliable water supply. Large-scale dam building began in the mid-nineteenth century and continued for over a hundred years, although the infrastructure was costly and often politically controversial and supply rarely managed to keep up with urban expansion. Nevertheless, very large cities would not have been possible without these ambitious nineteenth-century schemes for storing and delivering water. Earlier, it had been a matter of collecting rainwater in home tanks, drawing it from public hand-pumps, or paying handsomely to have it home-delivered by cart.

A perennial problem for the authorities was that urban Australians have always been relatively heavy users of water. There are various reasons for this, including our traditional love of gardens and our generally warm, dry weather. Curiously, we also embraced regular, all-over bathing with greater enthusiasm than people elsewhere. Perhaps this had something to do with the climate, and our passion for swimming. In any case, from the 1870s, bathrooms ceased to be a rarity in better-class Australian houses, while the respectable middle-classes took, with some trepidation, to weekly cleansing at public baths. This was a time when few in Britain or Europe ever washed themselves all over. We were, on the whole, unusually particular about personal hygiene, which is borne out by the fact that Australians became, and would remain for the following half-century, the world's largest per-capita users of soap. Not that this was entirely a good thing, according to some, for it was widely believed that too much bathing leached away the body's essential oils, leading to sickliness.[10]

Despite this enthusiasm, most suburban houses in the 1880s still lacked bathrooms, and even as they were introduced over the following twenty years or so, they were invariably severely utilitarian enclosures off the back verandah,

THE EROTIC CURVES OF
GEORGE BELL'S NUDE, ECHOED
IN THE CABRIOLE LEGS OF HER
DRESSING TABLE AND CHAIR,
WERE PERHAPS INTENDED
AS A GENTLE REBUKE TO THE
PRUDERY OF MIDDLE-CLASS
SUBURBAN LIFE.

GEORGE BELL
THE MIRROR 1956
OIL ON PLYWOOD
34.5 X 26.6 CM
NATIONAL GALLERY OF
AUSTRALIA

BOILING WATER

obtained with the utmost ease from

GAS AUTOMATIC WATER HEATER

You simply have to turn the tap to obtain BOILING WATER. "BRIAR" Heaters are made in sizes ranging from 1¼ gallons to 50 gallons storage capacity—and are capable of supplying their own capacity of BOILING WATER approximately each half-hour.

Sold by all gas companies and merchants, and manufactured wholly in Australia by

THE BRIAR MANUFACTURES Pty. Ltd.
28 ST. FRANCIS STREET, MELBOURNE

IN THE EARLY 1930S, THE BRIAR GAS HOT WATER HEATER WAS PROMOTED IN A DRYLY INFORMATIVE RATHER THAN ENTICING MANNER, BUT THEN THE BRIAR WAS HARDLY A STYLISH ADDITION TO THE HOME. THIS WOMAN APPEARS TO BE FILLING HER TEAPOT IN THE BATHROOM OR LAUNDRY.

equipped with cold water only. The bathroom was the man's domain, for, despite warnings about the dangers of overdoing it, a cold bath or shower first thing in the morning was thought necessary to stiffen his resolve. Women, who had no need of such stiffening, continued to sponge themselves at the bedroom wash-stand, although, if there were servants to bring kettles of hot water from the stove, and if privacy could be guaranteed, either sex might enjoy an occasional hip-bath in front of the parlour fire as a special treat.

Not that bathing was meant to be enjoyed. A bath or shower was strictly for hygiene and had to be taken seriously. Those who saw discipline and privation as moral imperatives were quick to quash any suggestion of the erotic. *Home and Health* recommended a cold hand-bath every morning, by which was meant a vigorous all-over scrubbing, using a basin of water, while standing. It should not last longer than five minutes and should comprise 'one part water, four parts rough towel-rubbing, and five parts friction with the bare hand'.[11] That the towel-rubbing should be rough was vital. Smooth cotton or linen towels were insufficiently stimulating (in other words, not self-punishing enough). Once a week, the book suggests, a hot bath should be taken, using a bath powder made from starch, orris root and camphor, ground to a powder and wrapped in a cheesecloth bag. Just in case you were tempted to enjoy this too much, however, you were strongly advised to finish with cold water 'to close the pores'.

It must be kept in mind that, in the early 1900s, preparing a hot bath was a major undertaking involving much careful preparation, despite considerable progress during this period, which saw the introduction of the enamelled cast-iron bath,* the porcelain pedestal wash basin and the free-standing shower stall (although the last mentioned would not appear in Australian homes until the late 1920s, and then only those of the wealthy). After that, there would be very few important innovations, other than stylistic ones, until the invention of the spa bath in the 1960s and the mixer tap a decade later.

Everything depended on the availability of affordable hot water, and that presented a problem. Although gas and electric water heaters were not unknown (The General Gordon, a riveted tinplate monster with an array of gas burners beneath it—not unlike the cauldrons that cartoon cannibals cooked their missionaries in—had been advertised in London as early as 1865 and came complete with a towel-warmer[12]), they were not commonly found in the suburban bathroom until well after World War I. Meanwhile, bathwater had to be heated by a pipe fed through the wood-fire stove in the kitchen, or by a kerosene or chip heater mounted over the tub.

Rose Harrex, growing up in Melbourne's Richmond in the late 1920s, was 'not allowed to use the chip heater because it was too dangerous. I remember being scalded by it once'. Her elder brother was responsible for keeping up the supply of kindling, which was piled on the floor next to the bath, but only mother was allowed to light the fire and keep an eye on it. 'It was likely to boil if you left it, and make a terrible booming noise as if it was going to explode.'[13] Kerosene bath heaters proved just as unpredictable.

In 1924, the makers of 'The Rapid' bath heater, which took just ten minutes to get the water up to temperature once the gas had been lit, claimed that it was 'well within the reach of all gas consumers', although at £9, it was still something most people would have to save for, especially considering the added cost of installing the gas pipes. The hot water it produced was so precious that the kids were forced to share the weekly bath in turns, eldest first and the unfortunate youngest left to slosh about in the others' filth. There was always the horrible suspicion that an elder sibling, to whom you had caused some minor offence earlier in the day, had peed in the water as an act of silent revenge.

* The cast-iron bath was invented in England around 1880, but until a method was devised to enamel it, its surface was rough and prone to rust, making it necessary to protect the skin with a cotton bath-sheet.

HOME BEAUTIFUL, IN 1927,
ENTHUSED THAT 'IT IS A
PLEASURE TO BATHE IN THESE
SURROUNDINGS'.

'What a joy to the housewife and mother', enthused an advertisement for the THM Electric Bath Heater in 1927, 'to know that when a hot bath is needed she has merely to turn on the bath heater tap and the steaming hot water is there!'[14] A joy indeed, but one that most housewives and mothers could only dream about as they shovelled another load of filthy black coke into their Boska Hot Water Boiler and waited.[15]

At least the general appearance of the room had improved, which may have been some consolation. The public health and hygiene campaigns of the early twentieth century had given rise to the minimalist white-tiled bathroom still familiar to us today. Hard, shiny, easy-to-clean surfaces replaced the dark wood panelling and Persian carpets that had previously added grace, dignity and mould to the bathrooms of the rich. The new style was more practical, of course, particularly now that housewives were having to do their own cleaning, but it also *looked* healthy and efficient, which was now a very important consideration. Minimalist modern design was manifested in the bathroom long before it became acceptable elsewhere in the house. Since the bathroom had rarely been associated with comfort anyway, being a purely utilitarian facility, there was no reason it should not look the part.

A Bath for Comfort

As the practical difficulties of delivering hot water were overcome, bathing began to take on a softer, more luxurious image. Bathrooms became more attractive and stylish, and taking a bath or shower could be an indulgence. This was not necessarily incompatible with simplicity and practicality of bathroom design. A crisp, white-tiled, linoleum-floored bathroom that *Home Beautiful* presented in 1927 as a model for the modern small house is basically like any modern bathroom today, apart from superficial differences of style. It has a glass shower screen over the bath, a pedestal wash basin, a glass shelf for the toothbrush holder, a shaving mirror and (presumably, out of the picture) a lavatory. 'It is a pleasure to bathe in these surroundings',[16] reads the caption—a comment that could not have been made twenty years earlier, both because bathrooms were not likely to have been a pleasure and because it would not have been proper to suggest they should be.

Hollywood had a big part to play in the change of attitude. Movie producers quickly discovered that they could indulge in a little titillation without incurring the wrath of the censors by showing attractive starlets up to their necks in suds. In 1919, Cecil B DeMille had Gloria Swanson bathing glamorously in *Male and Female*, and, as time went on, bathroom scenes became increasingly scandalous. George Cukor's *The Women*, made in 1939, features a young Joan Crawford lounging seductively in a translucent crystal bath fitted with gold dolphin taps and a matching crystal bath tray containing her perfumes, mirror and telephone.

A BATHROOM OF COMFORT
AND GLAMOUR FOR THOSE
WHO WANTED TO BE JOAN
CRAWFORD

Manufactured by
DRAFFIN BROS. PTY. LTD.
45 City Rd., Melb.
MX 3287

Lucky Mrs Wilson

Mr. & Mrs. Wilson built their house just prior to the war and installed an electric hot water system. Mrs. Wilson says she is lucky now for although clothes, food and petrol are rationed she still has really hot water whenever she turns on the tap. The Everhot system in Mrs. Wilson's home hasn't once let her down.

There are 11,999 other lucky housewives with Everhot hot water services getting really hot water day and night right through the war.

When you dream of your post-war home, plan it with an Everhot. Just now we're busy at Draffin Bros on war contracts, and we can't build you an Everhot, but when the war ends we'll be back on the job building the best hot water service for the new and not-so-new homes of Melbourne.

Would you like more information about Everhot? Write now for a leaflet.

EVERHOT
Electric
HOT WATER SERVICE D2.27

THIS RATHER TOUCHING 1944 ADVERTISEMENT TRIES HARD TO PUT A POSITIVE SPIN ON THE FACT THAT THE COMPANY'S HOT WATER SYSTEMS, LIKE MOST OTHER HOUSEHOLD GOODS, ARE UNAVAILABLE DUE TO WARTIME RESTRICTIONS.

It was hardly a coincidence that such fantasies began to take hold as dark economic and political clouds gathered outside. A hot bath was a protective womb. 'If the bathwater is hot and plentiful', wrote a *Sydney Morning Herald* columnist in 1934, 'if the towels are large and warm, no business depression, no private worries can harm me! ... I am an Empress in my own right'.[17] So what if your bathroom was not quite up to Joan Crawford's standard? You could still soak away the troubles of the world in a steamy tub.

A select few could even afford to bring the movies to life. This was how the bathroom of one Potts Point mansion was described in the *Sydney Morning Herald* on the eve of World War II:

The bath is sunk into the tiled floor, with every imaginable tap and spray, and down at it look three stained glass windows. Should you wish at night for direct lighting, a large lalique lamp sheds it upon you, and if you desire an indirect glow a button pressed will give you amber, blue, or rose at will ... A shower cabinet with every conceivable spray, a foot bath, three enormous marble hand-basins, with shampoo sprays, and a drinking water filter wait upon your desire! Gleaming white tiles have a lapis lazuli relief, while panels of cameo tiles in black and white and of green marble, with golden dancing figures, break the white surface ... beneath the side windows [are] three inset glass tanks in which living goldfish swim serenely through coral and seaweed, while under the centre windows a white marble fountain is guarded by four bronze nymphs.[18]

No vigorous towel-rubbing in this temple of indolence.

It was hardly a coincidence that such fantasies began to take hold as dark economic and political clouds gathered outside.

Yet the envy of many *Herald* readers would no doubt have been tempered by the suspicion that this bathroom, however splendid, was too much the public spectacle. It was the very point of Joan Crawford's crystalline tub that it wasn't real. It was a way for ordinary folk to indulge their fantasies. There was something bogus about a wealthy merchant in Potts Point trying to bring it all to life. Most people didn't want to be on display. They wanted privacy. A lock on the inside and a frosted-glass window were bathroom essentials. To sexually reticent middle-class Protestants, public bathing, of the kind familiar in the Middle East or Japan, was little short of barbarism. If we think of the home as a protective shell, shielding us from the pressures of social life, then the bathroom is its inner kernel, a private space within a private space, but private because it is associated with embarrassment, even shame. Fear of nakedness led to an uneasy ambivalence: scandalised admiration of the Hollywood fantasy existing side-by-side with everyday puritanism. Had we been more accustomed to public bathing, we might have been less conflicted, but niggling guilt has always tended to spoil our enjoyment of this solitary pleasure.

The Modern Bathroom

The kind of extravagance that might have aroused envy before the war was likely to prompt only resentment after it, when a general mood of solemn restraint was more in order. Although optimistic, people were wary of flamboyance, even when experienced vicariously.

The watchword was standardisation, for by no other means was it thought possible to cope with the post-war building boom. Many schemes were devised to standardise and manufacture off-site not only the individual fittings but entire bathrooms—indeed entire houses. One idea, outlined in *Home Beautiful*, was for pre-fabricated steel bathrooms that could be delivered complete. 'All the little extra things which we have come to regard as essential to bathroom comfort will be included in the standard unit', the article maintained, the shaving cabinet and mirror, the recesses for soap, the drinking glass and tooth brush holder, towel rails (probably heated), and possibly provision for a small gas or electric wall fire, a comfort which no one who has ever had one would want to be without. The built-in bath will have its shower screen, and possibly an additional shower cabinet unit will be evolved for those who desire that extra accommodation.[19]

Although it sounded eminently practical in theory, Australian industry simply wasn't tooled up for such ventures and the market was too small to justify the expense. In any case, the result, as pictured in *Home Beautiful*, was too stark and industrial-looking to have much appeal.

One noticeable absence from this ultra-efficient little bathroom was the water heater, for technical improvements meant that hot water could now be stored in a centrally-located hot water service. Originally developed for flats in the early 1930s, it was only gradually brought within the financial reach of individual homeowners. At last the ugly device could be hidden in the ceiling or outdoors, simultaneously serving kitchen, laundry and any number of bathrooms. Hot water now flowed, as if by magic, at the turn of a tap. At last the suburban bathroom had taken on the appearance of a fully self-functioning entity, with no mechanical operation exposed to view, which would eventually permit everyone to take this minor miracle entirely for granted.

Home Beautiful's mention of an optional shower cabinet unit is an indication that showers were increasingly coming into favour. Although never especially popular in England, they gained early acceptance in Australia during the nineteenth century, perhaps because of the milder climate. A worker arriving home filthy from a long shift at the factory might rinse himself in the backyard under a Boston shower, comprising a bucket at ground level from which the water was pumped to an overhead rose by a hand lever. It was hardly comfortable, but it did the job, so long as you were quick, for a bucket of water didn't last long. Twentieth-century bathrooms usually had a shower above the tub, because that was the cheapest option. But the fact that it was a mere accessory to the bath also indicated its lesser status. It took a long time for showers to shake off their masculine, working-class associations. Showers were particularly unsuited to women, for the very idea of them standing naked to wash, even in private, was thought indecent. Showers were active, baths passive.

Nevertheless, if you had to catch the 8.15 to the city, a bath was probably out of the question, and the fact that, from the 1930s, more women were joining the workforce was one reason that showers slowly gained acceptance.

A separate recess was ideal, being more intimate, private and comfortable, but it was also more expensive, even if you did have the space. In the early 1950s, you could buy a concrete shower base and build a recess around it using Masonite Lustrtile. Pressed-steel shower bases were also available, although the authorities in some cities stipulated concrete.

With or without a shower recess, a bathroom with hot and cold running water was now considered standard in any suburban house, although still by no means universal. For example, in 1956, the year Melbourne hosted the Olympic Games, just over 84 per cent of homes in Victoria had a bathroom. Tasmania had the lowest percentage of 75.6. But that was still a lot more than in London, where it was less than 35 per cent.[20]

Adventurous project-home designers in the mid 1950s started moving the bathroom from its customary position at the back to the middle of the house, even beside the front door, where it was more accessible to the livingroom than to the bedrooms. While this made the kids' nocturnal excursions more wearisome and prone to mishap, mum and dad might well have had the convenience of a private en-suite, so what did they care? *Women's Weekly* had heralded the arrival of the en-suite– this 'new idea from overseas'–in 1945.[21] Only a very small space was needed and the convenience of it more than justified the expense. But not until the development of moulded acrylics a decade or so later would the idea become really practical. Acrylics allowed for light-weight, compact fittings in a wide range of shapes and sizes, including shower recesses that could be bought off the shelf and simply placed into position. In the mid-1950s, an acrylic bath cost around £33, while the much more popular pressed-steel ones were £22 in white or £26 in pink (as with almost everything else around the home, colour cost more).[22] Yet the price of acrylics came down quickly as their ease and flexibility earned them a dominant market share. By 1967, *Home Beautiful* could claim, perhaps with some exaggeration, that 'most new homes these days have at least one-and-a-half bathrooms. Many have a private suite off the main bedroom for the

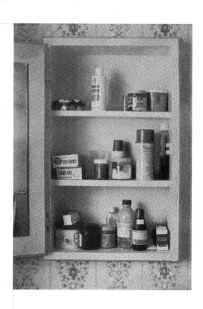

ARTIST ROBIN WHITE'S
PHOTO-ETCHING OF A HOME
MEDICINE CABINET

ROBIN WHITE
NEW ZEALAND 1946
MEDICINE CABINET 1988
PHOTO-ETCHING
NATIONAL GALLERY OF
AUSTRALIA

parents and another bathroom for the children...'[23] As one designer put it at the time, 'you can get a shower, toilet and handbasin into an area of about 10-ft. by 3-ft., or square equivalent. They work well, and for the man who's showered, shaved, dressed and breakfasted and on his way to work in 40 minutes are pretty well ideal'.[24]

This didn't mean that luxury and indulgence had been sacrificed altogether, only that bronze nymphs and lapis lazuli were no longer the favoured way of expressing them. Now it was lightness and brightness that mattered, and having everything close to hand. A view of the garden, a drift of fresh air, or a shaft of sunshine through a skylight counted for more than gold-plated taps. To ensure maximum bodily ease, ergonomics was introduced in the late 1960s courtesy of the influential Kira Report, a scientific study of bathroom design conducted by the Centre for Housing and Environmental Studies at Cornell University.[25] Its maze of graphs and charts reduced every detail of human well-being to a rational formula, with little consideration given to the vagaries of individual taste. The result was bathrooms that were undoubtedly more physically comfortable than the marble and crystal fantasies of Hollywood, although lacking their erotic charge.

By this stage, even Hollywood had given up on glamorously decadent bathing. Movie bathrooms were now more likely to be the scenes of grisly murders or melancholy suicides, an uncomfortable reminder of shaving cuts and the dressing of wounds, with which this little room, with its medicine cabinet above the sink, had always been associated. The final straw came in 1960, with Hitchcock's *Psycho* ensuring that the long hot shower could never again be enjoyed with complete peace of mind. The symbolism was prescient, in its way, for more recently, water-conservation campaigns have reimposed upon the art of bathing some of the moral guilt with which it was encumbered a hundred years ago—this time not erotic but aquatic—which means a bath or shower is again something to be done with as quickly as possible with minimum enjoyment.

The Importance of Keeping Beautiful

What houseguest, alone behind the locked bathroom door, has not peeked surreptitiously into the cabinet? Even if it reveals nothing more sinister than what brand of perfume or pimple cream the hosts are using, there remains the thrill of encroaching on their intimate personal lives without fear of recrimination. There is deep satisfaction in knowing that their poise and physical perfection, seemingly so natural, are in fact dependent on a battery of gels, lotions and electrical devices. Haemorrhoid creams and prescriptions for urinary tract infections are a positive godsend. Although intensely personal, the bathroom is, paradoxically, one of the most likely rooms in the house to be seen by visitors, alone and without supervision. The bathroom cabinet or shelf is where the boundaries between private and public life are put to the test.

It is a fair assumption that, in suburban bathrooms before World War II, patent medicines far outnumbered beauty aids, whereas the opposite is likely

THE COSMETICS AND
TOILETRIES COUNTER AT
AHERNS DEPARTMENT STORE,
PERTH, IN 1950

to be true today. The spectacular rise of the cosmetics industry over the past fifty years or so has crammed our shelves with expensive potions to smooth, soften, condition and protect.

Pears Soap was one of the first products to be successfully mass-marketed in the modern manner—that is, as a brand name which people bought because they recognised it. Pears made marketing central to merchandising. Yet mass marketing could not reach its full flowering until the advent of electronic media, so only when most homes had a radio or TV did advertisers supplant the local shopkeeper, family member or friend as the main influence on what cosmetics and health-care products people bought.

At first, few were on offer. In the early 1900s, a woman was expected to keep herself nice for her husband simply by dressing neatly and washing regularly. She did not, of course, try to make herself alluring to other men. That would have been sluttish, or, if she were rich and did it well, coquettish, which was still unacceptable, although easier to forgive. *The Australian Housewives Manual* recommended daily washing with Pears, because it was guaranteed 'pure', that is, not contaminated with carbolic or even arsenic, as some other brands were. A daily dab of bay rum, eau-de-cologne or toilet vinegar would combat wrinkles around mouth and eyes. And that was about it. The best you could do was to preserve the attributes God had bestowed upon you. 'Personal cleanliness and neatness are the first requisites toward good housekeeping, and no woman who wishes to preserve her husband's affection, or to make him comfortable, should ever waver for one moment in those attentions to her own person which will preserve whatever share of beauty she may have.'[26]

As the social commentator Joanne Finkelstein has pointed out,

> it is a reflection of women's subordinate position that their physical appearance is a point of vulnerability. The status of men in industrialised society is more closely attached to their labour value (unlike in previous epochs when they were the fashion peacocks), and this means their appearance is less important.[27]

WAR MIGHT BE THREATENING, BUT THE DEPRESSION WAS WELL AND TRULY OVER BY 1938 AND SOME WOMEN, AT LEAST, HAD BOTH THE MEANS AND THE DESIRE TO MAKE THEMSELVES GLAMOROUS.

The only significant change to men's faces was that they shed their whiskers. By the time Europeans went to war in 1914, the American Gillette Safety Razor was a world-wide phenomenon, thanks to the company's canny advertising, which made men with beards and moustaches feel dirty and unkempt.[28] Gillette brilliantly exploited the era's passion for hygiene and, with the coming of hot

THE HOME

MICHAEL COLLINS

PRICE
1′3

PRICE
1′3

SPECIAL COLOUR PRINT FOR FRAMING
INCLUDED IN THIS NUMBER:
THE SPIT, MIDDLE HARBOUR—BY JAMES R. JACKSON

water to the home, quickly ensured that a smooth chin became the norm. In an age just coming to terms with Darwinian evolution, facial hair, which for the Victorians had signified dignity and authority, now seemed uncomfortably close to simian nature. A clean-shaven man was a cultured man.

A woman, on the other hand, was supposed to be close to nature, although of course only its dainty, not its brutish side. Her spring-like innocence and purity could be conveyed through the fresh scent of tea-rose, lily-of-the-valley or daphne. But she had to beware. As a boy in Sydney in the late 1940s, Bert Jones was taught to distrust his Cousin Beth whose habit of wearing perfume and painting her nails made her a bit of a hussy in the eyes of the family. 'Only Catholics paint their nails', his mother assured him.[29] As far as the respectable middle-classes were concerned, perfume and nail polish would become acceptable only when marketing campaigns had turned being a bit of a hussy into a harmless game.

The woman who wanted to make herself nice, for whatever reason, was often obliged to make her own powders and potions from ingredients she bought at the chemist or grocer. Even kitchen leftovers might come in handy. In her popular advice book, Mrs Lance Rawson advised ladies to save their chicken fat, render it, beat it, add some scented oil, then rub it into their faces before bedtime. 'It is best to prepare one's own oil', she added, 'as oils bought at the chemists are not always pure'.[30] She was right about that, although chicken fat might not have been the most attractive alternative.

A mixture of sulphur and milk, applied at night, was said to be good for freckles and blotches; a few drops of bitter apple added to Jamaica rum and left to stand a day or two made an excellent tonic for the hair, after you had washed it in beaten egg and borax; and a complex concoction of melted wax, honey, lemon juice and salad dressing was good for keeping arms and hands white.[31] How did women find the time to prepare all these unguents, given the multitude of demands they faced?

Liberated young women in the 1920s and 1930s would have none of it. During their lunch-hours, they flocked to David Jones' ground-floor cosmetics counter, where Ashes of Roses, Evening in Paris, Black Narcissus, Devon Lilac and that old favourite, 4711, enticed their salaries from them. This was all very well for the smart young things, but housewives had a hard enough time making ends meet as it was. As Lydia Gill recalls, 'We did an awful lot of looking in the thirties'.[32]

Advertisers knew exactly who were just looking and who were spending. Emphasis shifted towards the young, who needed to look glamorous, had the cash, and were easier to sway. Their role models were not those of their parents' generation. *The Home*, in 1936, could still proudly feature 'The Hon. Mrs. Peter Rodd, the eldest daughter of the second Baron Redesdale, taking Lotte, her white French Bulldog, to Hyde Park', but already this sort of thing was looking frightfully snooty.[33] The vice-royals and their high-society hangers-on, whose every move had in the past been faithfully recorded in the social pages, had now been abandoned in favour of film stars. Glamour trumped breeding. It was certainly more egalitarian. As the American historian Victoria de Grazia notes, celebrities, the creations of mass consumption, did not have any political or economic credentials. They were not decision-makers. 'Thus they could engage attention without provoking the class envy, resentment, or hierarchical patterns of emulation typically stimulated by the old elites. In sum, they were a resource like other commodities, offering new models of social belonging.'[34] That the movie star Barbara Stanwyck recommended Lux Toilet Soap as 'the best way I know to make sure of charm and daintiness'[35] was enough to recommend it to any woman, irrespective of social status.

As cosmetics were thus democratised, the women's pages in newspapers and magazines put increasing emphasis on beauty tips, which mainly consisted in how to choose the right products and the correct way to apply them. Now you didn't have to be satisfied with preserving what nature had bestowed upon you: now you could improve on it. Needless to say, the magazines' recommendations chimed very nicely with the interests of companies that purchased their advertising space.

Unless you were having a fling with a visiting US marine, lipsticks, powders and perfumes were hard to find during the war years. Even the chaps had to dig about in the back of the cupboard for dad's old cut-throat as razorblades disappeared from the shops. Then, as post-war economies picked up across the western world, the global cosmetics industry exploded. Like almost everything else, 'personal care', as it was now called, was slowly prised from the domestic sphere and professionalised. No longer was it enough for a woman to attend to herself at home in private. Her skin, like her hair, had to be cared for by experts. Beauty parlours, which had originated in the 1890s to pamper rich New Yorkers and which, for decades, had been considered just another yankee excess, started appearing in every suburban shopping centre, offering manicures, facials, leg waxing and perms.

Among the young, class was no longer the issue: lipstick, eye-shadow and powder, rather than singling you out as a person of breeding and sophistication—or, alternatively, as cheap—established your allegiance to group or tribe. In the 1950s, bodgies and widgies signalled their menacing demeanour by means of their hairstyles, clothes and makeup. A decade later, cosmetics, properly chosen and generously applied under a beehive hairdo, said, 'I have no sympathy with hippies. I do not soak myself in Patchouli oil and wear beads. I am respectable and responsible'. By the same token, if you overdid it, they might say something a little less flattering, which, in this age of youthful rebellion, was okay too.

Thus age overtook social stratum as the measure of status. Everyone had to look young, even if that meant seventy-year-olds strutting about like mummified teenagers. The medical profession, seeing an opening, moved in to declare that wrinkles, sagging chins and bags under the eyes were clinical conditions demanding the attention of properly qualified practitioners. Plastic surgery, originally developed for the rehabilitation of soldiers whose faces had been blown off in the trenches of Passchendaele and the Somme, was co-opted to help women (and, latterly, men) to correct God's minor errors.

Australian men were slower than their European and American counterparts to embrace after-shaves, colognes and shower gels. A little dab of Brylcream and a splash of Old Spice (a birthday gift from the suspiciously sophisticated Aunt Alice) was as far as most were prepared to go. This wasn't just knee-jerk conservatism. Aussie blokes took readily enough to Palmolive Rapid Shave in its revolutionary Pressure-Pak can from the moment it was introduced in 1955 because it was practical and saved time, both good masculine virtues. But skin-care products, they feared, signalled a loss of virility.

In the modern world, personal
appearance necessarily counts for
much more than it once did.

They were probably right about that, but there was no point in resisting. In the modern world, where people frequently change houses, jobs and spouses, personal appearance necessarily counts for much more than it once did. The much derided 'cult of the body' is no frivolous matter. If we move to a new city, start a new job, or find ourselves recently divorced and prowling singles bars at fifty, our inner strengths will not be of much immediate use. We need to make an impression quickly. 'The average college graduate entering the job market today', writes the American author Alex Kuczynski,

> will hold at least seven different jobs for seven different companies during his or her lifetime. You may spend your entire work life not knowing your colleagues well, passing from city to city, with only a handful of long-term friends and family members who know your foibles, your habits, and the qualities that make you special or remarkable.[36]

Unable to rely on your reputation, you must rely on your appearance in order to make your mark. Surveys have shown that even a good-looking motor mechanic will get a job in preference to an equally or more skilled one who happens to be less attractive.[37]

A hundred years ago, young people thought of 'self-improvement' as a question of character, morality, intelligence and manners. Today, they automatically think of their weight, their skin, or the size of their breasts. While this might be cause for regret, there are good practical reasons for it.

All of which has had the paradoxical effect of, on the one hand, increasing the symbolic status of the bathroom in the house, as the workshop for the body beautiful, while, on the other, diminishing its actual role, as the business of personal care is removed from the house altogether and entrusted to outside experts. Today the bathroom, along with the kitchen, is likely to be the most expensive part of the house to build and fit out, a remarkable turnaround from its earlier incarnation, not so long ago, as a tin shed in the backyard. It is no longer the bath or shower that holds centre stage, but the aptly named vanity unit with its large mirror, strategically placed lighting and luxury appointments, where narcissism, that most necessary of modern personal attributes, can be cultivated.

Keeping Healthy

If you lived in Victorian times, it didn't do to get sick. Hospitals were such a nightmare that being admitted to one was considered a death sentence. Colonial governments were not especially interested in building or funding hospitals, since religious charities were perfectly capable of doing that. There were few controls over their operation and never enough funds. When Lucy Osborne, a protégée of Florence Nightingale, took over as head nurse at Sydney Hospital in 1868, she found the place overrun with vermin. Patients lay on rotting mattresses with buckets of excreta beside them. The main hospital sewer overflowed under the floorboards, creating a fearful stink in the unventilated wards, and no fresh water was available for surgeons to wash their hands. Furthermore, patients with infectious diseases such as typhoid or tuberculosis were not quarantined, but lay with others in open wards. But it was no worse than any other hospital at the time. As late as 1874, it was reported that staff at the Melbourne laying-in hospital threw placentas under the beds, where they were left to rot. No wonder up to 10 per cent of women died during childbirth in 'that house of slaughter'.[38]

The medical profession's acceptance of Joseph Lister's discoveries in anti-sepsis, which led to the use of carbolic acid in operations, was painfully slow. Nevertheless, by 1900, hospitals, along with general standards of health, had improved immeasurably. With few effective ways of fighting bacterial infection, prevention came to be seen as everyone's moral responsibility, which led to the lively interest in cleanliness and fresh air described in previous chapters. It had an immediate effect. In 1901, the annual report of Melbourne's City

FIELD'S
CHAMOMILE POWDERS.
For Infants and Children Teething.
For the Various Disorders incident to this period these Powders will prove Invaluable.

They remove pain and soothe the child; check stomach disorders; correct the motions; and are invaluable in delayed dentition.

PREPARED ONLY BY

MRS. M. J. FIELD,
FIELD'S CHAMOMILE POWDER DEPOT,
210 ELIZABETH STREET, BRISBANE, Q.

TO PREVENT DISAPPOINTMENT ask for FIELD'S CHAMOMILE POWDERS. None Genuine unless the Label bears the Signature of the late Proprietor.

Health Officer boasted of 'an encouraging fall in the number of deaths due to disease: 953 for the year ended 1900, 42 fewer than in 1899' (out of a population of 811 100).[39]

Tuberculosis was the main killer, followed by typhoid, diphtheria, scarlet fever, measles, influenza and diarrhoea, and children were the chief sufferers, 'especially in summer, when the main article of their food, milk, easily deteriorates under the influence of high temperature. The drop [in deaths] is due to better milk handling and improvements in supply, and also owing to the use of pasteurising methods by some of the large suppliers.'[40]

Despite such progress, however, it was still a good idea to stay out of hospital if you possibly could, and a wide range of patent medicines was available to assist you in that aim. Beecham's Pills were a favourite for 'biliousness, nervous disorders, indigestion in all its forms, wind and pain in the stomach, sick headache and giddiness'. Hean's Tonic Nerve Nuts would cure 'headache, backache, insomnia, anaemia, neuralgia, brain fag,* breakdown, lassitude, dizziness, palpitation and hysteria'. Influenza was nothing to worry about with Heenzo Tonic on hand and French's Remedy made light work of epilepsy. 'Drunkenness, dipsomania, the Liquor Habit, etc.' were cured 'speedily, safely, permanently and (if desired) secretly by Eucracy. All particulars, testimonials etc., posted free (in sealed envelope)'.[41]

The active ingredients of most of these wondrous cures were those that doctors had been recommending to their patients for years: alcohol, opium and cocaine. As one American authority put it, 'Ordinary whisky, as dispensed in saloons, is scarcely stronger in alcoholic content than are most of these so-called remedies, and especially some of them that are recommended for the treatment of inebriates ...'[42] Cocaine and opium were common even in the soothing syrups mothers administered to their infants, a fact that was not revealed on the labels.

MRS FIELD'S CHAMOMILE POWDERS EASED CHILDREN'S PAIN, CHECKED STOMACH DISORDERS AND CORRECTED THE MOTIONS. NO INGREDIENTS ARE LISTED ON THE LABEL, SINCE NO LEGISLATION REQUIRED THEM TO BE, BUT IT IS PROBABLY SAFE TO ASSUME THAT MORE THAN JUST CHAMOMILE WAS INVOLVED.

* Brain fag, an abbreviation of 'brain fatigue', is an old term for mental exhaustion, still used today in parts of Africa.

A WINTER'S MORNING — by "STEVE"

NO 'CLOSED SEASON' FOR BODY ODOUR. THE STRIP CARTOON ADVERTISEMENT WAS ALMOST ALWAYS DIRECTED AT WOMEN, FOR IT WAS ASSUMED THAT ALL WOMEN RESPONDED TO A GOOD STORY.

Advertisements for patent medicines reflected the particular social concerns of the times, just as they do today. For instance, traumatised soldiers returning from the trenches in 1918 prompted a spate of remedies for nervous disorders. Clement's Tonic was promoted as 'the nurses' and soldiers' medicine', with a suitably vague testimonial from an anonymous nurse: 'I have used it with very beneficial results. Several of our nurses in France have also proved its worth. I can highly recommend it to anyone suffering from brain fag'.[43] Toward the end of the year, as the effects of the post-war flu epidemic began to be felt, influenza cures were all the rage. Returning soldiers also brought an epidemic of venereal diseases (which the army coyly referred to as 'self-inflicted wounds') although nobody advertised cures for them, at least not in the popular press.

Buyers needed to be assured that these potions were British or Australian made, which appealed to patriotism as well as supposedly ensuring quality. 'You can't treat your system in the Prussian way', warned the makers of Nujol Constipation Cure. 'If the Prussian is annoyed by something he destroys it. You may not like constipation, but you can't get rid of it by injuring your system. Don't be a Prussian to your digestion!'[44]

The sad fact was that many important medicines were German or made under German licence, and substitutes had to be found during wartime. When

Bayer Aspirin became unavailable in 1915, a couple of Melbourne chemists beat the rest of the allied world in discovering the German firm's secret recipe, and started marketing Aspro tablets. Just twenty years later, hardly a medicine cabinet in the country was without its distinctive pink Aspro box. On the front was a list of twenty complaints it would 'speedily relieve', including asthma, malaria, dengue fever, sciatica and, of course, headache.

General practitioners were relatively few and, in the absence of any government assistance, the poor could not afford them anyway. People didn't just pop off to the doctor whenever they felt a sniffle coming on, as they do today. So a home medicine kit was vital. Aside from old sheets and handkerchiefs that could be torn up for bandaging, it typically contained flax seed and hop leaves for making poultices, hot water bottles and ice bags, a thermometer, Vaseline, witch-hazel (for sprains and bruises), cold cream, bicarbonate of soda (for burns), olive oil, spirits of camphor, oil of cloves, ammonia water, turpentine, carbolic acid (an antiseptic), bichloride of mercury tablets, collodion (for dressing cuts), mustard, alcohol, hydrogen peroxide, Listerine and iodine. Alarmingly, a surgical knife and a needle and thread for sewing wounds were also recommended.[45]

Through the 1920s and 1930s, the Rawlings man went door-to-door with his suitcase full of powders, lotions and creams, and your well-thumbed *Pear's Medical Dictionary*, a companion to the popular *Pear's Cyclopaedia*, took care of the diagnosis. That book and the local chemist were far more likely to be consulted than a GP, particularly during the depression, when public health standards fell and the gap widened between those who could afford medical care and those who couldn't. Herbal remedies and those concocted at home from generic ingredients held their own against patent medicines, which, although now sold under stricter controls, were still widely distrusted.

World War II, like World War I, brought major medical breakthroughs that would have a profound effect on the way people dealt with their health problems. Sulpha drugs had been used before the war to treat bacterial infections, dramatically lowering the risk of surgery. For example, they had halved the death rate during childbirth. However, by the time the troops came home in 1945, a way had been found to mass produce penicillin, a miracle cure for almost everything. It took the terror out of rheumatic fever, syphilis, pneumonia and tuberculosis. As the medical historian Robert Bud notes, 'patients who had once turned to many kinds of alternative medicine, or refused treatment, now entrusted themselves to antibiotics. The clouds of moral disapproval of infection were dispelled'.[46]

Since antibiotics were available only on prescription, people got used to visiting doctors more often, even for minor complaints that they would previously have ignored or treated themselves at home. Prevention was no longer a moral responsibility now that there was a magic pill to fix every problem. Consequently, the number of general practitioners increased significantly.

Increasingly, too, Australians took to consulting the family doctor for non-physical complaints such as stress, fatigue and depression, once regarded as unavoidable responses to external conditions. Before psychiatric drugs came along, there was little you could do about depression or anxiety. Psychiatric therapy was out of the question for all but a tiny minority, and Heans Tonic Nerve Nuts clearly weren't going to do the trick. Alcohol was the most common way out, although that was more acceptable for men than for women. Almost everyone knew of some poor woman who had 'suffered a breakdown', when the stresses of motherhood and housework had proven too great to bear. From such shame, she was unlikely ever to recover her social standing, because to have had a breakdown marked her as a bad mother. Men, traumatised by war or economic failure, were expected to take it on the chin. Suffering was internalised, or taken out on the kids. One woman, quoted by historian Janet McCalman, remembers her father as:

> a man who used to hang on to his feelings until he could stand it no longer and then it would erupt in the most shocking temper tantrums. We grew up with those temper tantrums every now and again erupting and we never knew what they were about. They *terrified* us.[47]

The first of the psychiatric wonder drugs, marketed in America from the late 1950s, became available in this country a decade or so later. They were revolutionary in that they treated depression and anxiety as biological problems resulting from chemical imbalances in the brain and, in that sense at least, they appeared to overturn Freudian psychology. It wasn't long before Valium—'mother's little helper'—was Australia's most-prescribed drug and, as the dismissive nickname suggests, most of those prescriptions were being made out to middle-class women. Valium, and later psychiatric drugs such as Prozac, were supposed to help stressed-out mums to get back to normal, although what 'normal' actually meant was based on all kinds of assumptions about motherhood and the social expectations women were supposed to be fulfilling. As the American author Jonathan Metzl has shown, psychiatric drugs, even today, are usually prescribed for women to help them control their emotions in order to save their families, while men are more likely to take them to improve their performance at work.[48]

Psychiatric drugs have extended our ideas about what constitutes a medical condition. What would previously have been thought of as high-spirits or naughtiness in children, for example, is now given a name—hyperactivity—and treated with mood-altering substances. We are less likely to deal with the causes so long as the quick-fix is readily available. Yet, while there are abuses, such drugs allow doctors to treat people for conditions that were untreatable in the past, and to be able to properly assess the results.

Computers and the products of the international pharmaceuticals industry have altered our relationships with GPs to the point where we no longer need to establish a personal bond with a local family doctor who is fully conversant with our medical histories. We go to the doctor—any doctor will do—with preconceived expectations that we expect him or her to fulfil. We outline our symptoms, the doctor writes a prescription for something that has been expensively promoted by a drug company, and we treat ourselves at home without fuss.

No more needles and thread in the bathroom cabinet for the sewing of wounds. No more poultices, ammonia water or collodion. The 24-hour clinic is just five minutes drive away and health insurance or government subsidies will help with the cost. Accidents or illnesses no longer need to be dreaded. Hence the patent medicines we keep at home will more than likely be limited to aspirin, a packet of adhesive bandages, a tube of antiseptic cream and a box of cough-drops. All the rest will be prescription medicines with official-looking typed paper labels for the sole use of a particular individual.

The Worst
Day of
the Week

The Battle against Drudgery

Traditionally, Monday was washing day. For women, it was the worst day of the week. Washing was drudgery, pure and simple— tedious, back-breaking, hand- and soul-destroying slog. Cooking was hard work too, but at least it had a certain creative element and might even draw the occasional compliment. Laundry offered no such consolations.

Initially, women gathered by a stream, as they had done for centuries, to rub shirts and sheets and shifts on stones or wooden washboards. If the water didn't come to you, then you had to go to the water. In their book *Australians at Home*, Terence Lane and Jessie Serle quote Elizabeth King, the first white child born in Terang in northern Victoria, who remembered helping to:

> carry the family's clothes to the lake, where a busy crowd of women
> and children converged each week with scrub-boards and home-made
> soap. There was gossip and chatter as clothes were soaped and rinsed
> in the water, children played, and the natives came out of their mia-
> mias along the banks to join the entertainment.[1]

This might explain why a particular day of the week was initially agreed upon, but why Monday and why did the habit stick? Perhaps in order that the family's Sunday-best could be washed, dried, ironed and folded in time for the following week's service; or so that dad or eldest son could chop wood for the copper over the weekend and have it stacked in readiness; or because inner-city air was a little cleaner on Monday after factories had been closed for the Sabbath; or was it just that women were determined to get it over and done with as early as possible? Whatever the reason, it helped that, after an exhausting day of washing, the remains of the Sunday roast were on hand as a labour-saving evening meal.

Apparently this was a peculiarly Australian custom. Women in Britain and Europe didn't necessarily wash on Mondays. Even here there was no hard and fast rule about it. And, over the years, as housework became less demanding and hot water more readily available, smaller washes could be done more frequently. Today, about a third of all households machine-wash more than five times a week.[2]

Of all the rooms in the house, the wash-house remained in a primitive state the longest, longer even than the bathroom. For most of the nineteenth century (and well into the twentieth in some areas), it was not a room at all, just a patch of bare earth near the back door, with perhaps a few sheets of corrugated iron over it to keep off the rain. Although pictures of nineteenth-century clothes-washing are rare, since this was hardly a worthy subject for the photographer, the one above, taken in 1935 in the inner-Melbourne suburb of Collingwood, indicates what it would have been like: no more than a galvanised-iron tub on a plank of wood amid piles of backyard refuse, with

FOR MANY WOMEN IN THE 1930S, ESPECIALLY THOSE IN THE INNER SUBURBS, WASH DAY WAS MUCH THE SAME AS IT HAD BEEN IN THE NINETEENTH CENTURY.

a grim-faced woman, sleeves rolled up to her elbows, bent to her task. She has no protection from the weather and the kids, who she must keep an eye on, are getting underfoot. As each garment is cleaned and rinsed, she hangs it directly on the line overhead.

She is, of course, working-class, but her chore would not have been markedly different from that of middle-class women of earlier generations. She does, in fact, enjoy two advantages over them. For one thing, she has a tap over a gully trap nearby where she can fill and empty her tub (although it's not clear how she heats the water). For another, clothing in the 1930s was a lot simpler and easier to manage than it had been earlier. 'Our enveloping nighties had dozens of pleats, cascades of lace and frills at neck and wrists', recalls Eugénie McNeil of her 1890s childhood. 'Petticoats were threaded with ribbon that had to be taken out before washing and threaded back after.'[3] In the days of brittle bone buttons, they too had to be removed before garments were put through the wringer, then laboriously resewn after the ironing had been completed.

Nevertheless, in 1894, Mrs Lance Rawson assured the young housewife without a servant that washing was not as bad as it seemed so long as it was approached methodically. To tackle a large wash, comprising around twelve dozen white articles (!), it is first necessary, she says, to separate them: handkerchiefs, collars, frilled pillow cases, table linen, muslin wrappers and aprons in one pile; shirts, sheets and plain pillow cases in another; and towels, singlets and other robust items in a third. Ideally, each lot should be assigned its own tub. That done, it is time to light the fire under the boiler, adding to the water half-a-bar of shredded soap and two tablespoons of soda. Once warm, the water can be ladled into the tubs and the clothes left to soak overnight.

Having soaked your clothes you start your washing as early as you can next morning. If you are quick you will get a boilerful on before breakfast so they can be boiling while you are at the meal and will be ready to come out when you have washed up and put your kitchen tidy.

TOO GOOD TO BE TRUE? FOR
JUST 15 SHILLINGS IN 1920,
A SWIFT VACUUM CLOTHES
WASHER WAS THE BEST WASH-
DAY FRIEND YOU WOULD
EVER HAVE, SO LONG AS YOU
DIDN'T EXPECT MIRACLES.

That's the easy part: now for the scrubbing. Each article must be lifted from the water, laid on a corrugated washboard and vigorously rubbed with soap, taking care, of course, not to scrape the skin off your knuckles. 'If it is a long article rub away, up and down, gradually rolling up or turning over the part you have done till you have come to the end of it and have turned it completely over, then rub that side in the same way … ' As each article is washed, it must be wrung out, then returned to the boiler, which has meanwhile been filled with fresh water, soap, soda and some kerosene for dissolving grease.

When your clothes have boiled the half hour and been properly poked under with the 'pot stick' so that everything has been boiled, they are ready to come out. Place a tub close to the boiler, I am persuming [sic] that you have no proper copper but merely the large oval boiler placed on a few bricks out in the back yard. Put a couple of clean boards across the tub, a basket on it or anything so that you can drain the clothes. Leave them to drain while you are preparing the blue water … Now pour back into the boiler the water that has drained from the clothes, let them down into the tub, cover with clear cold water and rinse well up and down to get all the soapy water out, then wring out each piece, shake it, turn it, and plunge into the blue water, rinse about in it and wring out again, shake, and throw into your basket to be hung out on the line to dry.[4]

And when you've done that to each and every one of your twelve-dozen white things (not to mention the coloureds), you'll be ready for a nice cuppa before getting on with the rest of the day's chores. What could be simpler?

WOMAN, O WOMAN!

WHY TOIL LIKE THIS?
WHY RUIN YOUR HANDS?
WHY RUIN YOUR HEALTH?
ONLY BECAUSE OF PREJUDICE

You fancy the only way to get clothes clean is by needless toil. We will send you a

SWIFT VACUUM CLOTHES WASHER

in return for **15/-**, and guarantee it to be the surest wash-day friend you ever had, if you don't expect miracles.

WRITE NOW!

If you haven't the money handy pay us when you can. We will trust you.

J. K. POWELL & CO.,
Freedman's Chambers, Hay Street, Perth.

* Blue—potassium ferric ferrocyanide—was purchased in blocks. It had to be cut into pieces and wrapped in little muslin bags tied with string. Dissolved in the rinse water, it prevented white cottons from yellowing. Later, no laundry would be without a box of Reckitt's Blue, which was purchased ready-wrapped. Reckitt's blue bags were also commonly used to treat bee stings.

Well, some sort of mechanical device to share the workload perhaps. A plethora of them came and went over the years: Mrs Lang's Patent Economical Domestic Washing Table, for instance, was little more than a glorified washboard that allowed you to sit down on the job. The fashionably dressed young lady in the advertisement looked as though she was playing a waltz on the harpsichord. The Wolter and Echberg Washing Machine, patented in Victoria in 1877, consisted of a tin tub on a spindle that was agitated back and forth by means of a lever. In addition, there were numerous British and American machines, most of which employed some sort of mechanical paddles.

But turning their handles and tugging on their levers was really no less arduous than scrubbing on the washboard, and nothing could be devised to deal with the whole complicated process from beginning to end. The heavy lifting of wet clothes could not be avoided, nor the lighting of fires, and the filling and emptying still had to be tediously carried out with bucket and ladle.

In the case of one-fire kitchen stoves and sewing machines, it had been a matter of discovering the basic working principle, to which all subsequent models could more or less adhere. These devices could then be manufactured in commercial quantities and the relative merits of differing models assessed by potential customers. Since washing involved a series of widely differing tasks, nobody had come up with an overriding working principle on which a mechanical device could be based.

Historian Kimberley Webber posits an additional reason for the painfully slow development of laundry technologies, which is that the low status of laundry work provided little incentive. 'Money spent on the laundry meant taking resources away from the domestic circle, rather than reinforcing it', she says.[5] Most women, resigned to the fact that washing was always going to be a hateful chore anyway, preferred to spend their money on things that would benefit the entire household. Nevertheless, even if you had no other domestic help, you set aside a shilling or so, if you possibly could, for a woman to come in once a week to make washing day a little less arduous. (Washer-women were at the very bottom of the social scale, even less well-paid than other domestics.)

The mangle was the one mechanical device that did survive, both because it was genuinely labour- and time-saving and because it could be incorporated seamlessly into the washing process without disrupting its natural working rhythms. In 1909, *Home and Health* very sensibly insisted on 'a first-class wringer'. 'Do not wring the clothes out by hand. If you do, you will pay a high price for your folly later on, out of your own strength and life.'[6] The wringer-type mangle, which squeezes water from clothes by passing them through a pair of

IN 1912, VIDA LAHEY
PROPPED HER CANVAS
ON THE MANGLE IN THE
FAMILY'S WASH HOUSE
IN INDOOROOPILLY,
QUEENSLAND, TO RECORD
A REGULAR MONDAY
MORNING CHORE.

VIDA LAHEY
MONDAY MORNING 1912
OIL ON CANVAS
153 X 122.7 CM
QUEENSLAND ART GALLERY

rollers, was an eighteenth-century invention. After the iron, it remained the most commonly used piece of domestic laundry equipment until the late 1940s.

By the time Vida Lahey painted her sister and another woman doing the washing in their Brisbane home in 1912, the terrors of washday had lessened considerably. First, those fussy, frilly fashions of the past, which had demanded so much unnecessary care and attention, had been supplanted by more practical clothing. Second, families were a lot smaller, so piles of twelve dozen white articles became a thing of the past. And, finally, the environment of the wash-house had improved.

The passing of the years has given this painting a romantic air but Lahey was depicting a thoroughly modern scene. These women work in relative comfort indoors. In fact, their wash-house appears to be a good deal more substantial than most at the time. One of them uses a laundry pole to lift a steaming garment from the built-in copper (or boiler) which would have had an enclosed firebox beneath. The other stands at the trough attending to a stain with a bar of yellow Velvet Soap. Beside her, the coloureds have been separated out for a cold soak. There are three troughs—quite a luxury, since two were the norm—each with its own cold-water tap. To this day, many older houses in Tasmania retain their solid Huon-pine wash troughs, but tin and cast-concrete were the more common materials. The painting shows no sign of a mangle. The Laheys had a freestanding one on cast-iron legs, which the artist was using as an easel, but more usual, and more convenient, were those that clamped onto the side of the trough.

Yet, despite such minor improvements, there remained something almost wilfully self-punishing about the state of most domestic wash-houses. There was no logical justification for their unlined walls, bare timber floors and cobwebby corners, nor for the aggressive utilitarianism of their appliances. George Simpson and Son, who advertised their laundry copper, boiler stand and flue stack in *Australian Home Builder* in the early 1920s, were apparently quite unembarrassed about its appearance, confident that plug-ugliness would have no negative effect on sales[7]—this at a time when kitchen stoves were being enamelled and decorated and baths and basins came in a range of appealing colours. 'In many cases', complained *Home Beautiful* in 1928, 'the operations of washing are rendered more

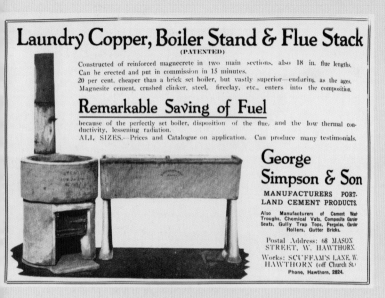

Laundry Copper, Boiler Stand & Flue Stack
(PATENTED)

Constructed of reinforced magnecrete in two main sections, also 18 in. flue lengths.
Can be erected and put in commission in 15 minutes.
20 per cent. cheaper than a brick set boiler, but vastly superior—enduring, as the ages.
Magnesite cement, crushed clinker, steel, fireclay, etc., enters into the composition.

Remarkable Saving of Fuel

because of the perfectly set boiler, disposition of the flue, and the low thermal conductivity, lessening radiation.
ALL SIZES.—Prices and Catalogue on application. Can produce many testimonials.

George Simpson & Son

MANUFACTURERS PORTLAND CEMENT PRODUCTS.

Also Manufacturers of Cement Wash Troughs, Chemical Vats, Composite Garden Seats, Gully Trap Tops, Pergolas, Garden Rollers, Gutter Bricks.

Postal Address: 68 MASON STREET, W. HAWTHORN.
Works: SCUFFAM'S LANE, W. HAWTHORN (off Church St.)
Phone, Hawthorn, 2824.

GEORGE SIMPSON AND SON, WHO ADVERTISED THEIR WASH-HOUSE EQUIPMENT IN THE MID 1920S, WERE APPARENTLY QUITE UNEMBARRASSED ABOUT ITS COMPLETE LACK OF CHARM, CONFIDENT THAT PLUG-UGLINESS WOULD HAVE NO NEGATIVE EFFECT ON SALES.

arduous by the fact that the washing appliances do not appear to have been deemed worthy of attention by the designer of the house'.[8]

However, gas and electricity were prompting a change of attitude, not only to the labour of washing but to the environment in which it was done, although the change would be painfully slow to take effect. The Western Electric Washer, it was boldly claimed in 1924,

> does away with the necessity for rubbing and boiling clothes. These, placed in the cylinder with plenty of hot, soapy water, are cleansed thoroughly in about fifteen minutes after the power has been switched on. An attached wringer, which is run by the same motor that operates the cylinder, swings and locks into any of five operating positions.[9]

It sounds good. So why were large numbers of women still lighting fires under their old coppers until well into the 1950s? It was partly because the wash-

THE AMERICAN-MADE 'EASY' WASHING MACHINE WAS SUPPOSED TO KEEP YOUR WIFE 'FRESH, YOUTHFUL AND HAPPY', BUT IT LOOKED ANYTHING BUT EASY TO OPERATE.

IN 1947, *HOME BEAUTIFUL* TEASED ITS READERS WITH 'THE VERY LATEST AMERICAN LAUNDRY', KNOWING THAT SUCH FANTASIES WERE ALMOST TOTALLY BEYOND THE REALMS OF POSSIBILITY HERE.

A WASH HOUSE IN THE 1930S, WITH CONCRETE TROUGHS, COPPER AND BENCH. THERE HAS BEEN NO ATTEMPT TO MAKE IT AN ATTRACTIVE PLACE TO WORK.

house remained the household's lowest priority when it came to spending. At between £35 and £50, gas and electric washing machines were strictly for the rich, although gas coppers cost a good deal less. As well, many houses in the 1920s, even those with electric lighting, had no electric power supply or hot water service, and laying gas pipes to the wash-house in the backyard would have entailed considerable extra expense. Ultimately, however, the claims made for washing machines just sounded too good to be true. No housewife believed you could get clothes really clean without boiling and rubbing. Paradoxically, it was precisely because washing was so laborious and time-consuming that women refused to accept that there might be an easier way of getting it done. New technologies constantly came up against ingrained conservatism and distrust, not all of which was unwarranted.

Realising that it was the man of the house who had to be convinced to part with his hard-earned cash, advertisers of the Easy Electric Washer appealed directly to his vanity: 'To husbands ... who want their wives to stay young—When you say "This is my wife", you want to introduce a woman who looks fresh, youthful and happy—not old or worn or tired.'[10] Nice try, but the girl in the ad looked so fresh, youthful and happy that many husbands would have failed to make the connection. Besides, the Easy, with its complicated array of tanks, belts and bulky exposed motor, looked anything but easy.

Yet, although they remained a distant dream for the majority, electric washing machines dramatically improved the status of the wash-house, if only by proxy. It would have been unthinkable, after all, to consign a state-of-the-art appliance costing three months' wages to a shed out the back. There was even talk of bringing washing facilities into the kitchen or bathroom to make best use of the hot-water heater and drainage pipes, although to most people that sounded unhealthy. For obvious reasons, builders and developers rather liked the idea, but home-help magazines usually advised against it.[11] Nevertheless, the overall effect of the new machines would be, finally, to lend a touch of status to what had been the most neglected part of the house.

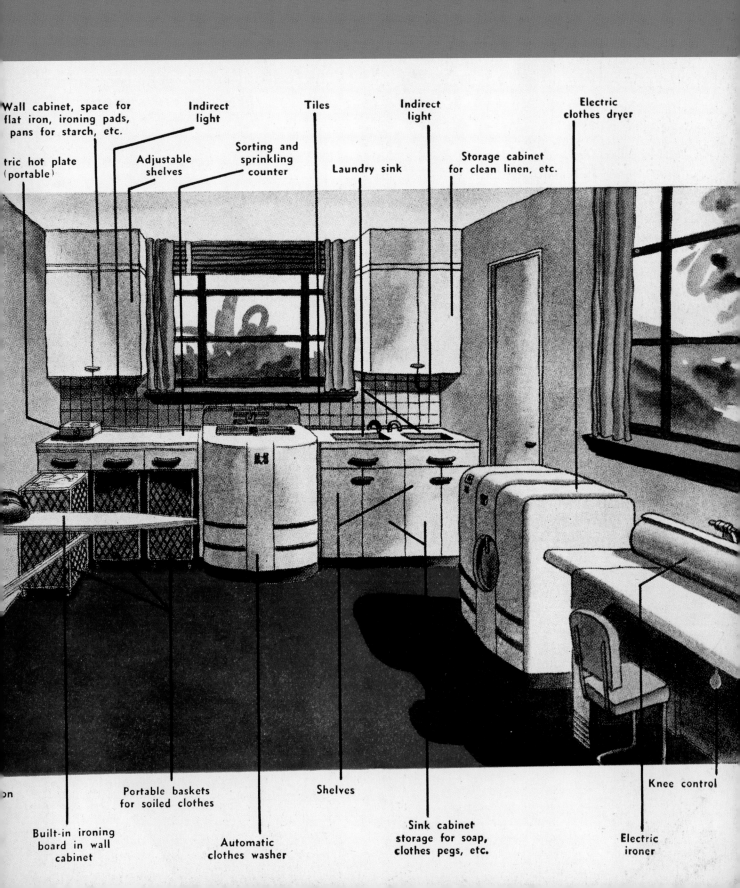

Wall cabinet, space for flat iron, ironing pads, pans for starch, etc.

Indirect light

Tiles

Indirect light

Electric clothes dryer

tric hot plate (portable)

Adjustable shelves

Sorting and sprinkling counter

Laundry sink

Storage cabinet for clean linen, etc.

on

Built-in ironing board in wall cabinet

Portable baskets for soiled clothes

Automatic clothes washer

Shelves

Sink cabinet storage for soap, clothes pegs, etc.

Knee control

Electric ironer

THE WILKINS SERVIS, WITH ITS INTEGRATED STYLING AND ELECTRIC WRINGER, WAS A PRACTICAL, REASONABLY PRICED AUSTRALIAN MACHINE IN 1952, YET STILL BEYOND THE REACH OF MANY MIDDLE-CLASS FAMILIES.

If a more attractive workspace was what you wanted, however, you had to roll up your sleeves and do it yourself. 'When showing visitors round, do you say in front of the shut door, "Oh that's the wash-house," or do your throw open the door and exclaim, "And here's my laundry!"' asked *Home Beautiful* a little too enthusiastically in 1930. 'A tin or two of paint, and a short length of cheap curtain material, a medium amount of energy, and you can have a laundry that you are not only proud of, but glad to work in.'[12] Note the terminology: the transformation of the 'wash-house' into the 'laundry' had begun. A gas or electric copper meant no more ash and smoke or risk of fire, so your bright new laundry could be incorporated under the main roof of the house, although you still had to haul baskets of wet clothes to the line, so a door directly onto the yard was essential.

Yet however attractive the surroundings, washing played havoc with a woman's appearance. *Women's Weekly*'s feature, 'How to Keep Lovely in Spite of Washday', was no doubt read with interest, although any sensible woman would already have known to wear a hair net and apply a dab of moisturiser.[13] The article's real purpose, it appears, was to recommend Persil as being safe for hands (the Persil advertisement on a nearby page being entirely coincidental).

Except for those who could afford to send it out, washing remained the great bugbear of the flat-dweller. Only very expensive units had their own laundries. An electric copper and a couple of concrete troughs in the basement were

IT WAS THE DESIGNERS OF DISPLAY HOMES, DRIVEN BY A NEED FOR DOMESTIC EFFICIENCY AND COST-CUTTING, WHO FINALLY BROUGHT THE LAUNDRY IN FROM THE COLD.

THERE WERE TWO MAIN
ADVANTAGES OF WASHING
POWDER, ACCORDING TO
THE MANUFACTURERS:
THEY MADE WASHING
EASIER BY ELIMINATING
HARD SCRUBBING ON
THE WASHBOARD, WHICH
BENEFITTED THE HOUSEWIFE,
AND THEY KEPT SHIRTS
WHITER FOR LONGER, WHICH
PLEASED HER HUSBAND. THIS
AD IS FROM 1931.

the best most residents could expect, with washdays having to be allocated by roster, a source of many in-house disputes.

These were the people who might have benefited from the Bendix fully automatic washing machine, had it not been for an unfortunate accident of timing. The Bendix took care of the washing, rinsing and spin-drying, then turned itself off, which was nothing short of miraculous. But at £100 who could afford it (the average male wage at the time being £4 7s 6d a week[14])? Cleverly, it was marketed not to potential consumers but to the designers and builders of flats. 'The unit is ideal for fitting in the modern kitchen', the ad in a building industry journal pointed out, 'while the cost is more than offset by elimination of the cost of a laundry—now rendered unnecessary'.[15] And, of course, by the higher rents that could be charged. Sadly, the Bendix was released in 1939, just as war was declared, when flat-building came to a halt.

In fact almost everything came to a halt on the domestic front. But hope was kept alive by exciting predictions of what lay just around the corner. The Hotpoint company looked forward to 'the laundry of the future', with electric washer and wringer, tumble dryer and something optimistically referred to as an 'ironing centre', all of which would, of course, be available 'when Victory comes'. Already the Americans were marketing an iron that released steam through tiny holes in its base, to save the time and bother of damping down, and it, too, was promised in due course. The steam-iron was, incidentally, the first major advance in ironing since the mid 1920s, when someone had had the bright idea of regulating the iron's temperature with a thermostat. 'The Post-War laundry will be a very different place from the dull and cheerless room in which we have spent our washing days', forecast *Home Beautiful* in 1944. 'Optimists believe that every home will contain a mechanical washer. We shall press the button, or pull the lever, and the Washing Machine will do the rest—we hope!'

Such predictions indeed sounded hopeful, but these were grim times and there was no harm in dreaming. Eventually they would come true, beyond even the wildest dreams of the pre-war generation. Even so, a full decade later

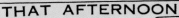

(Thousands write us letters like this)

AND *"Washing day never bothers me,"*
says Mrs. Sarah Long,
of Clifton Hill.

"Once I used to dread Monday but washing day never bothers me now! Rinso makes such great suds that all the dirt floats right off by itself. Take even the badly soiled parts — why, just a gentle rub and they're snow-white.

"Rinso is great for other cleaning too. Grease soaks right off dishes. Give them a hot rinse, let them dry by themselves, and just see how they shine!"

MRS. SARAH LONG,
466 Wellington St., Clifton Hill, Vic.

Whitest clothes you ever saw!

Once you see a gleaming white Rinso wash — you'll never use any other laundry soap. And it's so economical! Cupful for cupful, it goes twice as far as ordinary soaps — because it's granulated, compact. Get a packet of Rinso to-day.

LEVER BROTHERS LIMITED

Rinso
in tub or washer
for safety - for whiter clothes

IN THE LEAD-UP TO
FEDERATION, NATIONAL
PRIDE COULD BE HARNESSED
TO SELL ALMOST ANYTHING.
THE UNION JACK, THE
SOUTHERN CROSS AND
A MAP OF AUSTRALIA
ANNOUNCED SILVER STAR
STARCH AS A TRUE PRODUCT
OF THE NATION.

the magazine was still complaining that this essential little room was being entirely neglected by architects and builders. Washing just couldn't shake off its shabby reputation.

In the end, it was the designers of project homes, driven by a need for domestic efficiency and cost-cutting, who precipitated the change. And their message was not lost on the thousands of people who trooped through their latest models every weekend. How smart, modern and practical the bright little laundry space in AV Jennings' Ashburn must have looked to the housewife accustomed to a lean-to in the backyard. Conveniently sandwiched between kitchen and bathroom, directly off the main hallway, it came complete with black and white linoleum tiles, a stainless steel trough in a white enamelled cabinet, hot and cold taps and those evocative little pipes sticking out of the wall above the skirting board, just begging to be hooked up to a machine.[18] At last, the laundry had come in from the cold.

In 1960, *Home Beautiful* published a survey of 83 imported and locally made washers, priced from a modest 65 guineas for a Hoover with hand-operated wringer up to £221 for a fully automatic Westinghouse with spin-dry.[19] Since most were completely plumbed-in, eliminating the risk of water spills, you could put them just about anywhere, provided the building regulations were obeyed. In Western Australia, a separate laundry room was still required for all new houses, while Victoria forbade washing machines in kitchens. Other states were more relaxed, vaguely stipulating some 'provision for laundry facilities' without saying where, although local councils could be the sticking point. Sydney's Lane Cove Council angrily rejected what it saw as a preposterous proposal for a house with its laundry next to the front door, relenting only after much spirited confrontation from the architect.[20] As usual, the authorities had trouble keeping up with progress.

And no wonder. For within little more than a decade, a revolution had taken place. This most hated and demanding of all domestic chores, an embarrassment to architects, builders and social planners and long regarded by housewives as just an awful, inescapable fact of life, had at last been conquered by affordable machinery. It was a turning point in the history of domestic life because, coming at a time of unprecedented economic prosperity, it created a completely new mindset. In the quest to relieve women of their slavery, the final and most difficult hurdle had been overcome and, in that sense, eliminating the tyranny of washday was a major symbolic step towards the liberation of women. It also signalled the definitive victory of mass consumerism over the old ideals of self-reliance. Henceforth it would generally be taken for granted that the solution to any domestic labour problem lay in the purchase of some new item of mass-produced equipment.

Detergent Wars

Mrs Sarah Long of Clifton Hill, Victoria, wrote in especially to say that, 'Once I used to dread Monday but washing day never bothers me now! Rinso makes such great suds that all the dirt floats right off by itself. Take even the badly soiled parts—why, just a gentle rub and they're snow white.'[21] The good folk at Lever Brothers Ltd received thousands of appreciative letters like this, or so they claimed. Whiter whites: that's what all these women were so grateful for, because that's what Lever Brothers had convinced them they needed. Already by the mid 1920s, when Mrs Long supposedly put pen to paper, press advertisements for washing detergents were the brightest, best designed and most inventive of all. Yet they were a mere foretaste of what was to come.

Powdered detergents, really nothing more than dried soap-flakes, provided little benefit in the days of the washboard. Scrubbing demanded a solid cake of soap. In the 1890s, Mrs Lance Rawson expressed her contempt for:

> washing powders and fluids of which there are so many on the market. I think I have tried all or most of them and I do not believe any one of them has saved me half an hour's labour or made my clothes any whiter than I could get them with the ordinary soap and soda.[22]

Velvet Soap, first marketed in 1906, quickly became a wash-house staple. It was sold in long, segmented bars, rather like blocks of chocolate, from which individual cakes could be snapped off as required.* And no great difficulty was involved in shredding it into the copper with a cheese grater for the pre-scrub boiling. Many women, however, inherently suspicious of all brand-name products, or needing to count the pennies, considered even this a luxury, preferring to make their own soap. In an era when recycling was an ingrained habit rather than a conscious statement of good intentions, this was an effective way of using up animal fats from the kitchen. They were boiled in a big pot on the stove with borax, washing soda, slaked lime or caustic soda until the mixture turned glutinous, whereupon it was poured into a shallow box, allowed to dry, and cut into blocks. Only after a month or two in a cool, dry place would they be mature enough for use. In addition, all manner of special concoctions were laboriously prepared from herbs, vinegar, kerosene, ammonia and other more lethal substances to deal with specific stains.

Whether purchased or home-made, soaps demanded a lot of heavy rubbing, which was not kind to fabrics. They refused to lather in hard water, and their residues coagulated into slimy, stinking deposits around household grease-traps and drainpipes. The search was on for better alternatives. Persil, a German product introduced in 1907, was promoted as the world's first 'self-acting' washing powder, because it included chemical bleaching agents, a boon in a country where the sun could not always be relied on.[23] But, like so many other twentieth-century innovations, true detergents—synthetic surfactants whose molecular structure draws grease out of clothing and suspends it in water to be rinsed away—resulted from wartime research. They were developed by German scientists as a way of using waste petroleum products after World War I, when natural oils were in short supply.

Nevertheless, the cost of production remained high until after World War II, when three giant US corporations—Unilever, Procter and Gamble and Colgate-Palmolive—exploited Germany's economic weakness to secure

* School teachers often required their pupils to bring a cake of Velvet to their art classes for soap-carving.

patents on virtually all new detergent-making techniques and thus corner the world market. It was, writes the historian Victoria de Grazia,

> pure marketing genius: they had easy access to the basic raw material, petroleum, and plenty of capital to spend on research and design; they already had a century of experience promoting soaps, a fine art calling for carefully designed packaging, aggressive distribution, and massive advertising. Moreover, the need for the substance, if new standards of equipment and hygiene prevailed, was practically limitless.[24]

New standards of equipment would not be long in coming, as we have seen. New standards of hygiene would have to be imposed.

Thus began one of the biggest and most expensive global advertising blitzes in history. In the press, advertisements continued the time-honoured

WASHING POWDERS WERE BIG BUSINESS IN THE 1950S AND 1960S. THE PITCH WAS ALWAYS THE SAME: WHITER WHITES AND SOFTER HANDS.

conventions of the strip-cartoon narrative, since it was assumed that all women responded to a good story. Typically, a naive young woman, beset by a problem that darkens her relationship with her husband, is enlightened by a more experienced female friend about the washing product in question. 'You're right!', exclaims the wide-eyed beauty in one ad, 'The New Improved Rinso <u>does</u> get whites absolutely snowy!' to which her knowledgeable friend, gesturing towards the dazzling bedlinen, replies, 'It's the extra rich suds that get that extra-whiteness!'[25] By the 1960s, washing detergents (along with cigarettes) dominated television and radio commercial timeslots. Entire supermarket aisles were devoted to the numerous brands, almost all of which were manufactured by the big three companies. In fact, it was the new medium of television, with its wide reach and prestige, and new shopping trends created by supermarkets that helped to make it all possible.

With more women employed outside the home and a lowering of the social status of housework, detergents that effortlessly made the wash 'whiter than white' provided a convenient measure of one's care and sense of domestic responsibility. Of course your husband would get that promotion, because his shirt was so much whiter than that of his rival. And little Freddy's footy jumper, which looked as good as new, made you the envy of all the other mums. Yet your triumph as wife and mother had involved nothing more arduous than switching to Omo or Rinso or Surf.

At the same time as they were encouraging competitiveness, the advertisements were fostering a strong sense of group identity based on mass-market imperatives. A product that had hardly existed just two decades earlier was now one of life's indispensables. Washing powders came to have a symbolic value that far outweighed their actual benefits. They illustrated, in spectacular fashion, what marketing experts had known since the 1920s: 'that the family unit was central to mass consumption, that women were the busy bees of innovative family oriented shopping, and that family love was a ubiquitous and fundamental bond that salesmanship could exploit for profit'.[26]

As the market for laundry detergents became saturated, the advertising blitz waned. After all, there was a limit to how much whiter white could get. Besides, in these less formal times, dad was probably setting off to work in a blue or striped shirt, while the sheets on the bed and the towels in the bathroom were coloured to match the decor. Whiteness, that symbol of purity and cleanliness, that barometer of housewifely devotion, was losing its shine. 'Although white (properly laundered so that it really does look white) must always have an appeal,' observed *Home Beautiful* in 1967, 'there is now a wealth of color to choose from in the Manchester (household linen) department of any store. Well chosen, it can strike a dominant note in the color schemes of most rooms'.[27]

Marketers turned their attentions to offshoots of the detergent industry such as surface-cleaners, floor and car polishes and disinfectants. The new obsession was about killing germs in the home, which was necessary to maintain 'a healthy lifestyle'. They were invisible, but that only made them more insidious. As cities have become (or at least are perceived as being) dirtier and more threatening, a clean, spick-and-span, germfree house is a refuge from the squalor outside—a pristine oasis—just as a cosy, lavishly decorated house was in Victorian times.

If washing powder advertisements of the 1960s look quaint to us today, it is because they represented the last gasp of an attitude that has now almost passed into history: that the labour of the housewife was a noble expression of her love and devotion to an ideal of domestic life: father, the breadwinner, at the head, mother taking care of the home, and a couple of kids dependent on them for material needs, education and nurture. It was an ideal largely created and fostered by mass-marketing and, for economic reasons, aggressively promoted by politicians. It is one of life's endearing oddities that it should have found its fullest expression in the marketing of soap powders.

Conclusion

Picture this: dad, at his workbench, is re-soleing the kids' school shoes, watching through the shed door for blackbirds digging up his lettuces. Mum is shelling peas and basting the Sunday roast in the kitchen, flames flickering in the cast-iron stove behind her. In the parlour, Olive, still in her Sunday-school frock, is failing to master 'Chopsticks' while her sister curls on the sofa with the latest issue of *Girls' Own*. The lads, Frank and Johnny, are constructing a crystal set in the sleepout, listening intently through bakelite headphones for any hint of static. Soon they will have to wash their hands and change back into their good clothes, because grandma and grandpa will be arriving for lunch.

These happy, contented folk live in a mythical, indeterminate time we call 'the old days'. For some, they present an attractive picture of innocence and simple pleasures (people invariably believe that previous eras were more innocent than their own), while others will condemn them as the embodiment of suburban dreariness and conformity.

There are variations, of course, over the years. Go back a bit further, and grandma and grandpa might be living-in, rather than just visiting. Forward to the present, and they are taking their lunch alone in the 'village' where they live out their days trying not to be a nuisance. A century ago, the children may have numbered six or eight, whereas today there will typically be two (or one-and-a-half, to be precise). Today, too, Frank and Johnny (rechristened Ben and Jason) will be holed up in their separate rooms texting their friends and searching the internet. No leg of lamb will be roasting in the automatic electric oven. In fact, the family will not be eating lunch together at all. Mum is at her Pilates class and dad will grab something to eat on his way to the cricket, quite oblivious of how novel this is, Sunday sport (and any other kind of Sunday entertainment) having been forbidden to earlier generations. Our modern family will, in all probability, be immune to the rituals of institutionalised religion.

The kids now are far more independent, more 'grown up', than their predecessors ever were. The pressure on them to mature (if that's the right word) is so great that they hardly have a chance to be kids. While they are no longer expected to conform to the values of their parents and teachers, they are, however, ensnared in mass culture, which demands conformity of a different and more insidious kind. At the same time, if they are inquisitive and imaginative—if, for example, they want to learn ballet, to travel overseas, to rescue sea-eagles or write a book—they will find encouragement rather than hindrance and ridicule. Life is no longer an uphill battle for those with breadth of vision.

Something fundamental is missing from the idyllic picture of traditional family life outlined above: in a word, *toil*. Until quite recently, living in a suburban house meant, above all, hard, grinding, unrelenting work. The sanctuary that nurtured could also imprison. At the very least, the kids had to set the table, make their beds, wash the dishes, mow the lawns and chop wood. They also had to master the skills they would need in adulthood, such as sewing, cooking, woodwork and home maintenance.

Surrounded as we are with automatic washers, fridges and freezers, stocking up as we do at the supermarket each week, popping out in the car whenever the mood takes us, and skipping off to the beach-house at weekends, how can we possibly appreciate how difficult it once was to maintain a functioning household, how much effort and heartache was involved? Our houses today practically look after themselves, so long as we can afford it, of course. Until quite recently, the provision of basic needs such as hot water, lighting, heating and food, was virtually a full-time job. For women, domestic life was especially hard, but men had the added burden of long working hours and the stress of having to keep the money coming in. There were many casualties, both male and female. They were failures who could expect little sympathy or support.

In light of this, it seems especially cruel that these people were so often the victims of hostility from writers, artists and others who thought themselves superior. The historian Alan Gilbert has pointed out that suburbia was, in effect, a compromise between the excitements and dangers of city life and the impracticalities of rural alternatives, embracing the best of both worlds. 'But, like all compromises,' he adds,

> it was also exposed to two distinct types of negative criticism. Indeed, it could be seen to have the worst of both worlds: sharing the tendency of urban living to destroy traditional forms of community, and at the same time destroying the freedoms of choice and association characteristic of authentic city life.[1]

Hostility towards the suburbs reached its apogee in the 1960s. Young people led the revolt, fleeing the suburbs as soon as they could—those of an existential bent to inner-city digs and those more romantically inclined to rural communes. Australian society changed fundamentally. In a word (the buzzword of the time), it was all about *freedom*: freedom from social convention, religious dogma, material deprivation and domestic responsibility. It was a time of reckless optimism and energy, fuelled by economic prosperity, a plentiful supply of jobs and improved welfare and tertiary education systems. New mass communications, along with the introduction of labour-saving devices and a wide range of service industries, eased the way.

The result was a society that was richer in spirit, more diverse, more intellectually interesting, more tolerant and more fun, although also more divided. There were casualties, not least a bewildered and resentful older generation, whose hard work and self-sacrifice had made it all possible in the first place.

Since that time, for better or for worse, living as part of a nuclear family in a suburban house has been largely a matter of choice rather than necessity. It is a choice many still make, of course, but they are no longer the majority and they no longer set the agenda. Yet even these people can remain fairly confident that, whatever their economic circumstances and however realistic their domestic dream turns out to have been, their house need never become a prison. They need never be tied to it, as their grandparents were. They may reasonably expect that it will adequately serve their material needs without having its physical demands wear them down. And they know they can move whenever necessary, or whenever they choose, which is something their ancestors found far more difficult to do.

Today, even government bureaucrats talk about 'providing accommodation', whereas once they would have said 'providing houses'. It's an acknowledgement that our basic need for a roof over our heads must be satisfied, while all the rest—our notion of home, our domestic arrangements and the way we think of community—may safely be left to us as individuals. It's a coldly unsentimental word, 'accommodation', but one that is, nevertheless, accommodating. If, as TS Eliot claimed, home is where we start from, then for many of us that's all it is, and all it need be. Peer groups outside the home have replaced the family as our points of reference. Today we live in our houses more lightly than ever before. We are dependent on them more for status, prestige and image than for subsistence.

Yet the contrast between the old days and now can easily be overplayed. You have only to venture to the outskirts of any Australian city, where new housing estates are sweeping up former farmland, or to visit one of countless homemakers' super-stores with endless aisles of lounge suites, appliances and home-theatre systems, to appreciate that the comfort and security of the suburban house is still the main preoccupation of countless Australians. Home renovation is now one of Australia's biggest industries. Many of us are still prepared to sacrifice almost everything to own a house, the larger and more impressive the better. The big difference is that, although the suburban dream is alive and well, it is no longer the only permissible dream.

Notes and
Bibliography

Notes

1. Fortress or Fishbowl

1 Quoted in Wakely, *Dream Home*, p. 96.
2 *Builders' and Contractors' News*, Sydney, May 1887, quoted in Archer, *Building a Nation*, pp. 118–19.
3 Gardiner, *The House*, p. 227.
4 Quoted in Wakely, *Dream Home*, p. 72.
5 *Home and Health*, pp. 99–100.
6 McCalman, *Journeyings*, p. 74.
7 Kingsley Ussher, 'Common Faults in House Planning', *Australian Home Beautiful*, 1 May 1934, p. 16.
8 'The Window Wall Revolution', *Australian Home Beautiful*, February 1959, pp. 70–1, 73–5.
9 '90% Visit Display Homes', *Australian Home Beautiful*, March 1964, pp. 6–23.
10 'The Houses People Want', *Australian Home Beautiful*, January 1967, p. 31.

2. The Border Zones

1 For a spirited description of Victorian city streetlife, see Cannon, *Australia in the Victorian Age,* vol. 3: *Life in the Cities*.
2 Malouf, *12 Edmondstone Street*, p. 20.
3 Irving, *The History and Design of the Australian House*, pp. 51–2.
4 Baglin and Moffitt, *The Australian Verandah*, p. 5.
5 Boyd, *Australia's Home*, p. 7.
6 R Chandler, 'Community Thoughts on Home-Building', *Australian Home Beautiful*, 1 October 1927, p. 27.
7 'The Advantages of the Small House Occupant', *Australian Home Beautiful*, 1 June 1927, p. 30.
8 Archer, *Your Home*, p. 27.
9 'Practical points in home design', *The Australian Home Builder*, 15 December 1924, p. 28.
10 Robert B Hamilton, 'How to Bring the Old Home Up-to-date', *Australian Home Beautiful*, 1 June 1928, p. 14.
11 *Home and Health*, p. 50.
12 Cathie May, 'The Self-Built Home, Sudlow Street, Embleton Western Australia', on *Australian Heritage Places Inventory* website.
13 'Two Small Houses by Home Builders', *Australian Home Beautiful*, 1 June 1927, p. 31.
14 'How to Bring the Old Home Up-to-date', *Australian Home Beautiful*, 1 June 1928, pp. 13–14.
15 Nora Cooper, 'Modernism Moving Outwards', *Australian Home Beautiful*, September 1939, p. 21.
16 'The Highway of Australian Architecture', *Australian Home Beautiful*, January 1934, pp. 16–17.
17 Best Overend, 'The House of 1960', *Australian Home Beautiful*, August 1938, pp. 14–15.
18 Mark Thomson on *George Negus Tonight*, ABC Radio, 5 May 2003.
19 Feifer, *Going Places*, p. 216.
20 'A Timber Residence for £892', *Australian Home Beautiful*, 1 June 1928, p. 15.
21 'Eating in the Garden', *Australian Women's Weekly*, 24 November 1945, p. 30.
22 'Now Meet a Family whose Backyard is (almost) Indoors', *Australian Home Beautiful*, October 1959, p. 43.
23 'Swim in Your Garden', *Australian Home Beautiful*, January 1959, pp. 48–9.

3. Once Inside

1 Boyd, *Outbreak of Love*, p. 96.
2 Quoted in Reiger, *The Disenchantment of the Home*, p. 49.

3   *Age*, 11 May 1901, p. 17.
4   Cliff Page, unpublished notes on his childhood, given to the author by his daughter, Helen.
5   Boyd, *Australia's Home*, p. 56.
6   'Home Furniture and Artistic Interiors', *Australian Home Builder*, May 1924, pp. 42–3.
7   'Let the Hall be an Index to Your Home', *Australian Home Beautiful*, July 1931, pp. 28–9.
8   ibid.
9   Cannon, *Australia in the Victorian Age,* vol. 3: *Life in the Cities*, p. 120.
10 *Argus*, 1 August 1912, reprinted in Crowley (ed.), *Select Documents in Australian History, 1901–1939*, p. 189.
11 In conversation with the author.
12 Judy Wajcman, 'Technology', in Beilharz and Hogan, *Sociology,* pp. 307–11.
13 *Commonwealth Year Book*, 1938, p. 195.
14 Advertisement for Beale and Company Ltd, *The Home*, October 1936, p. 7.
15 In conversation with the author.
16 Beaton and Wajcman, 'Patterns of Use of Mobile Telecommunications', *The Impact of the Mobile Telephone in Australia*, p. 15.
17 In conversation with the author.
18 Ruth Lane-Poole, 'The Linen Cupboard', *Australian Home Beautiful*, January 1928, pp. 34–5.
19 ibid.
20 Maria Tence and Elizabeth Triarico, 'La Dote: Preparing for a Family', in Epstein (ed.), *The Australian Family*, pp. 73–82.
21 David McNicoll, 'Decline and Fall of Sydney', *The Home*, December 1939, pp. 40–1.
22 '"Birtley Towers", Elizabeth Bay, Sydney: A Striking Addition to Sydney's Flat-Land', *Building*, 12 July 1934, pp. 14–20.
23 Jarrett Walker, in conversation with the author
24 'Boom in Project Housing', *Australian Home Beautiful*, December 1968, pp. 58–9.
25 'The Houses People Want', *Australian Home Beautiful*, January 1967, pp. 31–5.
26 Australian Bureau of Statistics, *Australian Social Trends, 2007.*
27 Advertisement for AV Jennings, *Home and Apartment Trends*, vol. 22, no. 17, n.d. (c. 2006), p. 165.

4. Come into the Parlour

1   *Australian Housewives' Manual*, p. 95.
2   Rybczynski, *Home*, p. 48.
3   Schama, *The Embarrassment of Riches*, p. 386.
4   Mark Peel, Introduction to Epstein (ed.), *The Australian Family*, p. 3.
5   Harold Bloom, 'The Family Pool', *Your Garden*, May 1964, pp. 42–3.
6   Australian Bureau of Statistics, 2006 census.
7   Maclehose, *Picture of Sydney*, p. 64.
8   See Nicholas Brown, 'Making Oneself Comfortable', in Troy (ed.), *A History of European Housing* , pp. 110–11.
9   Australian Bureau of Statistics, *Australian Housing Survey*, 1999.
10 *Argus*, 6 October 1909, p. 9.
11 *Age*, 9 January 1923, p. 10.
12 *The Australian Housewives' Manual*, p. 12.
13 Arnold Grodski, in conversation with the author.
14 Best Overend, 'The Desirable House', *Australian Home Beautiful*, June 1938, p. 21.
15 'Home Furniture and Artistic Interiors', *Australian Home Builder*, May 1924, pp. 42–3.
16 'An Experiment in Modernism', *Australian Home Beautiful*, February 1931, pp. 14–15.

17   '£.s.d. of Small House Heating', *Australian Home Beautiful*, July 1951, p. 14.
18   *Australian Home Builder*, March 1924, p. 48.
19   *Australian Home Beautiful*, January 1971, pp. 8–10
20   'Colors for 1967', *Australian Home Beautiful*, January 1967, p. 19.
21   'Home Furniture and Artistic Interiors', *Australian Home Builder*, May 1924, pp. 42–3.
22   'Avoid Those Dreadful Cousins "Clutter" and "Chaos"', *Australian Home Beautiful*, May 1967, p. 11.
23   *Australian Housewives' Manual*, p. 19.
24   *Home and Health*, p. 78.
25   Archer, *Your Home*, p. 11.
26   'An Electric Day', *Australian Home Beautiful*, September 1927, p. 46.
27   *Australian Home Beautiful*, January 1956, p. 22.
28   *Age*, 9 January 1923, p. 10.
29   *Australian Home Beautiful*, January 1944, p. 11.
30   Advertisement in *Australian Women's Weekly*, 20 January 1945, p. 26.
31   *Age*, 7 December 1918, p. 5.
32   'The Modern Music Room', *Australian Home Builder*, March 1924, p. 58.
33   Advertisement for Kiernan's Player Pianos in *Australian Home Beautiful*, May 1927, back cover.
34   *Australian Home Builder*, May 1924, p. 17.
35   Molony, *The Penguin Bicentennial History of Australia*, p. 281.
36   'The Youth Show', *The Home*, May 1941, pp. 63–4.
37   'The Promise of Radio', *Building*, 26 April 1938.
38   'TV in Your Home', *Australian Home Beautiful*, November 1956, p. 23.
39   *Australian Broadcasting Control Board Annual Report*, 1958, quoted in McKee, *Australian Television*, p. 23.
40   'TV in Your Home', *Australian Home Beautiful*, November 1956, p. 25.

5. May I Leave the Table?

1   *The Australian Housewives' Manual*, p. 25.
2   McNeil, *A Bunyip Close Behind Me*, p. 36.
3   *The Australian Housewives' Manual*, p. 25.
4   Nicholas Brown, 'Making Oneself Comfortable', in Troy (ed.), *A History of European Housing in Australia*, p. 114.
5   Quoted in Buckberry (ed.), *Padd, Paddo, Paddington*, p. 25.
6   'The Heyday of the Small Diningroom', *Australian Home Beautiful*, May 1931, pp. 14–15.
7   'In the Modern Small Home, do you Require a Dining Room?', *Australian Home Beautiful*, January 1945, pp. 7–10.
8   ibid.
9   Greig, *Home Magazines and Modernist Dreams*, p. 6.
10   Nora Cooper, 'A Little Forecasting about Furniture', *Australian Home Beautiful*, June 1944, p. 16.
11   'Furnish with Aluminium', *Australian Home Beautiful*, March 1947, p. 27.
12   'Furnishing to a Plan', *Australian Home Beautiful*, March 1951, pp. 22–3.
13   ibid.
14   *Women's Weekly*, 13 January 1945, p. 2.
15   Advertisement for Masonite, *Women's Weekly*, 1 December 1945, p. 38.
16   Advertisement for Laminex, *Australian Home Beautiful*, December 1953, p. 2.
17   Advertisement for Aristoc furniture, *Australian Home Beautiful*, February 1967, p. 53.

18   Quoted in Bannerman, *Acquired Tastes*, p. 24.
19   Quoted in Elias, *The History of Manners*, p. 121
20   ibid, p. 120.
21   Judith Martin, quoted in Miller, *Conversation*, pp. 24–5.
22   Vansittart, *In the Fifties*, p. 154.

6. The Heart of the Home

1   Blainey, *A History of Camberwell*, pp. 55–71.
2   Vesta, 'Women to Women', *Argus*, 2 February 1910. This particular issue of the *Argus'* regular column for women includes a description of a reader's Melbourne kitchen. I have used it as the basis for Mrs Ridley's kitchen, with additional material from other contemporary sources.
3   See 'The Administration of the Home', in Reiger, *The Disenchantment of the Home*, pp. 56–82, for an account of the domestic economy movement.
4   Advertisement for Wincarnis Restorative, *Argus*, 12 January 1910, p. 5.
5   *Home and Health*, p. 110.
6   *Age*, 4 May 1901, p. 17.
7   Vesta, 'The ANA exhibition', *Argus*, 9 February 1910, p. 9.
8   Blainey, *A History of Camberwell*, p. 70.
9   *Argus*, 3 July 1909, p. 8.
10   *Argus*, 19 March 1910, p. 8.
11   *Home and Health*, p. 269.
12   'Fighting the Heat', *Argus*, 26 February 1910, p. 7.
13   Mrs Ridley's is an amalgam of three suggested work schedules published in: Mrs Lance Rawson, *The Australian Enquiry Book of Household and General Management*, pp. 13-14; *Home and Health*, pp. 79-80; Vesta, 'Houses and Heat', *The Argus*, 5 January 1910, p. 9.
14   Vesta, 'Diet in Summer: Salads and Salad Dressings', *Argus*, 6 October 1909, p. 9.
15   'Plan of Bright Promise', *Telegraph*, 7 February 1934, p. 6.
16   'Women and Unemployment', *Sydney Morning Herald Women's Supplement*, 6 December 1934, p. 2.
17   Gill, *My Town*, p. 159.
18   Advertisement for Romano's Gala Dinner Dance, *Telegraph*, 20 November 1934, p. 14.
19   '"Chesterfield" Flats, Edgecliff, Sydney', *Building*, 12 July 1934, pp. 23–5, and '"Birtley Towers", Elizabeth Bay, Sydney', *Building*, 12 July 1934, pp. 15–20.
20   Grace and Dennis' flat is loosely based on a description of Beverley Flats in Bondi, Sydney, in *Building*, 12 February 1934, with additional features suggested by other contemporary sources.
21   'Planning a Kitchen', *Telegraph Home and Building Section*, 5 December 1934, p. 13.
22   'Birtley Towers Electrical Installation', *Building*, 12 July 1934, p. 20.
23   General Electric advertisement, *Building*, 12 December 1933, and 'Electricity Ends Home Drudgery', *Telegraph*, 5 April 1933, p. 8.
24   'Beverley Flats, Bondi, NSW', *Building*, 12 February 1934, p. 30.
25   'Cooking without Looking', *Telegraph*, 14 November 1934, p. 13.
26   Advertisement for Mark Foy's, *Telegraph*, 5 December 1934, p. 13.
27   'New Aids to Ease: Efficiency in the Kitchen', *Telegraph*, 10 May 1933, p. 6.
28   *Age*, 25 July 1931, p. 8.
29   Dorcas Day, 'The Alphabet of Homecraft: Asbestos', *Australian Home Beautiful*, January 1934, p. 12.

30 For some of the background to this section, I am grateful to Betty Salomon, who moved to a Housing Trust bungalow in Klemsig in 1956 with her German husband.

31 'Dutch Carnival at Easter', *Advertiser*, 31 January 1956, p. 4.

32 Peters, *The Dutch Down Under*, pp. 248–9.

33 'Wood Competes with Steel for Kitchen Smartness', *Advertiser*, 12 July 1956, p. 15.

34 'Transfer Decoration Gay and Amusing', *Advertiser*, 13 January 1956, p. 9.

35 Peters, *The Dutch Down Under*, p. 250.

36 ibid.

37 'Living Cost Rises 2/- in Adelaide', *Advertiser*, 19 January 1956, p. 3.

38 'Butter To Go Up 4d. lb., Cheese 2d.', *Advertiser*, 20 July 1956, p. 1.

39 *Advertiser*, 19 July 1956, p. 1.

40 'Snails—And Shells—Vie With Steak and Eggs', *Advertiser*, 9 March 1955, p. 5.

41 ibid.

42 Advertisement for Hains Hunkin Ltd, *Advertiser*, 12 April 1955, p. 4.

43 'New Washable Wallpaper', *Advertiser*, 15 March 1955, p. 9.

44 'Storage is key to good kitchens', *Australian Home Beautiful*, September 1956, p. 23.

45 Advertisement for Kelvinator refrigerator, *Australian Home Beautiful*, September 1956, p. 30.

46 Advertisement for Woden Plaza, *Canberra Times*, 14 September 1974, p. 9.

47 Election advertisement for Australian Labor Party, *Canberra Times*, 15 May 1974, p. 9.

48 'Kitchen Remodelling', *Canberra Times*, 8 October 1974, p. 21.

49 Advertisement for Frigidaire Caprice oven, *Canberra Times*, 18 March 1975, p. 10.

50 Letters to the editor about Bankcard, *Canberra Times*, 22 June 1974, p. 2 and 15 November 1974, p. 6.

51 For a full account of the development of the frozen and fast food industries, see Symons, *One Continuous Picnic*, pp. 224–47.

52 *Canberra Times*, 13 June 1974, p. 17.

53 *Canberra Times*, 28 September 1974, p. 13.

54 Symons, *One Continuous Picnic*, p. 253.

55 ibid., p. 252

56 ibid., p. 266.

57 Melissa's kitchen is drawn from articles in various contemporary homemaker magazines. Some of the descriptive passages are taken from Susan Breen, *Creating Your Dream Kitchen*.

58 Miele promotion, *Home and Apartment Trends*, vol. 22, no. 17, n.d., p. 173.

59 ibid.

60 Breen, 'The Smart Kitchen', in *Creating Your Dream Kitchen*, pp. 30–1.

7. Go to Your Room

1 Advertisement for Sharps Bedrooms, *House Beautiful* (UK), November 2005, p. 5.

2 Malouf, *12 Edmondstone Street*, p. 24.

3 Lane and Serle, *Australians at Home*, p. 196.

4 *The Australian Housewives' Manual*, p. 26.

5 Quoted in Archer, *Your Home*, p. 175.

6 ibid., p. 33.

7 Rawson, *The Australian Enquiry Book of Household and General Information*, p. 153.

8 *Home and Health*, p. 72.

9   AH Beard Bedding Pty Ltd, *History of Sleep in Australia*, website.
10   Advertisement for Dunlopillo foam-rubber mattresses, *Australian Home Beautiful*, March 1951, back cover.
11   'Daybeds', *Australian Home Beautiful*, July 1956, p. 48.
12   *Women's Weekly*, 24 June 1933, p. 38.
13   ibid.
14   Advertisement for Warrnambool Blankets, *Women's Weekly*, 25 August 1945, p. 25.
15   In conversation with the author.
16   In conversation with the author.
17   Quoted in Buckberry (ed.), *Padd, Paddo, Paddington*, p. 17.
18   Reiger, *The Disenchantment of the Home*, p. 153.
19   *Argus*, 4 September 1909, p. 8.
20   *Home and Health*, pp. 365–6.
21   *Argus*, 19 February 1910, p. 8.
22   'How to Keep Them At Home', *Australian Home Builder*, 16 June 1924, p. 32.
23   ibid.
24   Erica Harcourt, 'A Room for Your Son', *Australian Home Beautiful*, February 1948, pp. 7–8, 46.
25   Erica Harcourt, 'A Room for Your Daughter', *Australian Home Beautiful*, February 1948, p. 9.
26   Buller-Murphy, *Lady Hackett's Household Guide*, p. 71.
27   Reiger, *The Disenchantment of the Home*, p. 188.
28   In conversation with the author.
29   'This is How You, or your Children, will Live in 31 Years' Time', *Australian Home Beautiful*, April 1968, pp. 12–17.
30   Conrad, *Modern Times, Modern Places*, p. 547.
31   Kohák, *The Embers and the Stars*, p. 213.

8. The Facilities

1   Jones, *Cleanliness is Next to Godliness*, p. 11.
2   Cannon, *Australia in the Victorian Age*, vol. 3: *Life in the Cities*, p. 158.
3   Quoted in Archer, *Your Home*, p. 131.
4   Cowan, *From Wattle and Daub to Concrete and Steel*, p. 156.
5   *Home and Health*, p. 106.
6   Advertisement for R Fowler Ltd, *Building*, 12 December 1933, p. 96.
7   Advertisement for the Delmatic cistern, *Australian Home Beautiful*, August 1955, p. 92.
8   Website of Green Building Supply, http://www.greenbuildingsupply.com/utility/
9   *The WaterLogue*, newsletter of the California Urban Water Conservation Council, vol. 2, no. 5, Fall 2003, p. 3.
10   McNeil, *A Bunyip Close Behind Me*, p. 41.
11   *Home and Health*, p. 370.
12   'An Antique Bath', *Building*, 24 August 1939, p. 79.
13   In conversation with the author.
14   Advertisement for THM Electric Bath Heater, *Australian Home Beautiful*, July 1927, p. 71.
15   Advertisement for Boska Hot Water Boiler, *Australian Home Builder*, July 1924, p. 8.
16   *Australian Home Beautiful*, November 1928, p. 16.
17   'Bathrooms', *Sydney Morning Herald* Women's Supplement, 23 August 1934, p. 10.
18   ibid.

19   Nora Cooper, 'When Peace Comes, What About the Bathroom?', *Australian Home Beautiful*, November 1944, p. 19.
20   '160 Ideas for your Bathroom', *Australian Home Beautiful*, February 1956, p. 25.
21   Advertisement for Masonite, *Australian Women's Weekly*, 22 September 1945, p. 16.
22   '160 Ideas for your Bathroom', op. cit.
23   'Bathrooms Galore', *Australian Home Beautiful*, August 1967, p. 6.
24   ibid.
25   Kira, *The Bathroom*, passim.
26   *Australian Housewives' Manual*, p. 77.
27   Finkelstein, *Slaves of Chic*, p. 23.
28   de Grazia, *Irresistible Empire*, pp. 4 and 197.
29   In conversation with the author.
30   Rawson, *The Australian Enquiry Book of Household and General Information*, p. 139.
31   ibid, pp. 139–45.
32   Gill, *My Town*, p. 22.
33   *The Home*, July 1936, p. 52.
34   de Grazia, *Irresistible Empire*, p. 363.
35   Advertisement for Lux soap, *Truth*, 20 January 1940, p. 15.
36   Kuczynski, *Beauty Junkies*, p. 85.
37   Ellen Berscheid, 'Overview of the Psychological Effects of Physical Attractiveness', quoted in Kuczynski, p. 86.
38   For a full description of hospital conditions in the nineteenth century, see Cannon, *Australia in the Victorian Age*, vol. 3: *Life in the Cities*, pp. 133–53.
39   Quoted in the *Age*, 30 May 1901, p. 7.
40   ibid.
41   Advertisements in various issues of the *Age* between 1899 and 1914.
42   Quoted in *Home and Health*, p. 510.
43   *Age*, 2 January 1918, p. 8.
44   *Age*, 25 November 1918, p. 10.
45   *Home and Health*, p. 529.
46   Robert Bud, 'The History of Antibiotics', on the website of the Wellcome Trust, http://www.wellcome.ac.uk/docWTX026108.html
47   McCalman, *Journeyings*, p. 84.
48   Metzl, *Prozac on the Couch*, passim.

9. The Worst Day of the Week

1   Lane and Serle, *Australians at Home*, p. 389.
2   Australian Bureau of Statistics, *General Social Survey,* Summary Results, 2002.
3   McNeil, *A Bunyip Close Behind Me*, p. 61.
4   Rawson, *The Australian Enquiry Book of Household and General Information*, pp. 103–4.
5   Kimberly Webber, 'Embracing the New', in Troy (ed.), *A History of European Housing in Australia*, p. 101.
6   *Home and Health*, p. 131.
7   Advertisement for George Simpson & Son, *Australian Home Builder*, March 1924, p. 8.
8   'Drudgery in the Australian Home', *Australian Home Beautiful*, 2 July 1928, p. 59.
9   'The Electric Servant', *The Australian Home Builder,* December 1924, p. 64.
10 Advertisement for the Easy Electric Washer, *Australian Home Beautiful*, March 1928, p. 9.

11   See, for example, 'Electricity in the Small Home', *Australian Home Beautiful*, 1 August 1928, p. 48; and 'How to fit up a convenient Bathroom-Laundry', *Australian Home Beautiful*, 1 February 1928, p. 50.

12   'Why Not a Pleasant Laundry?', *Australian Home Beautiful*, 1 October 1930, p. 63.

13   'How to Keep Lovely in Spite of Washday', *Australian Women's Weekly*, 2 May 1942, p. 16.

14   *Commonwealth Year Book*, 1940, p. 691.

15   Advertisement for Bendix Automatic Washing Machine, *Building*, 24 October 1939, p. 117.

16   Advertisement for Hotpoint, *Australian Women's Weekly*, 5 September 1942, p. 32.

17   ibid.

18   Review of AV Jennings' Ashburn project home, *Australian Home Beautiful*, September 1964, pp. 48–9.

19   'Electric Washers–83 to Pick From', *Australian Home Beautiful*, May 1960, pp. 36–7.

20   'Well-Known Before it was Built!', *Australian Home Beautiful*, June 1955, pp. 16–17.

21   Advertisement for Rinso, *Australian Home Beautiful*, 1 January 1931, p. 3.

22   Rawson, *The Australian Enquiry Book of Household and General Information*, p. 103.

23   see website of Deutsches Verpackungs-Museum: http://www.verpackungsmuseum.de/Objects/persil-en.htm, and 'History and Chemistry of the Laundry' at: http://chemistry.co.nz/framed/stain_laundry.html.

24   de Grazia, *Irresistible Empire*, p. 422.

25   Advertisement for Rinso, *Truth*, 20 January 1940, p. 16.

26   de Grazia, *Irresistible Empire*, p. 433.

27   *Australian Home Beautiful*, June 1967, p. 103.

Conclusion

1   Alan Gilbert, 'The Roots of Anti-Suburbanism in Australia', in Goldberg and Smith (eds), *Australian Cultural History*, p. 39.

Bibliography

Newspapers and Periodicals

Advertiser, Adelaide, 1 January 1955 – 30 December 1956.
Age, Melbourne, 4 September 1899 – 8 August 1910 and selected other issues.
Argus, Melbourne, 1 June 1909 – 30 December 1910 and selected other issues.
Australian Home Beautiful, Melbourne, October 1925 – November 1972.
Australian Home Builder, Melbourne, August 1922 – September 1925.
Australian Home Journal, Sydney, September 1945 – December 1952.
Australian Women's Weekly, Sydney, 10 June 1933 – 29 December 1971.
Building, Sydney, September 1907 – September 1942.
Canberra Times, 1 May 1974 – 30 December 1975.
Commonwealth Year Book, Australian Government Publishing Service, Melbourne and Canberra, selected issues from 1920.
Herald, Melbourne, selected issues between 1939 and 1941.
The Home: An Australian Quarterly, Sydney, January 1936 – September 1942.
Home and Apartment Trends, Sydney, vol. 22, no. 17, n.d.
Mercury, Hobart, selected issues.
Telegraph, Sydney, 1 April 1933 – 31 December 1934 and selected other issues.
Truth, Melbourne, selected issues of the early 1940s.
Sydney Morning Herald, 6 June 1933 – 30 March 1935, and selected other issues.

Books, Catalogues, Pamphlets, Reports

Apperly, Richard, Irving, Robert and Reynolds, Peter, *A Pictorial Guide to Identifying Australian Architecture: Styles and Terms from 1788 to the Present*, Angus & Robertson, Sydney, 1989.

Archer, John, *Building a Nation: A history of the Australian House*, William Collins, Sydney, 1987 (republished in 1996 by William Collins, Sydney, as *The Australian Dream: The History of the Australian House*).

Archer, John, *Your Home: The Inside Story of the Australian House*, Lothian, Melbourne, 1998.

The Australian Home Beautiful: From Hills Hoist to High Rise, Hardie Grant, Sydney, 1999.

Australian Homes, vol. 1, no. 1, Ramsay, Melbourne, 1927.

The Australian Housewives' Manual: A Book for Beginners and People with Small Incomes, AH Massina and Co., Melbourne, 1885.

Baglin, Douglass and Moffitt, Peter, *The Australian Verandah*, Ure Smith, Sydney, 1976.

Bannerman, Colin, *Acquired Tastes: Celebrating Australia's Culinary History*, National Library of Australia, Canberra, 1998.

Beaton, John and Wajcman, Judy, *The Impact of the Mobile Telephone in Australia* (discussion paper), Australian Mobile Telecommunications Association and Academy of the Social Sciences, Canberra, 2004 (available online at: http://www.assa.edu.au/Publications/mobile-phone.pdf).

Beilharz, Peter and Hogan, Trevor, *Sociology: Place, Time and Division*, Oxford University Press, Melbourne, 2006.

Benjamin, Zoë, *You and Your Children*, vol. 1: *The Young Child*, Gayle Publishing, Sydney, 1944.

Blainey, Geoffrey, *A History of Camberwell*, Lothian Publishing, Melbourne and Sydney, 1980.

Boyd, Martin, *Outbreak of Love*, Penguin, Melbourne, 1993 (first published 1957).

Boyd, Robin, *The Australian Ugliness*, Melbourne, Penguin, 1968.

Boyd, Robin, *Australia's Home*, Melbourne University Press, Melbourne, 1987 (first published 1952).

Breen, Susan, *Creating Your Dream Kitchen*, Sterling Publishing Co., New York, 2005.

Brown, Nicholas, *A Cliff of White Cleanliness: Decorating the Home, Defining the Self*, Urban Research Program, Research School of Social Sciences, Australian National University, Canberra, 1995.

Buckberry, Dawn (ed.), *Padd, Paddo, Paddington: An Oral and Visual History of Early Paddington. Living Memories from the Heart of Brisbane*, Red Hill Paddington Community Centre and Paddington History Group, Brisbane, 1999.

Buller-Murphy, Deborah (Lady Hackett), *Lady Hackett's Household Guide*, Robertson & Mullens, Melbourne, 1940.

Cannon, Michael, *Australia in the Victorian Age,* vol. 3: *Life in the Cities*, Thomas Nelson, Melbourne, 1975.

Cathcart, Michael (ed.), *Manning Clark's History of Australia, Abridged by Michael Cathcart*, Melbourne University Press, Melbourne, 1993.

Clark, Rosemary, *The Home Front: Life in Australia during World War II*, Australia Post, n.d. (about 1991).

Committee for Economic Development of Australia, *Home Building for the 80s* (forum report), Melbourne, 1980.

Conrad, Peter, *Modern Times, Modern Places: Life and Art in the 20th Century*, Thames and Hudson, London, 1998.

Conway, Ronald, *The Great Australian Stupor: An Interpretation of the Australian Way of Life*, Sun Books, Melbourne, 1971.

Cowan, Henry J, *From Wattle and Daub to Concrete and Steel: The Engineering Heritage of Australia's Buildings*, Melbourne University Press, Melbourne, 1998.

Crowley, FK (ed.), *Select Documents in Australian History, 1901–1939*, Melbourne, Wren Publishing, 1973.

Cushman, EM, *Management in Homes*, Macmillan, New York, 1945.

Davison, Graeme, *What Makes a Building Historic?*, Historic Buildings Council, Melbourne, 1986.

de Bonneville, Françoise, *The Book of the Bath*, Thames and Hudson, London, 1998.

de Botton, Alain, *The Architecture of Happiness*, Hamish Hamilton, London, 2006.

de Grazia, Victoria, *Irresistible Empire: America's Advance through 20th-century Europe*, Harvard University Press, Cambridge, MA and London, 2005.

Dupain, Max, Herman, Morton, Barnard, Marjorie and Thomas, Daniel, *Georgian Architecture in Australia*, Ure Smith, Sydney, 1974.

Elder, Bruce, Atkinson, Ann and O'Keefe, Daniel, *Australian Family Album: The Australian Family in Photographs, 1860 to 1980s*, Daniel O'Keefe Publishing, Sydney, 1983.

Elias, Norbert, *The History of Manners*, Basil Blackwell, London, 1983 (first published in German in 1939).

Epstein, Anna (ed.), *The Australian Family: Images and Essays*, Scribe, Melbourne, 1998.

Evans, Ian, *The Australian Home*, Flannel Flower Press, Sydney, 1983.

Evans, Ian, *Furnishing Old Houses: A Guide to Interior Restoration*, Sun Books, Melbourne, 1983.

Evans, Ian, *The Australian Old House Catalogue*, Methuen Haynes, Sydney, 1984.

Feifer, Maxine, *Going Places: The Ways of the Tourist from Imperial Rome to the Present Day*, Macmillan, London, 1985.

Ferber, Sarah, Healy, Chris and McAuliffe, Chris (eds), *Beasts of Suburbia: Interpreting Cultures in Australian Suburbs*, Melbourne University Press, Melbourne, 1994.

Finkelstein, Joanne, *Slaves of Chic: An A to Z of Consumer Pleasures*, Minerva, Melbourne, 1994.

Franks, Thetta Quay, *Household Organisation for War Service*, GP Putman's Sons, New York and London, 1918.

Fraser, Bryce, *The Macquarie Book of Events*, Macquarie Library, Sydney, 1983.

Fraser, H and Joyce, R, *The Federation House: Australia's Own Style*, Lansdown Press, Sydney, 1986.

Freeland, JM, *Architecture in Australia: A History*, Penguin, Melbourne, 1974.

Gardiner, Stephen, *The House: Its Origins and Evolution*, Constable, London, 2002.

Gerster, Robin and Bassett, Jan, *Seizures of Youth: The Sixties and Australia*, Hyland House, Melbourne, 1991.

Gill, Lydia, *My Town: Sydney in the 1930s*, State Library of New South Wales, Sydney, 2000.

Goldberg, SL, and Smith, FB (eds), *Australian Cultural History*, Cambridge University Press, Cambridge, 1989.

Gould, Nat, *Town and Bush*, Penguin, Melbourne, 1974 (facsimile edition of 1896 original).

Greig, Alastair Whyte, *Home Magazines and Modernist Dreams: Designing the 1950s House*, Urban Research Program, Research School of Social Sciences, Australian National University, Canberra, 1995.

Hemingway, Wayne, *Mass-Market Classics: A Celebration of Everyday Design: The Home*, Rotovision, Hove, UK, 2003.

Home and Health: A Household Manual, Signs Publishing, Melbourne, 1909.

Horne, Donald, *The Lucky Country*, Penguin, Melbourne, 1964.

Horne, Donald, *The Lucky Country Revisited*, Dent, Melbourne and London, 1987.

Irving, Robert, *The History and Design of the Australian House*, Oxford University Press, Melbourne, 1985.

Jones, Shar, *Cleanliness is Next to Godliness: Personal Hygiene in New South Wales 1788–1901*, Historic Houses Trust, Sydney, 1984.

Jones, Shar, *Let There be Light: the development of domestic lighting in New South Wales 1788–1904*, Historic Houses Trust, Sydney, 1984.

Kinglake, Edward, *The Australian at Home: notes and anecdotes of life at the Antipodes, including useful hints to those intending to settle in Australia*, Leadenhall, London, 1892.

Kira, Alexander, *The Bathroom: Criteria for Design*, Bantam, New York, 1967.

Knight, Stephen, *The Selling of the Australian Mind: From First Fleet to Third Mercedes*, William Heinemann, Melbourne, 1990.

Kohák, Erazim, *The Embers and the Stars: A Philosophical Enquiry into the Moral Sense of Nature*, University of Chicago Press, Chicago and London, 1984.

Kuczynski, Alex, *Beauty Junkies: Under the Skin of the Cosmetic Surgery Industry*, Vermilion, London, 2007.

Lane, Terence and Serle, Jessie, *Australians at Home: A Documentary History of Australian Domestic Interiors from 1788 to 1914*, Oxford University Press, Melbourne, 1990.

Luck, Peter, *Australian Icons: Things That Make Us What We Are*, William Heinemann, Melbourne, 1992.

Maclehose, James, *Picture of Sydney and Strangers' Guide in NSW for 1839*, John Ferguson, Sydney, in association with the Royal Australian Historical Society, 1977 (facsimile of original 1839 edition).

Malouf, David, *12 Edmonstone Street*, Penguin, Melbourne, 1986.

McCalman, Janet, *Journeyings: The Biography of a Middle-Class Generation, 1920–1990*, Melbourne University Press, Melbourne, 1993.

McCalman, Janet, *Janet McCalman On the World of the Sixty-Nine Tram*, Melbourne University Press, Melbourne, 2006.

McFadden, David Revere (ed.), *Scandinavian Modern Design, 1880–1980*, Harry N Abrams, New York, 1982.

McKee, Alan, *Australian Television: A Genealogy of Great Moments*, Oxford University Press, Melbourne, 2001.

McKinlay, Brian, *Sweet and Simple Pleasures: Australian Entertainment in Colonial Times*, Collins Dove, Melbourne, 1988.

McNeil, Eugénie, *A Bunyip Close Behind Me: Recollections of the Nineties*, Hawthorn Press, Melbourne, 1972.

McQueen, Humphrey, *Social Sketches of Australia 1888–1975*, Penguin, Melbourne, 1978.

Metzl, Jonathan, *Prozac on the Couch: Prescribing Gender in the Era of Wonder Drugs*, Duke University Press, New York, 2003.

Miller, Stephen, *Conversation: A History of a Declining Art*, Yale University Press, New Haven and London, 2006.

Molony, John, *The Penguin Bicentennial History of Australia*, Viking, Melbourne, 1987.

Murphy, John and Norris, Kathryn, *'The Most Useful Art': Architecture in Australia 1788–1985*, Library Council of NSW, Sydney, 1985.

Murray, Mary, *A Home of my Own: Handy Hints and Images from Domestic Life in Australia in the 1940s and 1950s*, Mallon, Melbourne, 2001.

Nicholas, Joanna, *And So To Bed* (exhibition guide), Historic Houses Trust of New South Wales, Sydney, 2002.

O'Callaghan, Judith (ed.), *The Australian Dream: Design of the Fifties*, Powerhouse Publishing, Sydney, 1993.

Peters, Nonja (coordinating author), *The Dutch Down Under: 1606–2006*, Sydney, Wolters Kluwer, 2006.

Pickett, Charles, *The Fibro Frontier: A Different History of Australian Architecture*, Powerhouse Publishing and Doubleday, Sydney, 1997.

Planel, Philippe, *Locks and Lavatories: The Architecture of Privacy*, English Heritage, London, 2000.

Pratt, Richard, *Ladies' Home Journal Book of Landscaping and Outdoor Living*, M Evans and Co., New York, 1963.

Rawson, Mrs Lance, *The Australian Enquiry Book of Household and General Information*, Kangaroo Press, Sydney, 1984 (facsimile edition of 1894 original).

Reiger, Kerreen, *The Disenchantment of the Home: Modernising the Australian Family, 1880–1940*, Oxford University Press, Melbourne, 1985.

Rowley, Anthony, *The Book of Kitchens*, Flammarion, Paris, 2000.

Rybczynski, Witold, *Home: A Short History of an Idea*, Viking, New York, 1986.

Rybczynski, Witold, *The Look of Architecture*, Oxford University Press, New York, 2001.

Schama, Simon, *The Embarrassment of Riches: An Interpretation of Dutch Culture in the Golden Age*, Collins, London, 1987.

Sharpe, Alan, *Years of Change: A Nostalgic View of Australia in the 20s, 30s and 40s*, Currawong Press, Sydney, 1981.

Slessor, Catherine, *Contemporary Doorways: Architectural Entrances, Transitions, and Thresholds*, Mitchell Beazley, London, 2002.

Spearritt, Peter and Walker, David, *Australian Popular Culture*, George Allen and Unwin, Sydney, 1979.

Stretton, Hugh, *Housing and Government* (1974 Boyer Lectures), Griffin Press, Adelaide, 1974.

Sudjic, Deyan, *Home: The Twentieth-century House*, Laurence King, London, 1999.

Symons, Michael, *One Continuous Picnic: A Gastronomic History of Australia*, second edition, Melbourne University Press, Melbourne, 2007.

Tanner, Howard, *Australian Housing in the Seventies*, Ure Smith, Sydney, 1976.

Troy, Patrick (ed.), *A History of European Housing in Australia*, Cambridge University Press, Cambridge, 2000.

Unstead, RJ, and Henderson, WF, *Pioneer Home Life in Australia*, Edward Arnold, Melbourne, 1971.

Vansittart, Peter, *In the Fifties*, John Murray, London, 1995.

Wakely, Mark, *Dream Home*, Allen & Unwin, Melbourne, 2003.

Wheeldon, Leigh (ed.), *Period Home Renovators Guide 1988*, Publicity Press, Melbourne, 1988.

Whitelock, Derek, *Adelaide: Sense of Difference*, Australian Scholarly Publishing, Melbourne, 2000.

Willes, Margaret, *And So To Bed*, National Trust, London, 1998.

Williams, Neville, *Chronology of the Modern World*, 1763–1965, Penguin, London, 1975.

Women's Work in the Home, 1850s–1950s, Powerhouse Museum, Sydney, n.d. (about 1991).

You Can Build Your Own Home! and save hundreds of pounds on the cost, The Home Builders' Advisory, Sydney, 1946.

Electronic Sources

AH Beard Bedding Pty Ltd, *History of Sleep in Australia*, http://www.ahbeard.com/info/sleep-australia.htm

About Inventors, http://inventors.about.com/

Australian Bureau of Statistics, http://www.abs.gov.au/

Australian Heritage Places Inventory, http://www.heritage.gov.au/ourhouse/

Caslon Analytics, www.caslon.com.au

Clark, Tim (writer/director), *In the Mind of the Architect*, DVD, ABC enterprises, Sydney, 1999.

Electrical and Electronics and Telecommunications History Milestones in Australia, http://www.ewh.ieee.org/

Picture Australia, http://www.pictureaustralia.org/

Powerhouse Museum Collection Search, http://www.powerhousemuseum.com/collection/database/

Technology in Australia, 1788–1988, http://www.austech.unimelb.edu.au/tia

Wellcome Trust, http://www.wellcome.ac.uk/doc/

Picture
Credits

Chapter 1

Chapter 2

Chapter 3

Chapter 4

1920-1930. Purchased 1986. Collection: Powerhouse Museum, Sydney.

Advertisement for Arnotts biscuits, *Daily Telegraph*, 16 February 1934, p. 16, Courtesy of the State Library of Victoria, Imaging by Greg Elms

Domestic interior, kitchen
Photographer unknown
NSW Police Forensic Photography Archive
Justice and Police Museum collection, Historic Houses Trust

Sunshine kitchens, *Australian Home Beautiful*, 1 October 1934, p. 54, Courtesy of the State Library of Victoria, Imaging by Greg Elms

Private residence – unidentified, c. 1940, Courtesy of the State Library of Victoria, image number a36949

Sylvia at refrigerator, 22 October 1941
Alan Evans
Caroline Simpson Library & Research Collection, Historic Houses Trust

Max Dupain
The Meat Queue, 1946
Gelatin silver print, 45.5 x 54.7 cm
Monash Gallery of Art, City of Monash Collection

Mrs Adriana Zevenbergen polishing her Dutch solid oak diningroom dresser, 1958, Courtesy of the National Archives of Australia, image 4748283

Migrants in the community, 1964, Courtesy of the National Archives of Australia, image 7529967

Simpson E6 enamelled electric stove, 1952. Collection: Powerhouse Museum, Sydney. Photo: Sotha Bourn

Hotpoint cooking range, *Australian Home Beautiful*, January 1951, p. 55, Courtesy of the State Library of Victoria, Imaging by Greg Elms

Advertisement for New World supermarket, Courtesy of the Coburg Historical Society

New World Supermarket, Courtesy of the Redcliffe City Library

1970s kitchen, *Australian Home Beautiful*, June 1971, p. 16, Courtesy of the State Library of New South Wales

Kitchen and dining room of Toorak house, showing ceiling lighting, 1968, Harold Paynting Collection, Courtesy of the State Library of Victoria, image number a47425

Advertisement for Corning Ware, *Australian Home Beautiful*, July 1972, p. 36, Courtesy of the State Library of Victoria, Imaging by Greg Elms

Breville 'Easy Living' advertising pamphlet, Summer 05, published by Breville (part of Housewares International) in 2004. Gift of Breville Design – Housewares International, 2006. Collection: Powerhouse Museum, Sydney.

Chapter 7

Wallach Brothers, *Complete design book : furniture, bedsteads, pianos &c.*, [Melbourne, ca. 1880]. Lithographs by Troedel and Co.,

Collection of The Shaw Research Library, National Gallery of Victoria

Messrs. WH Rocke and Co.'s Exhibits, 1880, Courtesy of the State Library of Victoria, image number mp004467

Advertisement for Marcus Clark's furniture, *Sydney Morning Herald* Royal Visit Souvenir Supplement, Thursday 22 November 1934, p. 19, Courtesy of the State Library of Victoria, Imaging by Greg Elms

Bedroom as sitting room, *Australian Home Beautiful*, August 1971, p. 52, Courtesy of the State Library of Victoria, Imaging by Greg Elms

Alarm clock, *Women's Weekly*, 10 June 1933, p. 3, Courtesy of the State Library of New South Wales

David Moore
Australia 1927–2003
Redfern Interior
gelatin silver photograph
30.0 x 40.3 cm
National Gallery of Victoria, Melbourne
Purchased, 1991

How to house a boy, *Australian Home Beautiful*, August 1964, p. 26, Courtesy of the State Library of Victoria, Imaging by Greg Elms

Crowd outside the paramount Theatre in Bundaberg which was screening a sex education film called 'Secrets of Life', 1950s, Courtesy of the State Library of Queensland, image number 64547

Apple Mac (Macintosh 128) computer

designed and manufactured by Apple Corporation, USA/Japan, 1984. Gift of Peter Henderson, 1997. Collection: Powerhouse Museum, Sydney. Photo: Nitsa Yioupros.

Chapter 8

Chapter 9

Index

The Miegunyah Press

This book was designed and typeset by Peter Long
The text was set in 10 point Berthold
Baskerville Book with 14 points leading
The text is printed on 130 gsm matt art paper

This book was edited by Carla Taines

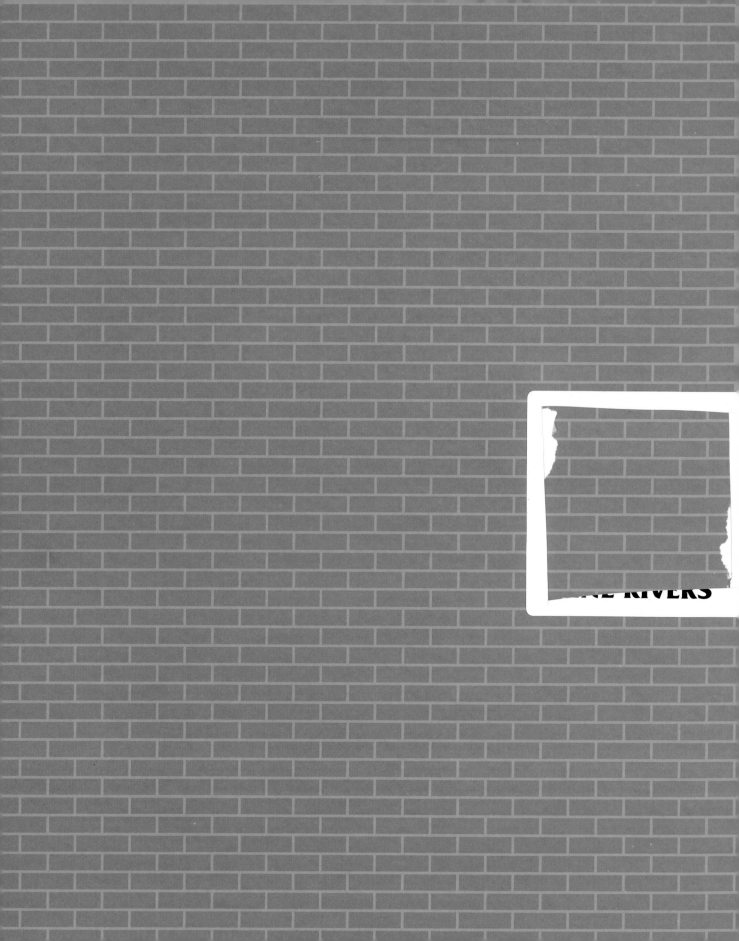